South-Western
ENTREPRENEURSHIP
IDEAS IN ACTION

CYNTHIA L. GREENE

VISIT US ON THE INTERNET
www.swep.com

South-Western Educational Publishing

an International Thomson Publishing company I(T)P®

www.thomson.com

Cincinnati • Albany, NY • Belmont, CA • Bonn • Boston • Detroit • Johannesburg • London • Madrid
Melbourne • Mexico City • New York • Paris • Singapore • Tokyo • Toronto • Washington

Team Leader	Eve Lewis
Managing Editor	Enid Nagel
Marketing Manager	Nancy A. Long
Editor	Tina Edmondson
Art and Design Coordinator	Bill Spencer
Production Coordinator	Patricia Matthews Boies
Marketing Coordinator	Christian L. McNamee
Manufacturing Coordinator	Kathy Shaut
Team Assistant	Linda Adams
Marketing Assistant	Yvonne Patton

About the Author

Cynthia L. Greene has taught business education at the high school level for more than 20 years. She is employed by the Fulton County School System at Centennial High School in Roswell, Georgia, where she is Cooperative Business Education Coordinator and chair of the business and career technology department. She has been active in the National Business Education Association, serving on the Entrepreneurship Standards Committee and as a writer for the Entrepreneurship Lesson Plans. She recently served as president of the Southern Business Education Association.

ISBN 0-538-68268-X

6 7 8 9 0 D 05 04 03 02 01 00
Printed in the United States of America

South-Western Educational Publishing is a division of International Thomson Publishing Inc. The ITP Logo is a registered trademark used herein under License by South-Western Educational Publishing.

Reviewers

Contents

1 **Should You Become an Entrepreneur?** 2

Build a Business
Delia's Dilemma 3

1.1 Entrepreneurs: Present and Past 4

1.2 Is Entrepreneurship Right for You? 9

1.3 Identify Business Opportunities and Set Goals 14

What Went Wrong?
Be Sharp or Fall Flat 16
Entrepreneurial Timeline
The First Woman Millionaire 6

Chapter Review 18
This Is Your Business Project 21

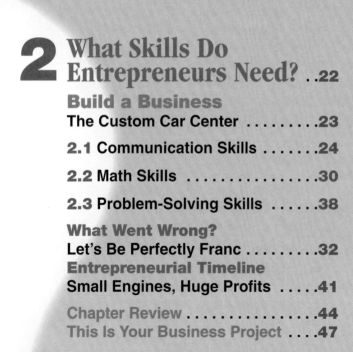

2 **What Skills Do Entrepreneurs Need?** ..22

Build a Business
The Custom Car Center 23

2.1 Communication Skills 24

2.2 Math Skills 30

2.3 Problem-Solving Skills 38

What Went Wrong?
Let's Be Perfectly Franc 32
Entrepreneurial Timeline
Small Engines, Huge Profits 41

Chapter Review 44
This Is Your Business Project 47

3 Entrepreneurs in a Market Economy 48

Build a Business
Darrell's Digs 49

3.1 What Is an Economy? 50

3.2 The Concept of Cost 55

3.3 Government in a
Market Economy 59

What Went Wrong?
The Case of the Failed
Ice Cream Shop 62
Entrepreneurial Timeline
Making Money in
Colonial America 51

Chapter Review 64
This Is Your Business Project 67

4 Select a Type of Ownership 68
Build a Business
The Pastry Shop 69

4.1 Run an Existing Business ...70
4.2 Own a Franchise or Start
a Business 75
4.3 Choose the Legal Form of
Your Business 82

What Went Wrong?
With a Friend Like This 73
Entrepreneurial Timeline
Stop the Presses! 76

Chapter Review 88
This Is Your Business Project 91

5 Develop a Business Plan 92
Build a Business
The Importance of a Plan 93

5.1 Why Do You Need a
Business Plan? 94
5.2 What Goes into a
Business Plan? 98
5.3 Create an Effective
Business Plan 103

What Went Wrong?
Pop Goes the Planning 104
Entrepreneurial Timeline
British Business in the 18th
and 19th Centuries 96

Chapter Review 110
This Is Your Business Project ...113

7 Finance, Protect, and Insure Your Business ..136

Build a Business
One Day at a Time 137

7.1 Put Together a
   Financial Plan 138
7.2 Obtain Financing for
   Your Business 146
7.3 Theft Proof Your
   Business 153
7.4 Insure Your Business 157

What Went Wrong?
Things Change 144
Entrepreneurial Timeline
Airing Good Business Practices . . .154

Chapter Review 160
This Is Your Business Project . . .163

6 Identify and Meet a Market Need 114

Build a Business
Cheryl's Day Spa 115

6.1 The Value of Market
   Research 116
6.2 How to Perform Market
   Research 122
6.3 Identify Your Competition . . .127

What Went Wrong?
Price Wars 125
Entrepreneurial Timeline
Vegetables Are Good for You . . .128

Chapter Review 132
This Is Your Business Project . . .135

9 Market Your Business ..188

Build a Business
Mixing Up the School Store 189

9.1 The Marketing Mix—Product,
Distribution, Price 190
9.2 The Marketing
Mix—Promotion 196
9.3 Set Marketing Goals 204

What Went Wrong?
Toothless in Seattle 202
Entrepreneurial Timeline
A Business with
Automatic Gains 206

Chapter Review 208
This Is Your Business Project ...211

8 Choose Your Location and Set Up for Business ...164

Build a Business
Expanding and Moving 165

8.1 Choose a Retail
Business Location 166
8.2 Choose a Location for a
Non-Retail Business 171
8.3 Obtain Space and Design the
Physical Layout 174
8.4 Purchase Equipment,
Supplies, and Inventory ...180

What Went Wrong?
Right Space, Wrong Place 175
Entrepreneurial Timeline
An Electric Career
(In More Ways than One) 182

Chapter Review 184
This Is Your Business Project ...187

10 Hire and Manage a Staff 212

Build a Business
The Frazzled Photographer 213

10.1 Hire Employees 214
10.2 Create a Compensation
Package 221
10.3 Manage Your Staff 225

What Went Wrong?
Who Do You Trust? 226
Entrepreneurial Timeline
A Pattern for Good Business ...218

Chapter Review 232
This Is Your Business Project ...235

11 Record Keeping and Accounting 236

Build a Business
CDs and Records 237

11.1 Set Up a Record
     Keeping System 238
11.2 Understand
     Basic Accounting 244
11.3 Track Your Inventory 248

What Went Wrong?
All Your Eggs in One Basket 242
Entrepreneurial Timeline
An Empire Built on Soap
and Candles 246

Chapter Review 252
This Is Your Business Project ...255

12 Financial Management 256

Build a Business
Financing and Web Pages 257

12.1 Manage Your Cash Flow ...258
12.2 Analyze Your Financial
     Performance 262
12.3 Hire Experts 268

What Went Wrong?
That Takes the Cake 270
Entrepreneurial Timeline
More Than Gold in California ...265

Chapter Review 272
This Is Your Business Project ...275

13 Use Technology 276

Build a Business
Getting Up to Date 277

13.1 Technology and
     Your Business 278
13.2 Learn about the Internet ..284
13.3 Purchase Technology 289

What Went Wrong?
Ice-Cold 281
Entrepreneurial Timeline
From Computers to Clothing ...286

Chapter Review 292
This Is Your Business Project ...295

14 Meet Your Legal, Ethical, and Social Obligations 296

Build a Business
Reasons for Regulations 297

14.1 Understand Your Legal
     Requirements 298
14.2 Ethical Issues in Business ...305
14.3 Meet Your Social
     Responsibilities 309

What Went Wrong?
Modern Day Pirates? 307
Entrepreneurial Timeline
A Beautiful Empire 310

Chapter Review 314
This Is Your Business Project ...317

15 Growth in Today's Marketplace 318

Build a Business
Gavin's Business Grows 319

15.1 Develop a Strategy
     for Growth 320
15.2 Global Trends
     and Opportunities 324
15.3 Culture and Business ...330

What Went Wrong?
Make–Up Test 331
Entrepreneurial Timeline
Music to His Ears 322

Chapter Review 334
This Is Your Business Project ...337

Glossary 338
Index 343
Photo Credits 356

To the Student

Welcome to *Entrepreneurship: Ideas In Action!* What brings you to the exciting world of entrepreneurship? Do you know someone who owns his or her own business? Do you want to be your own boss? Do you have the goal of owning a highly successful company? These are only a few of the reasons why thousands of people in the United States become entrepreneurs.

This textbook will take you on a step-by-step journey through the entire process of owning your own business. You will select a product or service to sell, determine who your customers are, learn how to market your business, obtain financing, manage your employees, and more. You will also learn how to put together a business plan and will have created a complete plan by the end of the text.

Entrepreneurship: Ideas In Action is easy to learn from, with every chapter broken into three or four lessons. Throughout the text, concepts are further explained through the use of real-world examples. These examples illustrate how entrepreneurs might use a concept or idea in their own business.

There are numerous special features in *Entrepreneurship: Ideas In Action* to make learning how to run your own business even more interesting:

- Each chapter begins with **Build a Business,** a thought-provoking real-world case that introduces you to the important concepts you will learn in the chapter.

- **What Do You Know?** immediately follows Build a Business and asks you some questions about the case. You will see how much you've learned after you've studied the chapter when you answer these questions once more.

- The pitfalls of actual entrepreneurs are profiled in **What Went Wrong?** These interesting stories may help you determine what not to do or what to avoid when you open your own business.

- The tales of entrepreneurs in history are included in the **Entrepreneurial Timeline.** You'll learn about the first African American millionaire, the beginnings of cable television, how people made money during the California Gold Rush without even using a shovel, and more!

- **This Is Your Business Project,** an activity at the end of each chapter, will help you develop a complete business plan by the end of the textbook.

- Read inspirational quotations from people involved in entrepreneurship in **You Can Say That Again!**

- **Did You Know?** provides additional information that you'll find interesting.

- Explore the Internet with **Net Worth.** First you'll come to a web site designed for this special feature. Then you'll be directed to visit other sites to answer questions and find out lots of interesting facts.

- An **In Class Activity** in each lesson provides opportunities for you to work with your classmates on projects and exercises.

   There are also a number of other books and supplementary items that can make it even easier and more fun to learn the world of entrepreneurship:

- A **Workbook** with exercises for every lesson, plus chapter reviews with fun activities such as crossword puzzles and word jumbles.

- A **CNN Video** with interesting clips about entrepreneurs and business from the well-known cable news station. An accompanying Discussion Guide helps you and your classmates get the most from the video.

- **Activity Masters** that include in class visits from entrepreneurial professionals, interesting research opportunities, creative writing exercises, and more.

   Entrepreneurship: Ideas In Action will provide you with an interesting introduction to launching and owning your own business. Becoming an entrepreneur is an exciting adventure that many people take. Not everyone is successful at it. If you combine this text with other business courses, it is possible for you to realize your dreams of owning your own business.

Chapter 1

SHOULD
YOU BECOME
AN ENTREPRENEUR?

LESSONS

1.1 Entrepreneurship: Present and Past

1.2 Is Entreprenuership Right For You?

1.3 Identify Business Opportunities and Set Goals

BUILD A BUSINESS

Delia's Dilemma

"**I**'m so tired of someone telling me what to do all the time," Delia said to her friend Gloria.

"I know what you mean," Gloria answered. "I get the same thing."

"It seems like there should be somewhere we could be in charge," Delia said. "There's got to be a better way."

"I've got an idea," Gloria said, "let's be entrepreneurs."

"Entrepre . . . what?" questioned Delia.

"Entrepreneurs," Gloria answered. "Mr. Rivera talked about them in my business class last week. They are people who start and run their own businesses. We could do that!"

"What would we have to do? Would we make a lot of money? Would it be fun? Would we get to do whatever we wanted?" Delia's mind was overflowing with questions.

Gloria was getting very excited as she replied, "We could be our own boss! If we were the owners, we would be in charge! We'd get to make all the decisions!"

"This is starting to sound pretty good," Delia replied as she began to share Gloria's excitement. "We could decide when we work, what we do, how we do it, and make lots of money! I can't wait. When do we start?"

Gloria thought for a second before answering, "Well, Delia, it's not really that easy. When we talked about this in class, Mr. Rivera said that there are a lot of things to consider before starting a business. First, we need to decide what we like to do and what we are good at. Then we have to do a lot of research and planning if we want to be successful."

Thinking about what Mr. Riviera told her in class, Delia sighed, "This entrepreneur thing sounds like a lot of work. What do you think we should do?"

Gloria could understand Delia's dilemma. There are many advantages of owning your own business, but there are also many responsibilities and challenges that a business owner has to face. Gloria knew that she and Delia had their work cut out for them, but she knew they could do it if they put their minds to it. "Delia, I think we need to get to the library as soon as possible. We've got a lot of work to do!"

What Do You Know?

1. Who are some famous entrepreneurs in our country? Name some in your local community.
2. What kinds of things do you think Delia and Gloria should consider before they decide to start a business?
3. What resources do you think Delia and Gloria will find in the library?
4. Where else could they go to get help in making their decision about starting their own business?

Entrepreneurs: Present *and* Past

The United States economy includes thousands of small businesses. Many of these small businesses are owned and operated by men and women who created their own companies. But what makes someone an entrepreneur? What impact have entrepreneurs had in history, and today?

WHAT IS AN ENTREPRENEUR?

People who own, operate, and take the risk of a business venture are called **entrepreneurs.** They are engaged in **entrepreneurship,** the process of running a business of one's own. Entrepreneurs come from all types of backgrounds and create all kinds of businesses. All ages of people choose to become entrepreneurs. Some own tiny craft shops, while others own huge construction companies. Entrepreneurs try to identify the needs of the marketplace and to meet those needs by supplying a service or product. When they succeed their businesses flourish and the profits go to them. When they fail their companies decline and they may have to go out of business.

EMPLOYEES VS. ENTREPRENEURS Entrepreneurs assume risk. This makes them different from **employees,** who are people who work for someone else. Both may make decisions, but only the entrepreneur is directly affected by the consequences of those decisions. Sam Jones manages a record store owned by Felipe Santiago. Sam decides to keep the store open until midnight during the week. If the additional hours bring in customers and increase profits, Sam may be praised by Felipe. He may even get a raise. However, Sam won't directly receive any of the profits because he is an employee. The earnings will flow to Felipe, the owner.

WHY DO PEOPLE BECOME ENTREPRENEURS? People go into business for themselves for many reasons. Some want to leave the fast-paced corporate environment. Others want to be at home but still earn an income. Others want to pursue a personal dream. The reason you might become an entrepreneur may be completely different than these.

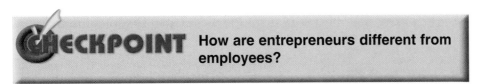

CHECKPOINT How are entrepreneurs different from employees?

Types of Entrepreneurial Businesses

There are many opportunities for entrepreneurs in each type of business *Manufacturing businesses* actually produce the products they sell. Using resources and supplies, they create everything from automobiles to paper. *Wholesaling businesses* sell products to people other than the final customer. For example, a wholesaler supplies your local greeting card store with items such as cards and wrapping paper. *Retailing businesses* sell products directly to the people who use or consume them. *Service businesses* sell services rather than products. They include hotels, hairdressers, and repair shops.

In Class Activity

Gather in small groups. List reasons you would like to be an employee. List reasons you would like to be an entrepreneur. Compare and discuss the reasons.

Manufacturing	Wholesaling	Retailing	Service
Apparel and other textile products	Apparel	Auto and home supply stores	Appliance repair
Chemicals and related products	Electrical goods	Building materials and supply stores	Automotive repair
Electronics and other electrical equipment	Groceries and related products	Clothing stores	Babysitting
Fabricated metal products	Hardware, plumbing, heating equipment	Florists	Bookkeeping
Food products	Lumber, construction materials	Furniture stores	Consulting
Industrial machinery and equipment	Machinery, equipment, supplies	Gift, novelty, and souvenir stores	Dance instruction
Printing and publishing	Motor vehicles, automotive equipment	Grocery stores	Exterminators
Rubber and miscellaneous plastic products	Paper, paper products	Hardware stores	Electrical services
Stone, clay, and glass products	Petroleum, petroleum products	Jewelry stores	Flower decorating
		Retail bakeries	House cleaning
		Shoe stores	Lawn care
		Sporting goods and, bicycle stores	Painting
			Plumbing
			Translating
			Travel agency
			Tutoring

Source: Small Business Administration

OTHER BUSINESS AREAS Two other categories of businesses are (1) agricultural and (2) mining and extracting businesses. *Agricultural businesses* generate fresh produce and other farm products, such as wheat. *Mining and extracting businesses* take resources like coal out of the ground so they can be consumed.

CHECKPOINT Describe different kinds of entrepreneurial businesses.

ENTREPRENEURS IN UNITED STATES HISTORY

During the colonial years, entrepreneurship flourished. Entrepreneurs raised crops such as rice and tobacco. They also worked as bankers, merchants, silversmiths, and candlemakers, to name a few career choices. After the American Revolution, the United States began to industrialize. Entrepreneurs invented machines that increased productivity and helped the economy grow.

Entrepreneurs Who Changed America

Entrepreneurs change American business decade after decade. They establish huge companies or fill unmet needs. They constantly change how things are done and contribute to the overall good of the nation. In each chapter, you will learn something about

Entrepreneurial Timeline

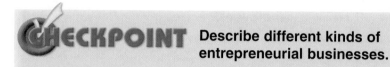

| 1880 | 1900 | 1920 | 1940 |

The First Woman Millionaire

Many entrepreneurs start by offering something they themselves need. That's exactly what made Madam C. J. Walker a millionaire. Walker began making her own hair treatments in 1904. The treatments worked well, so Walker began offering them to other African-American women. She sold her products door-to-door and bought ad space in newspapers. Walker then opened Lelia College, where she and her daughter trained other women to use and sell the product line, which now included items such as complexion soap and dental cream. At least 20 women completed the program every six weeks. Besides becoming a millionaire from the sales of her products, Walker made a huge contribution to the African-American community by empowering women to take pride in their work.

entrepreneurs in history, because they are an important part of what the United States and the world have become today.

NINETEENTH CENTURY ENTREPRENEURS A machine that put a major boost in the United States economy was the reaper. In 1831, Cyrus McCormick took the reaper, which had already been invented, and used it to mechanize the job of harvesting crops. McCormick had $60 when he went to Chicago to set up a factory to manufacture reapers. In time, the company that marketed his reapers evolved into International Harvester, which produced farm equipment for many years. Today this company is called Navistar International Transportation Company and manufactures International brand trucks.

Lydia Moss Bradley, an entrepreneur from Peoria, Illinois, made millions of dollars in investments and real estate. She transformed seemingly unusable marshland into productive farm land. She also founded Bradley University in 1896.

John D. Rockefeller began working at the age of 16 as a clerk in a small produce company. At 23, he had saved enough money to enter the oil refinery business. By 1872, his company, Standard Oil, owned all of the main oil refineries in Cleveland, New York, Pittsburgh, and Philadelphia. Before long, Rockefeller controlled almost all oil distribution in the United States. Eventually, he became the richest man in the world.

EARLY 20TH CENTURY ENTREPRENEURS Entrepreneurs remained very important in the twentieth century. For example, Henry Ford developed and mass-produced the Model-T automobile, which he sold at a price many Americans could afford. A machinist from Detroit, Ford created one of the largest companies in the world. Also during the early part of the century, Olive Ann Beech co-founded the Beech Aircraft Company with her husband. She had always handled the financial aspects of the company and took part in major company decisions. She ran the business when her husband became ill in 1940. With Beech at the helm, the company continued to be a leader in the aviation industry until merging with the Raytheon Company in 1980.

Henry Ford

Clarence Birdseye pioneered the development of packaged frozen foods in the 1920s. His developments had a major impact on eating habits throughout the world. Rose Knox became another leader in the food industry when she took over the Knox Gelatine Company in 1908. Besides being an innovative business owner, she was the first to provide employees paid sick and vacation leave and a five-day work week.

CHECKPOINT **Name one historical entrepreneur and describe what he or she did.**

More than 6.5 million small businesses contribute billions of dollars every year to the United States economy. These small companies employ more workers than all of the country's large corporations combined. Small businesses are found in virtually every sector of the economy. Companies such as Microsoft, Intel, and Apple all started as small businesses. These companies have changed the workplace by making computers accessible to the world. Other entrepreneurial companies include Southwest Airlines, Mrs. Fields' Cookies, and Estée Lauder Cosmetics. These companies make life more pleasant for consumers and provide employment to hundreds of thousands of workers.

Small companies can be more creative and take more risks than large companies. Their experimentation and innovation leads to technological change and increased productivity. This makes small business a significant part of the American economy. For this reason, many experts believe that small companies will play an increasingly important role in the future.

CHECKPOINT Why are small businesses so important to our economy?

THINK CRITICALLY

1. What are your reasons for wanting to become an entrepreneur? Do you think they are common to all entrepreneurs, or are some of your reasons unique?

2. What other entrepreneurs in the 19th or 20th century have changed the American economy? How?

MAKE CONNECTIONS

3. MATH Suppose there are exactly 6,750,000 small businesses in the economy today. Approximately 27 percent of those businesses are service businesses. What is the number of service businesses in the economy?

4. COMMUNICATION Clarence Birdseye developed the first packaged frozen foods. He greatly influenced eating habits in the United States and throughout the world. What do you think a typical family's daily eating habits were like at the end of the nineteenth century? Write a short scenario describing them.

Is Entrepreneurship Right *for* You?

GOALS

IDENTIFY the characteristics of successful entrepreneurs.

ASSESS whether you have what it takes to succeed in your own business.

Many people dream of running their own businesses. They would like to become entrepreneurs. Entrepreneurship can be exciting. But running your own business is difficult. In fact, many companies started by entrepreneurs go out of business.

CHARACTERISTICS OF SUCCESSFUL ENTREPRENEURS

Researchers have identified several characteristics that distinguish successful entrepreneurs from those that fail.

1. ***Successful entrepreneurs are independent.*** They want to make their own decisions and do something they enjoy.

2. ***Successful entrepreneurs are self-confident.*** Entrepreneurs make all the decisions. They must have the confidence to make choices alone and bounce back when a decision they made was poor.

3. ***Successful entrepreneurs have determination and perseverance.*** Entrepreneurs persist through hard times until goals are met.

4. ***Successful entrepreneurs are goal-oriented.*** They know what they want, and they are able to focus on achieving it.

5. ***Successful entrepreneurs have a need to achieve and to set high standards for themselves.*** They are constantly setting challenging new goals.

6. ***Successful entrepreneurs are creative.*** They think of new ways to market their businesses, and are always looking for new solutions to problems.

7. ***Successful entrepreneurs are able to act quickly.*** They are not afraid to make quick decisions when necessary, which helps them beat their competitors.

The vast majority of businesses in the United States are small businesses that employ fewer than 20 people.

There are eight million women-owned businesses in the United States. These businesses employ more than 25 percent of American workers and contribute $23 trillion annually to the economy.

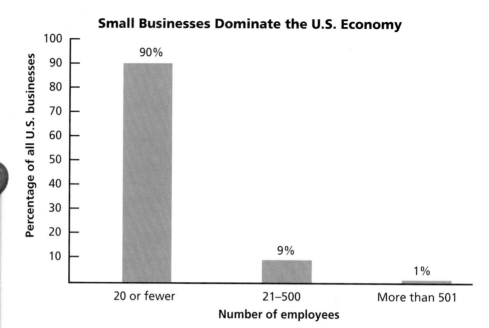

Small Businesses Dominate the U.S. Economy

Percentage of all U.S. businesses (y-axis: 10–100)

- 20 or fewer: 90%
- 21–500: 9%
- More than 501: 1%

Number of employees (x-axis)

Ryan Nelson has many entrepreneurial characteristics. Since he was 14, Ryan played for his high school basketball team. Other boys his height—just 5'8"—would not have enjoyed competing with much taller boys. Ryan accepted that he would have to work harder to win. He needed to be creative in handling the ball. Most of all, he had to believe in himself. He did, and became one of the top players on his team. If Ryan opened his own business, the characteristics he displayed as a ball player might help him succeed.

CHECKPOINT Name three important characteristics of entrepreneurs.

ASSESS YOUR SUITABILITY FOR ENTREPRENEURSHIP

Entrepreneurship is not for everyone. Some people lack the qualities needed to become successful entrepreneurs. Others lack the aptitude needed to run a business. For others, the benefits of entrepreneurship do not outweigh the disadvantages.

To determine if entrepreneurship is right for you, you first need to perform a **self-assessment,** an evaluation of your strengths and weaknesses. You can do this in a number of ways. You can list your strengths and weaknesses on a sheet of paper. You can ask others what they believe your strengths are and where your weaknesses lie. There are also tests you can take to assess your abilities.

Assess Your Interests

Success as an entrepreneur requires a strong commitment to a business and a lot of energy. To be able to commit yourself fully to a business, you should choose a field that interests you and that will provide you with an experience you will enjoy.

HOBBIES AND INTERESTS Many entrepreneurs center a business on an interest or hobby. Tricia Johnson loved reading mysteries and was interested in book collecting. Tricia created Royal Books, a company that buys and sells new, used, and rare books, especially mystery books. Making a list of hobbies and interests can help you decide what business is right for you.

PAST EXPERIENCES Analyzing past experiences and jobs can help you decide on a business you would enjoy owning. Samantha Rodriguez worked as a customer service representative for a large company. Recognizing that she wanted a job where she could spend time outdoors, Sam formed her own bicycle messenger service. She now earns less money than she did as a customer service representative, but she enjoys the work that she is doing.

 **CHECKPOINT** Name key factors that aid an entrepreneur's commitment to a business.

Assess Your Aptitude

Different jobs require different job aptitudes. **Aptitude** is the ability to learn a particular kind of job. Auto mechanics must possess an aptitude for solving mechanical problems. They also must be good with their hands. People who sell insurance must have good interpersonal skills. Answering questions like those in the Job Attributes Checklist can help you identify the kinds of entrepreneurial opportunities that might match your aptitudes and interests.

JOB ATTRIBUTES CHECKLIST

☐ 1. I enjoy working with numbers.
☐ 2. I enjoy working outdoors.
☐ 3. I enjoy working with my hands.
☐ 4. I enjoy selling.
☐ 5. I like working with people.
☐ 6. I prefer to work alone.
☐ 7. I like supervising other people.
☐ 8. I like knowing exactly what it is I am supposed to do.

In Class Activity

As a class, suggest ten possible jobs for each item on the job attributes checklist. Choose two people to write down all the suggestions on the chalkboard or on paper.

CHECKPOINT What does it mean to have an aptitude for something?

NET WORTH

Point your browser to

http://www.ideas-in-action.swep.com

Complete the activity for Chapter 1.

Assess the Advantages of Entrepreneurship

Many people see significant advantages in owning their own businesses.

1. *Entrepreneurs are their own bosses.* Nobody tells an entrepreneur what to do. Entrepreneurs control their own destinies.

2. *Entrepreneurs can choose a business that interests them.* Entrepreneurs work in fields that interest them. Many combine hobbies and interests with business.

3. *Entrepreneurs can be creative.* Entrepreneurs are always implementing creative ideas they come up with themselves.

4. *Entrepreneurs can make lots of money.* Entrepreneurship involves risk. This means that entrepreneurs can make a lot of money if their business succeeds.

Assess the Disadvantages of Entrepreneurship

There are also disadvantages to being an entrepreneur. They include the following:

1. *Entrepreneurship is risky.* All small businesses face the possibility of going out of business or of losing money.

2. *Entrepreneurs face uncertain and irregular incomes.* Entrepreneurs may make money one month and lose money the next.

3. ***Entrepreneurs work long hours.*** Entrepreneurs never really are finished with their jobs. They can work long, irregular hours. They receive no paid days off, and they may have to work evenings and weekends.

4. ***Entrepreneurs must make all decisions by themselves.*** Unless they have partners, entrepreneurs must make all the decisions alone.

 **What are advantages and disadvantages of entrepreneurship?**

YOU CAN SAY THAT AGAIN!
"The thing you have to remember is that you can't blame anyone else for your mistakes."

—Vinita Gupta, creator of Digital Link

THINK CRITICALLY

1. Entrepreneurs can fail even if they are committed and have the characteristics needed to be successful. Why do you think this can happen?

2. Why is it important for entrepreneurs to choose a field that they will enjoy?

3. Do you think the advantages of entrepreneurship outweigh the disadvantages? Why or why not?

MAKE CONNECTIONS

4. **MATH** One in four small companies begun this year will be out of business within the next two years. What percentage is this? Six years from now, nearly two-thirds of all businesses started this year will no longer be open. What percentage is this?

5. **COMMUNICATION** Rank the advantages of entrepreneurship in order of importance to you. The item ranked "1" is most important to you and the item ranked "4" is the least important. Write a paragraph explaining your rankings.

Lesson 1.3

Identify Business Opportunities and Set Goals

Millions of entrepreneurs in the United States start their own businesses. How did they decide what businesses to operate? How can you learn about the business opportunities available to you? What kinds of goals should you set for yourself?

INVESTIGATE OPPORTUNITIES

The library has resources that can help you examine different opportunities. These include books on entrepreneurship, magazines for entrepreneurs, trade magazines for certain businesses, and government publications. *County Business Patterns* is an annual series of publications providing economic profiles of counties, states, and the United States as a whole. Data include employment, payroll, and number of establishments by industry.

The library is not the only place to investigate opportunities. The Small Business Administration (SBA) is an organization that exists to help small businesses and their owners. It publishes information that may be helpful. Talking to entrepreneurs and attending **trade shows,** which are special meetings where companies display their products, can also be beneficial.

Luanda Williams wanted to use her love of sports and dancing to create her own company. She found books and magazine articles at the library that gave her information on various kinds of businesses. She also talked to owners of gymnastic centers, health clubs, and dance studios. Her research helped her come up with the idea of opening a gymnastics and fitness center for children.

CHECKPOINT How can you find out about various business opportunities?

Compare Different Opportunities

Once you find some appealing businesses, you need to identify which have the best chance for success. Now is the time to assess each business idea by asking yourself the following questions:

1. Is there a market in my community for this kind of business? Will people buy my product or service?
2. How much money would it take to start this business? Will I be able to borrow that much money?
3. How many hours a week is it likely to take to run this business? Am I willing to commit that much time?
4. What are the particular risks associated with this business? What is the rate of business failure?
5. Does my background prepare me to run this kind of business? Do most people who own this kind of business have more experience than I do?
6. How much money could I make running this business?

In Class Activity

In small groups, brainstorm a list of resources for finding information about a company that sells automobile accessories.

CHECKPOINT What are some questions you need to ask to help determine if the business opportunities you listed are realistic?

SETTING GOALS

For everything you do in life, you set goals. As an entrepreneur, you will need to set financial and non-financial goals.

FINANCIAL GOALS Financial goals can include how much money you will earn and how quickly you will pay off debts. Make sure your goals are realistic. They should be easily obtainable. If one of your first goals is to make lots of money early on, you almost certainly will be disappointed. It usually takes time for businesses to be financially viable. Most businesses begin operations by borrowing money. These debts usually are paid within one to five years. This means that at first, an entrepreneur may earn less than they would have earned working as an employee.

Setting specific financial goals before starting a business can ensure a business is able to earn the profits you want. Mo Yang wants to start a mail-order business for model trains, planes, and cars. He estimates that after expenses he would earn $9 for each item he sold. At this rate of profit, he would have to sell 3,000 models to meet an income goal of $27,000 a year. This showed Mo that he would have to lower his income goal or find another business idea, because he would probably not be able to sell that many models.

NON-FINANCIAL GOALS

Most people who own their own businesses do so for more than just monetary gain. They are looking for personal satisfaction. They may serve a community need, do something they like, or enjoy the personal independence of being an entrepreneur. You will want to specify what non-financial goals you want to get out of being an entrepreneur.

Mark and Cindy Baird own Outdoor Exploration, a company specializing in

What Went Wrong

Is Entrepreneurship Right for You?

Be Sharp or Fall Flat

Business: Print Here!, San Francisco, CA * Open for business 5 months

Louise was an opera singer, but it wasn't a financially viable career. She earned additional money working at a copy shop in San Francisco. The elderly couple who owned the shop gave flexible hours to employees with aspiring music careers. Sadly, the husband died and the wife decided to sell the business and go to Cincinnati. Louise grabbed the opportunity.

The former owner helped Louise gather financial information and put together a business plan. Louise's uncle co-signed on a bank loan, and she was in business. She modernized the décor of the shop. Louise contacted all the existing customers to assure equal or better service. Sales increased the first two months. But then...

The former owner left town earlier than planned. Then Louise's chief printer quit. With the schedules of her part-time employees, Louise was frantically trying to get large orders out on time. With no formal business training and no management experience, Louise couldn't begin to deal with all these problems, problems even a veteran would find difficult. She ended up selling the business at a $50,000 loss.

Think Critically

1. What characteristics did Louise possess that led her to become an entrepreneur?
2. What circumstances out of Louise's control led to the failure of this business?

backpacking, white-water rafting, and mountaineering trips. The Bairds had a dream to help disabled children experience the outdoors. Last year, they began offering inexpensive outdoor programs to children with Down's syndrome and cerebral palsy. Mark and Cindy experienced an enormous sense of satisfaction in seeing these children enjoy themselves outdoors.

 **CHECKPOINT** Why are financial goals important? Name some non-financial goals an entrepreneur may have.

THINK CRITICALLY

1. Choose a business idea that appeals to you. For this business, answer the six assessment questions listed in this lesson on a sheet of paper. Is this a realistic choice for you? Why or why not?

2. In terms of annual income, what financial goals have you set for yourself for five years after you graduate? What non-financial goals have you set that becoming an entrepreneur can help you achieve? Are financial or non-financial goals more important to you? Why?

MAKE CONNECTIONS

3. **MATH** You live near the beach and have a passion for snorkeling. Your dream is to give snorkeling lessons. You estimate that after expenses, you can earn $10 per lesson. Your income goal is $15,000 per year. How many lessons do you need to give to achieve this goal? Is this goal realistic?

4. **COMMUNICATION** Write a letter to the Small Business Administration. In your letter, indicate your interest in starting a small business. Be specific about the type of business you wish to start. Ask what specific services they provide to people who wish to start this type of business. Give your letter to your teacher.

5. **COMMUNICATION** Make a list of personal non-financial goals you would like to achieve through entrepreneurship. Choose one of these goals. Write an outline for a detailed plan you can follow to achieve this goal.

CHAPTER SUMMARY

Entrepreneurs:
Present
and **Past**

1. An entrepreneur is a person who owns, operates, and takes the risks of a business venture. Entrepreneurs try to identify and meet a need for a product or service.
2. Entrepreneurs come from all types of backgrounds, and they own all kinds of businesses including manufacturing, retailing and service businesses.
3. Throughout U.S. history, there have been many entrepreneurs who have contributed to the economy.
4. Today, more than 6.5 million small companies still contribute greatly to the U.S. economy.
5. Small businesses generally are more creative and willing to take risks than large corporations.

Is Entrepreneurship
Right *for*
You?

6. There are a number of characteristics successful entrepreneurs possess, such as independence and determination.
7. To determine whether entrepreneurship is for you, you will need to assess your strengths, weaknesses, interests, and aptitudes.
8. Advantages of owning your own business include being your own boss and working in a field that interests you. Disadvantages include uncertainty, risk, and the need to work very long hours.

Identify
Business
Opportunities
and **Set Goals**

9. There are many resources at your public library that can help you develop a list of business ideas. Trade shows can also give you valuable information.
10. Once you have identified several opportunities, ask yourself key questions to analyze each option and identify the kind of business that makes the most sense for you.
11. Financial goals should include how much money you want to earn from your business. Setting specific financial goals will help you determine if your business idea will make the profits you want.
12. Nonfinancial goals can include serving a community need, working at something you enjoy, or maintaining the independence that comes with entrepreneurship.

What Do You Know Now?

Read *Build a Business* again. Then answer the questions a second time. How have your responses changed?

VOCABULARY BUILDER

Choose the term that best fits the definition on the right. Write your answers on a separate sheet of paper.

1. People who work for someone else *B*
2. Evaluation of your strengths and weaknesses *E*
3. Special meetings at which companies display their products *F*
4. People who own, operate, and take the risk of a business venture *C*
5. The ability to learn a particular kind of job *A*
6. The process of running a business of one's own *D*

a. aptitude
b. employees
c. entrepreneurs
d. entrepreneurship
e. self-assessment
f. trade show

REVIEW YOUR KNOWLEDGE

7. How are entrepreneurs different from employees? *entrepreners own the business and employees work for them.*

8. Why do some people go into business for themselves? *To make good money*

9. Name all the different kinds of entrepreneurial businesses and describe what each produces.

10. Name two early American entrepreneurs and what they did.

11. Why are entrepreneurial companies important to our economy?

12. What are the seven characteristics of successful entrepreneurs?

13. Why is it important for a beginning entrepreneur to perform a personal assessment?

14. Why should entrepreneurs take past experiences into account when deciding to start their own business?

15. Why is it important to have an aptitude for the business you decide to own?

16. List the four advantages and four disadvantages of entrepreneurship.

17. What resources can you use to research business opportunities?

18. Why should you set both financial and non-financial goals for yourself as an entrepreneur?

APPLY WHAT YOU LEARNED

19. The five categories of privately owned businesses include manufacturing, agricultural, mining and extracting, retailing, wholesaling, and service. In small groups, brainstorm specific industries and companies that belong to each category of business. Make a list of industries and companies for each type. Share your results with the class.

20. In groups, brainstorm a list of jobs that relate to each aptitude given in Lesson 1.2. For each job listed, have members vote on which ones they would like to do. Are there any jobs that received more votes than the others? What are the aptitudes involved in these jobs? Share your results with the class.

THINK CRITICALLY

21. How is entrepreneurship today different from entrepreneurship during colonial times?

22. What is the relationship between interest in and aptitude for a particular field? Can interests and aptitudes be the same? Why or why not?

23. Other than going to the library and attending trade shows, can you think of other ways to investigate business opportunities?

24. Why is setting realistic financial goals important to creating a successful company?

MAKE CONNECTIONS

25. **MATH** Ellen Greenberg loves to make and fly kites. Ellen is planning to open a shop selling custom-made kites. She asks for your advice to help her set financial goals. Ellen estimates that after expenses, she can make a $15 profit on each kite she sells. If her annual income goal is $15,450, how many kites will she have to sell? Is this goal realistic?

26. **RESEARCH** Find information on the life and career of a famous historical entrepreneur. Find out information such as birthplace, the type of business started, and what effect the person had on the economy and history. Is the business still operating? Write a short report about your findings.

27. **COMMUNICATION** For the above Research question, find a creative way to present your findings to the class. Use visual aids, skits, costumes, games, etc.

This Is Your Business Project

This activity will help you identify a business opportunity that may be right for you. Once identified, you will use this business idea for the "This Is Your Business Project" throughout the book.

1. Divide a sheet of paper into two columns. In the first column list all your interests. In the second column, list business ideas that relate to each interest.

2. Make a list of your strengths and weaknesses. Compare this list with your list of business opportunities. For which business ideas would your strengths most apply? For which business ideas would your weaknesses hurt the most? Based on your strengths and weaknesses, cross out those business ideas that no longer seem suitable for you.

3. Assess your aptitude, using the checklist in Lesson 1.2. Put a checkmark next to the business opportunities that relate to your aptitudes.

4. For the business opportunities remaining on your list, assess the advantages and disadvantages of each. Cross out any whose disadvantages outweigh its advantages.

5. Using the library or Internet, find sources of information that relate to the business opportunities that remain on your list. Make a list of these sources. Locate at least one of these sources for each business opportunity. For each source, write a sentence stating the type of information that you can obtain from it. On your list, cross out business opportunities for which you could not find any information.

6. Choose one of the business opportunities remaining on your list. Answer the six Compare Different Opportunities questions based on this business opportunity.

7. Set personal financial goals for a five-year period based on the business opportunity you chose. Be realistic. Assume you will need to borrow money to get started. Estimate both your income and expenses to determine the amount of profit you can expect to make. Next, set non-financial goals you hope to achieve with this business. Be sure to include specific activities for each goal.

Chapter 2

WHAT SKILLS DO ENTREPRENEURS NEED?

LESSONS

2.1 **Communication Skills**
2.2 **Math Skills**
2.3 **Problem-Solving Skills**

BUILD A BUSINESS

The Custom Car Center

"You know, Sam, I think we're ready to get our car customization business going," Philip said one day at lunch.

"Yeah," Sam replied, "I think we've talked about it long enough. We need to get moving. I'm ready to be my own boss."

"Yesterday, I talked to a man with a garage for lease up the street," Philip said.

"Great! What did you find out?"

"Well, we talked about how much the rent would be, and he said that he would need the names of some references before we could sign a lease."

"I've got some people in mind, like my former business teacher. I know she would be glad to write a reference for me." Sam thought for a moment and asked, "Do you remember how to write a business letter?"

"I think we'd better look it up in a reference book," Philip answered. "If our letters aren't written correctly, we won't make a good impression. We want people to see that we are well prepared and know what we are doing. After we get our references for the lease, then we need to go to the bank to get a loan for our business."

"I know," Sam replied, "And before we go, we need a well-written business plan. The business plan and the presentation we do at the bank will be very important when the bank is deciding on our loan. We've got to be able to share our vision both orally and in written form if we want others to buy into it. I'm also glad we are good at math. We'll have to do a lot of calculations for our business plan. We sure don't want to make any mistakes," Sam cautioned.

"You're right," said Philip. "If the loan officer doesn't think we can work with money, there's no way the bank will loan us any. Plus, we'll be using math for lots of other things once we get our business going. You know, it's kind of funny, all of these things our teachers stressed in school turned out to be really important."

"They sure have," agreed Sam. "Communication and math skills are really important to entrepreneurs. If we did not have good basic skills, we couldn't get this business going."

"You know, Sam," Philip said, "as we get further into this we are going to have to make a lot of decisions about our business. It is important that we think things through carefully and make good decisions. If we don't, our 'Grand Opening' sign could change very quickly to a 'Going Out of Business' sign."

"You're so right!" Sam concluded. "We'll have to devise a decision-making method so we make the right choices for our business."

What Do You Know?

1. Why do you think a bank or other potential investors are concerned about how a business plan is written?
2. List all of the ways that math might be used by a business.
3. How would you go about making an important decision?

Communication *Skills*

Businesspeople communicate by writing letters and memos, talking on the telephone, and meeting with customers, suppliers, bankers, employees, and others. To succeed as an entrepreneur, you will need to develop your writing, speaking, and listening skills because you will use them every day.

WRITING SKILLS

As an entrepreneur, you will frequently communicate in writing with customers, suppliers, and employees, among others. To do so effectively, you will need to develop your business writing skills. Good business writing communicates ideas clearly. It also gets results by being positive and persuasive, and by convincing readers that they should accept what the writer is communicating.

Effective Business Letters

The most common form of business writing is the business letter. You might write letters to solicit business, respond to customer questions, negotiate purchases, or deal with suppliers. Writing a business letter is different from writing a letter to a friend. A certain level of formality is necessary, and certain standards must be respected. That doesn't mean business writing should be difficult to understand. If it is not understandable, the desired result may not happen. Good business writing is clear. It is concise and coherent, and it gets its message across simply and positively.

Certain basic rules should be followed in writing business letters.

1. *Key all formal correspondence.* Send handwritten letters only when they are intended as personal letters.
2. *Be sure to spell all names correctly and have the correct address.* No matter how well written your letter is, its effect will be dramatically reduced if you misspell the name of the person to whom you are writing or refer to his or her company by the wrong name. Addressing a letter incorrectly may cause it to arrive late or to be returned.

3. ***Always date your business correspondence.*** It may be necessary to refer to this date at a later time.

4. ***Use names and titles appropriately.*** Use the person's first name if you know him or her well. If you do not know the person or the letter is very formal, use the person's last name, along with the appropriate title (Dr., Mr., Mrs., Ms., or Miss).

5. ***Be direct and positive.*** Always maintain a positive tone and portray your business in an optimistic light, even if your letter contains bad news.

6. ***Be persuasive and specific.*** Make sure the action or result you want from the reader is clear. Use non-threatening language that will persuade the reader why this action or result is the most desirable.

7. ***Avoid using fancy language.*** Avoid showy phrases that you would not use while speaking. Use straightforward language that says exactly what you mean.

8. ***Be polite.*** Deal with complaints in a businesslike fashion. Don't whine or express outrage, and never become abusive or insulting. Be especially polite in writing rejection or bad news letters.

Did You Know?

Today, 25 percent of the students enrolled at America's top business schools are from foreign countries.

Andrews Electronics
10 E. 34th Street • Baltimore, MD 21218

April 11, 20—

Ms. Jane Cartright
6028 Sareva Drive
Baltimore, MD 21209

Dear Ms. Cartright

It was a pleasure discussing the assistant manager position with you last week. I enjoyed meeting you and was impressed by your enthusiasm for sales.

As you know, our products are highly technical, and selling them requires considerable product knowledge. Although your interpersonal skills seem outstanding and I have confidence that with time you could learn our line and become a successful salesperson, I need someone who can begin selling our products immediately. I have therefore decided to offer the position to another candidate.

Thank you again for giving me the opportunity to meet you. I wish you the best of luck in finding a position you will enjoy.

Sincerely

Mark A. Andrews

Mark A. Andrews
President

Sample business letter

9. *Use an appropriate closing.* There are many ways to close a letter. Make sure your close corresponds to the content of the letter you have written. If you have written a letter to a supplier complaining about poor service, do not use "With warmest regards."

Sincerely	Cordially
Sincerely yours	Cordially yours

Different ways to close a business letter

10. *Proofread for spelling and grammatical errors.* Even the most persuasive and positive letter can be ruined by a single mistake that you fail to correct.

Effective Business Memos

A **memorandum** is a short written form of business communication that has a set format. *Memo* is short for memorandum. The format of a memo contains who the memo is for, who it is from, the date, and the subject of the memo. Anyone who does business for or with a company, including suppliers and clients, can get memos. An **interoffice memo** is a memo from one person in a company to another. Interoffice memos can be written to one employee, to a group of employees, or to everyone in the company. They can be hand-delivered, e-mailed, sent by interoffice mail, or faxed.

In Class Activity

In small groups, brainstorm at least 20 situations for which a business letter is the appropriate form of communication, and 20 for which a memo is the best form of communication.

MEMORANDUM

To: All Employees
From: Jessica Myers
Date: January 13, 20—
Re: December Sales

Thanks to all of you for making December the best month in our company's history. I know how hard all of you worked during the busy holiday season and want you to know just how much I appreciate your efforts. Thank you all for a job well done!

Sample business memo

Memos, like business letters, should be clear, concise, persuasive, and positive. Memos are used for many purposes, such as communicating company policies and procedures, assigning tasks, or motivating staff. They are also used to congratulate employees or to announce changes in an employee's status.

 **What are some of the characteristics of good business writing?**

SPEAKING SKILLS

Much of your communication as a business owner will be conducted verbally either over the telephone or face-to-face. How you present yourself will have a big impact on the people with whom you deal.

Telephone Conversations

Business transactions can be made over the telephone. Use the following tips to make the most of your telephone conversations.

1. *Speak clearly, and talk directly into the receiver.*
2. *Be cheerful.* Everyone prefers to deal with a happy person rather than with someone who is sad or angry.
3. *Always speak politely.* Do not use improper language. Be respectful, and don't interrupt.
4. *Think about what you are going to say before you make a call.* Write down the questions you want to ask or the points you want to make. Consult your notes as you are talking to make sure you cover everything.
5. *Take notes.* You may forget important details unless you write them down.

 **Give three important tips you should keep in mind when conducting a business conversation on the telephone.**

Meetings with Customers and Suppliers

Some of the communication you have as an entrepreneur will be face-to-face rather than in writing or on the telephone. Meetings can be formal occasions, with agendas and handouts for all attendees. They can also be informal ways to discuss issues and keep everyone informed. How can you make the most of your personal contacts with customers and others?

1. *Shake hands and make eye contact with the person you are meeting.* If you know the person's name, use it.

2. *Show an interest in what the other person is saying.* Ask questions or provide appropriate responses to show that you are listening carefully and that you care about what the other person is telling you.

3. *Speak clearly.* Do not cover your mouth when you talk, and speak loud enough to be heard easily.

4. *Do not be rushed or anxious to be somewhere else.* If you do not have the time to meet with the person, apologize for having another commitment and schedule another time to meet.

5. *Thank the person at the end of the meeting.* Express your interest in seeing the person again.

 **CHECKPOINT** Give three important tips you should keep in mind when conducting a business meeting.

LISTENING SKILLS

Problems in business often occur because people fail to listen to each other. Ariel Martin, the owner of a neighborhood bakery, did not listen to her employees when they asked for an air conditioner in the back room. Ariel was preoccupied with other matters and failed to listen to their request. Angry over their working conditions, all four of her bakers walked off their jobs one afternoon. Ariel had to close the shop temporarily and deal with the conflict.

As a business owner, you will need to listen carefully to your employees. You also need to listen to bankers, suppliers, customers, and anyone else who may impact your business. What can you do to improve your listening skills?

1. ***Focus your attention on the person who is speaking.*** Concentrate exclusively on what the person is saying.
2. ***Think about and try to understand what the other person is saying.*** Resist the temptation to interrupt.
3. ***Ask questions to make sure you understand what the person is saying.***
4. ***Take notes to confirm what you are hearing.***

 Why is it important for entrepreneurs to listen carefully?

THINK CRITICALLY

1. How do writing a formal business letter and writing a letter to a friend differ? What elements in a business letter would not appear in the letter to your friend?

2. How is speaking with customers and suppliers on the telephone similar to speaking with them face-to-face? How is it different? Is it necessary to have both types of communication? Why or why not?

3. Why is it important for an entrepreneur to listen to employees? Why is it important to listen to customers?

MAKE CONNECTIONS

4. COMMUNICATION You own a shop that sells comic books. Write a business letter to your main supplier, a comic book wholesaler. Tell the supplier that you have not received the shipment you ordered of the most recent edition of a popular comic. Be sure to follow the basic rules for writing business letters. Make up names for your business and your supplier's business.

5. COMMUNICATION As the owner of a large manufacturing company, write a memo to all employees communicating a change in your vacation policy. In your memo state what the policy has been and what it will now be.

Math *Skills*

$\mathbf{Y}$ ou need a solid command of basic math skills to run a successful business. You should know how to use addition, subtraction, multiplication, and division. You also should know how to calculate simple averages and percentages.

BASIC MATH SKILLS

The basic skills of adding, subtracting, multiplying, and dividing are important in business.

Addition and Subtraction

Addition and subtraction skills are essential to running a business. Maria Ortega is the owner of Eastern Pharmacy. Maria's pharmacy fills prescriptions and sells other items like magazines, candy, greeting cards, and cosmetics. Last year, category 1, sales of prescription drugs totaled $135,000, category 2, sales of nonprescription drugs and related items totaled $114,000, and category 3, sales of magazines and newspapers totaled $15,000. Total sales for Eastern Pharmacy were $315,000. Maria keeps separate sales figures for only these three categories, but she would like to know what her total sales of other items were. Some of Maria's uncategorized items include candy, greeting cards, and grocery items.

Maria adds sales for the three categories for which she has data. This gives her the total category sales.

Category 1 + Category 2 + Category 3 = Total category sales
$135,000 + $114,000 + $15,000 = $264,000

The difference between the total sales and the total category sales represents the sales of items not in the categories. Maria now knows the total sales for all the items in her pharmacy that she does not categorize.

Total sales − Total category sales = Sales of non-categorized items
$315,000 − $264,000   = $51,000

Maria also uses subtraction to determine her profits for the year. Maria's total sales last year were $315,000 and her expenses were $266,000. Maria subtracts her expenses from her sales to find her profit, $49,000.

Total sales − Expenses = Profit
$315,000 − $266,000 = $49,000

Multiplication

Multiplication is used to solve a variety of business problems, such as figuring out how much profit is earned. Suppose Eastern Pharmacy sells 27 jars of hand cream a month, with a profit of $1.75 on every jar. How much profit does the store earn on hand cream every year?

Maria first needs to figure how many jars of hand cream she sells a year by multiplying the sales each month by the number of months.

Monthly sales × Months in a year = Jars sold a year
    27   ×   12   =   324

Then she must multiply the profit per jar by the number of jars sold.

Profit per jar × Jars sold in a year = Yearly profit
   $1.75   ×   324   = $567

The store earns $567 on hand cream every year.

Averages Using Division

Calculating an average involves adding all of the relevant data and dividing this sum by the number of data. If Maria sells 12 razors one month, 22 the next, and 14 the next, what is the average number of razors sold each month over the three-month period?

Add the sales for all three months.

Month 1 sales + Month 2 sales + Month 3 sales = Total sales
     12   +   22   +   14   =   48

Then divide the total sales by the number of months to find the average number of razors sold each month.

Sales total ÷ Number of months razors sold = Average
     48   ÷   3   =   16

On average, 16 razors were sold each month.

 **CHECKPOINT** **Give an example of when you might use addition, subtraction, or multiplication in business.**

As an entrepreneur, you will make sales transactions every day. The sales transactions you will deal with are purchase orders, invoices, sales tax, and sales slips.

Purchase Orders and Invoices

Purchase orders are used whenever goods or services are sold. They are a record of the fact that a buyer has placed an order with a company. They include information such as:

- the addresses of both the buyer and seller
- a purchase order number
- the date of the transaction
- a listing of each item purchased, the quantity of each item purchased, the cost of each item, and a total item cost
- the total amount due

What Went Wrong

Communication Problems

Let's Be Perfectly Franc

Business: Villette Renoir, Loire Valley, France * Never opened for business

John, Melodi, Don, and Arlene vacationed in the French countryside one summer. While exploring one day, Melodi and Arlene found a small mansion with a sign on the front gate: "for sale—built 1703." Converting from French francs, the printed price was $32,000.

By the end of a duck l'orange dinner, the women had the plans for an inn sketched out. Their husbands committed to explore the property with them the next morning. By lunch, the new entrepreneurs had agreed that it would probably cost about $20,000 to renovate. But once completed, "Villette Renoir" would be a nice income-producing rental property, as well as their own vacation home. Each couple put up $25,000. They consulted an attorney and started the legal paperwork.

Sacre bleu! Who would have known the international phone calls and shipping charges would be so high? Plus, there were renovation problems. Workers were hard to find when renova-tions started because everyone was harvesting grapes. Tools bought in the United States did not work in France because of the different electricity currents. Installing new wiring and plumbing through stone proved almost impossible.

All in all, the unplanned airfares and renovation costs easily doubled their original budget. What's more, Melodi wanted to furnish the home with antiques, while Arlene's taste ran more modern. They argued about every decision and then stopped talking to each other altogether. The project was abandoned, and three months later, sold at a substantial loss.

Think Critically

1. What type of communication problems led to the Villette Renoir's failure?
2. What problem-solving method were Melodi and Arlene unable to conduct due to their personality differences?

When determining the total item cost, the quantity of the item being ordered should be multiplied by the unit cost of the item.

Quantity × Unit cost = Amount due
5 × $4.99 = $23.96

Sales Tax

Retail sales transactions involve sales tax, which is a federal, state, or local government tax charged on goods. Sales tax varies from state to state, and may even vary from city to city. You'll need to find out how much sales tax to charge your customers because you will be fined if you do not pay the government this tax. Sales tax is a percentage and is calculated using the total price of an item being purchased. The amount of sales tax should be added to the purchase price to determine the total selling price. Shipping and delivery charges should not have sales tax applied to them.

Price of purchase × Tax rate = Amount of sales tax
$23.92 × 0.07 = $1.67

Price of purchase + Amount of sales tax = Total sales charge
$23.92 + $1.67 = $25.59

NET WORTH

Point your browser to

http://www.ideas-in-action.swep.com

Complete the activity for Chapter 2.

Sales Slips

You will complete sales slips for two kinds of sales transactions: cash sales and credit card sales. For cash sales, the total amount due is calculated in the same way as on a purchase order or invoice. Eva Sanchez owns Adventure World, a retail store that sells sporting and outdoor equipment. She fills out a form for all of her cash sales.

Credit card sales are very similar to cash sales, but additional information, such as a credit card number and expiration date, is also

Cash Sales Slip for Adventure World					
Stock No.	Qty.	Description		Unit Cost	Total
784	2	Skateboard		$32.50	$65.00
912	1	Helmet		$15.00	$15.00
				Subtotal	$80.00
				Sales Tax	$4.80
				Total	**$84.80**

recorded. Credit card sales are not as profitable to businesses as cash sales. Whenever a customer uses a credit card to pay for a purchase, a fee is assessed to the merchant. The bank that issues the credit card to the customer assesses this fee to the merchant because they are acting as the collection agent for the merchant.

Managing a Cash Drawer

Today most businesses use electronic cash registers to generate sales slips. The totals are automatically added up by a machine for each sales transaction. But you still need to verify the beginning cash amounts and balance the cash drawer at the end of the day.

To verify the starting cash in the cash drawer, you should manually count the money and record each amount on a form or piece of paper. Some businesses always begin with a set amount in their cash drawer, such as $50.00.

BALANCING THE CASH DRAWER When you balance the cash drawer, you need to add up all your receipts: paper money, checks, and credit slips. Subtract any cash refunds that were given during the day. Finally subtract the amount of cash you started with to determine your actual receipts for the day. The total receipts you calculate should match the

Cash	$348.62
Checks	$154.20
+ Credit sales	$218.98
Total receipts	$721.80
− Refunds	$ 21.47
Adjusted receipts	$700.33
− Opening cash	$ 50.00
Actual receipts	$650.33

register tape. If it doesn't, you need to find out where the mistake was made.

CHECKPOINT What are the four types of sales transactions? Describe how you balance a cash drawer.

PERCENTAGES

Percent calculations are used in many business applications. They are particularly important in calculating growth rates, interest payments, and markups and markdowns. Remember that percent means per hundred.

Working with percents usually requires converting the percents to decimals. To convert a percent to a decimal, remember that 100% in decimal form is 1.00.

To convert a percent to a decimal, move the decimal point two places to the left. Thus, 14% is 0.14 in decimal form, and 1% is 0.01 in decimal form.

To convert a decimal to a percent, move the decimal point two places to the right. So, 0.263 is 26.3%.

Remember when you need to round, round up numbers more than 5 and round down numbers less than 5. For example, round 0.66 to 0.7 and 0.64 to 0.6.

Growth Rates

To calculate sales growth, sales for one period are compared with sales in a different period. Maria wants to know how sales at her pharmacy business grew in August, when sales reached $26,710. Comparing August sales with July sales of $26,533, Maria finds that sales increased $177.

August sales − July sales = August increase
$26,710   − $26,533   = $177

Growth rates are usually given in percents. To determine what percentage increase $177 represents, Maria divides the dollar increase in August by total sales in July. The more than one-half percent increase represents the rate of sales growth in August.

August increase ÷ July sales = Percent increase
$177   ÷ $26,533 = 0.00667, or 0.7%

EASTERN PHARMACY SALES OVER PAST SIX MONTHS		
Month	Sales	Monthly Growth
July	$26,533	—
August	26,710	0.7%
September	26,977	1.0%
October	27,397	1.6%
November	27,600	0.7%
December	28,202	2.1%
TOTAL	$163,419	6.1%

AVERAGE MONTHLY GROWTH RATE To determine the average monthly growth rate, Maria must obtain an average using the total monthly growth and the number of months for which Maria has data.

Total monthly growth ÷ Number of months = Average monthly growth
0.061   ÷   5   =   0.0122, or 1.2%

USING MATH TO PROJECT SALES Maria uses the average monthly growth to project sales into the next year. She assumes that sales will continue to grow at the rate of 1.2% per month. She uses this growth rate to create sales projections for the next six months. She multiplies each month's sales by the growth rate to determine the projected sales increase.

Dec. sales × Growth rate = Projected Jan. increase
$28,202 ×   0.012   = $338

PROJECTED EASTERN PHARMACY SALES OVER NEXT SIX MONTHS	
Month	Sales
January	$28,540
February	28,882
March	29,229
April	29,580
May	29,935
June	30,294

Then she adds the increase to the December sales to determine the actual dollar amount she should make in January.

Dec. sales + Projected Jan. increase = Jan. projection
$28,202 + $338   = $28,540

Maria could also have calculated January sales directly. If January sales are projected to grow by 1.2%, then sales that month will be 101.2% as great as sales in December.

$28,202 × 1.012 = $28,540

 **Assuming the growth rate of 0.012, what will Eastern Pharmacy's sales be next December?**

Interest Payments

You will probably need to borrow money to start your business, and you will pay interest on that money. **Interest** is an amount charged for borrowing money. It is important to understand how interest payments are calculated.

If you take out a $25,000 loan from your local bank, the **principal** is the amount of money borrowed in a loan. Your loan agreement will indicate the **rate of interest,** or the percent that is the basis for interest earned or paid. The agreement will also indicate the **term** of the loan, or the number of years for which a loan is extended. How much simple interest will you pay on the loan if your rate of interest is 9.5% and your term is five years? Multiply the loan amount by the rate of interest to find the amount of simple interest.

Loan amount × Rate of interest = Interest paid
$25,000   ×   0.095   = $2,375

Suppose you borrowed the $25,000 for 5 years and only paid the interest. Then you would pay $2,375 in interest each year, or a total of $11,875 in interest.

Interest each year × Number of years = Total interest
$2,375   ×   5   = $11,875

 **CHECKPOINT** How much simple interest would you pay a year on a $30,000 loan at a rate of 8.25%?

Markups and Markdowns

A **markup** is an amount added to the cost price to determine the sales price. Markups allow you to cover expenses and earn a profit. A **markdown** is an amount deducted from the retail price to determine the sales price.

In Class Activity

In small groups, brainstorm a list of 10 items that might be sold in a media store. Assign a unit cost to each item. You will need a markup of 45 percent to cover your expenses and make a profit. What will be the price of each item to customers? Share and explain your results with the class.

CALCULATING MARKUPS You own an office supply store that sells desk lamps. You purchase the lamps for $14.00 each. You estimate that to cover your expenses and make a profit, you need to add a markup of 35 percent.

$14 × 0.35 = $4.90

Add the markup amount to your cost to get the selling price.

$14.00 + $4.90 = $18.90

CALCULATING MARKDOWNS To unload last year's file cabinets, which sold for $149.95, you decide to reduce their price to just $99.95 each. How large a percentage markdown are you offering? First, calculate the difference between the original price and the sale price.

$149.95 − $99.95 = $50.00

Then calculate what percentage that difference represents of the original price.

$50.00 ÷ $149.95 = 0.33

The result represents the percentage markdown of 33 percent.

Discounts

A **discount** is a reduction in the retail or wholesale price of a product or service. You may give employees discounts as incentives for working for you. You might get a discount if you buy a large number of items from a company that supplies your business. Calculating a discount is similar to calculating a markdown.

Retail price × Discount percent = Amount of discount
$54.99   ×   0.15   = $8.25

CHECKPOINT How much of a markup is there on an item that you purchase for $45 and sell for $54?

THINK CRITICALLY

1. How do you think multiplication and division are used in determining employee wages? Give specific examples in your answer.

2. Make a list of five ways averages can be used in business. Give a specific example for each item on your list.

3. What factors should you consider in calculating the percentage markdown for "sale" items you are offering? Why is it important to carefully consider these factors?

MAKE CONNECTIONS

4. MATH You are preparing a purchase order for a customer who has ordered 5 tape dispensers, 2 pairs of scissors, and 1 telephone. The tape dispensers are $2.35 a piece, the scissors $4.90 each, and the telephone is priced at $25.99. You must charge 5 percent sales tax. What is the total of the customer's order? If you give the customer a discount of 15 percent, what is the total of the order?

5. MATH Total sales for each month last year for your catering business averaged $13,500. Average total monthly sales so far this year are $15,200. If you maintain this average, what will be the percentage growth in sales from last year to this year? Project your average total sales per month for next year based on this percentage growth.

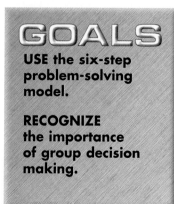

Problem-Solving *Skills*

Once you own your own business, you will have to make decisions and solve problems every day. Many entrepreneurs make decisions casually or base them on intuition. As a result, their decisions are based on faulty assumptions or illogical thinking. The best entrepreneurs use formal problem-solving mechanisms to gather information and evaluate different options.

For many kinds of problems, you will need to make decisions alone. For other kinds of decisions, however, involving other people in the company in brainstorming and consensus-building techniques can make the most of group decision making.

USE A PROBLEM-SOLVING PROCESS

A formal problem-solving model helps business people solve problems in a logical manner. The model consists of six steps: defining the problem, gathering information, identifying various solutions, evaluating the alternatives and selecting the best option, taking action, and evaluating the action taken.

Define the Problem

Before you can solve a problem, you need to diagnose it. Write down what the problem is and why it is a problem. Try to quantify the problem, too. For example, your store may be out of stock 14 times a month, costing you a total of $102 a month in lost revenue. Quantifying the problem helps you figure out how much it is worth to you to correct it.

Will Peterson knows what his problem is: his employees are using the photocopier for their personal use. Despite the sign above the machine indicating that it is to be used for business only, Will constantly sees employees photocopying everything from recipes to cartoons. Will is concerned about the problem for a couple of reasons. First, he feels that allowing employees to use company time to photocopy personal items takes them away from their work

and reduces productivity. Second, the personal photo-copying is costing Will about $80 a month in paper, toner, and wear on his photocopier.

Gather Information

Once the problem has been defined, you need to gather information that could help solve the problem. Relevant information may be obtained from company records, industry data, and interviews with customers, suppliers, and employees.

Will needed to identify whether all or just a few of his employees ignored the rules. He found that 3 of his 13 employees accounted for almost all of the personal photocopying. He also talked to other business owners to see if they had similar problems and how they handled them.

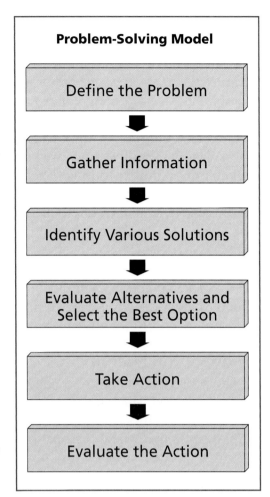

Problem-Solving Model

Define the Problem

Gather Information

Identify Various Solutions

Evaluate Alternatives and Select the Best Option

Take Action

Evaluate the Action

Identify Various Solutions

Most problems can be solved in various ways. Identify all possibilities before you settle on a particular solution. Will came up with several possible solutions to his problem.

1. Live with the problem and absorb the cost.
2. Reprimand problem employees and reinforce that the photocopier is to be used for business only.
3. Ask a manager to watch the photocopier and to report to him when an employee uses the machine inappropriately.
4. Allow the photocopier to be used for personal use after hours for a minimal charge and remind employees that no personal photocopying is permitted during business hours.

YOU CAN SAY THAT AGAIN!

"I felt there was a place for fresh hamburgers made just the way the customer wants....This philosophy sets us apart...and helped us to grow to 5,000 restaurants worldwide."

—*Dave Thomas, founder of Wendy's Old Fashioned Hamburgers Restaurants*

Evaluate Alternatives and Select the Best Option

The decision maker next needs to evaluate the alternatives to determine the best solution. In some cases, it may be possible to quantify the costs and benefits of each alternative. In other cases, quantifying each alternative may not be possible, and the decision maker may simply have to rank each alternative.

Will ranked option 3 the lowest, since he did not want any of his managers spending time away from other important duties. He ranked option 2 next to lowest because he did not want to upset his employees. He ranked option 1 second, because he wanted to fix the problem. Will decided option 4 was the best solution.

Take Action

Once you have selected the best solution to the problem, you need to take an action to implement it. Will decided to send out a memo to all of his employees, letting them know of the new company policy on photocopying.

Evaluate the Action

The problem-solving process is not complete until you have evaluated your action, since even a well thought out solution may not work. Will's solution seemed to solve the problem. For the most part, employees limited their personal photocopying to after the close of business. Personal usage of the photocopier dropped by 75 percent.

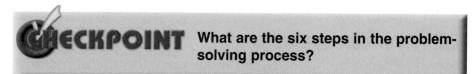

CHECKPOINT What are the six steps in the problem-solving process?

GROUP PROBLEM SOLVING

The problem-solving process just described assumes that you have to solve a problem alone. As a business owner, you will make many decisions by yourself. Sometimes, however, you may want to include employees in the problem-solving process. What kinds of problems call for group problem solving? What techniques can you use to make the most effective use of groups?

Brainstorming

Brainstorming is a creative group problem-solving technique that involves generating a large number of fresh ideas. In a brainstorming session, several people gather in a room to discuss a particular problem. The meeting is informal, and everyone is encouraged to volunteer possible solutions. A designated person writes down all of the ideas suggested. The person who called the meeting usually serves as the group moderator. The moderator maintains order during the brainstorming session, making sure that everyone has a chance to be heard. The moderator also makes sure the group does not stray too far from the problem being examined.

Ideas are not analyzed or critiqued at a brainstorming session. Instead, participants simply share creative ideas, regardless of how practical or impractical they may be. Following the brainstorming session, all of the ideas are carefully evaluated, and a list of ideas that are practical to implement is prepared.

Entrepreneurs often ask their employees to brainstorm when a new opportunity presents itself or a problem seems to demand new ideas. Kris Carpenter asked her employees to brainstorm when she decided to have a website created for her catering company, Bon Appetit. Together her four employees came up with 94 different items they felt could be used on the company's home page. After the brainstorming session, Kris examined each idea carefully, eventually reducing the list to 30 items.

Consensus-Based Decision Making

Consensus is agreement among a group of people. Consensus-based decision making is an effective way of solving problems when different groups in an organization are affected. Consensus building can be used to prevent and resolve conflicts. It can also be used to

Entrepreneurial Timeline

| 1930 | 1940 | 1950 | 1960 |

Small Engines, Huge Profits

In the late 1940s, entrepreneurship opportunities were plentiful for people living in Japan. One of the most notable entrepreneurs of that time was Soichiro Honda, who founded Honda Motors. He was one of the first people to see there was a need for inexpensive, reliable transportation in his country. Soichiro began producing a new kind of vehicle, one that used less gasoline and was affordable. His first venture was affixing war surplus engines to bicycles so they could be motorized. Then, in 1949, Honda Motors produced its first motorcycle, called the Dream D-Type. One motorcycle became many, and in 1952 Soichiro won an award for superior mini-size engine development. His cycles were exported and sold in the United States starting in 1959. Honda Motors is now a multimillion dollar company, and one of the world's foremost producers of motorcycles, automobiles, and scooters.

build trust among employees and to bring together different groups within a company. It can bridge communication problems and help employees accept changes they may see as threatening.

The aim of consensus building is to find a way of resolving a problem that is acceptable to all of the people involved. The process tries to eliminate anger and hostility by allowing employees with conflicting opinions to meet in an atmosphere of mutual respect.

Pete McWilliams used consensus building to smooth tensions between the graphic artists and the writers at his advertising agency, Image Plus. According to the artists, copywriters routinely rewrote copy after the artists had completed their work, sometimes causing them to spend hours recreating the designs. The artists resented the fact that the writers seemed indifferent to the effect of their changes on their workload. They wanted Pete to do something about it. The writers saw the problem a little differently. They admitted to making changes late in the process but claimed that the need for some of the changes was often not apparent earlier on. Through a consensus-building session, the writers agreed to spend more time checking their copy before submitting it to the art department. The artists gained an understanding of the importance of perfecting the ad copy, even if it meant reworking a design. Both sides agreed to try to improve the way they worked. Pete agreed to consider hiring a part-time artist if the writers' efforts did not succeed in reducing the workload in the art department.

 **CHECKPOINT** How does brainstorming differ from consensus building?

THINK CRITICALLY

1. What are some other benefits to using a formal problem-solving method that are not given in the text?

2. Must the six steps in the problem-solving model be performed in the order described? Why or why not?

3. What specific types of decisions could employees help with during group problem-solving sessions? Are there any disadvantages to involving employees in problem solving? If so, what are they?

MAKE CONNECTIONS

4. MATH In the Identify Various Solutions stage of the problem-solving model, you list a variety of possible solutions to a problem. For the four options listed in the text, assign a percentage weight to each. Give the decimal equivalent for each percentage. What must the decimal value of the four options total?

5. COMMUNICATION Write a letter to a local bank to find the current interest rate on small business loans. Use the company you selected in This Is Your Business Project and determine a specific use for the money. Apply the basic rules for drafting business letters described earlier in this chapter.

6. PROBLEM SOLVING You own a successful shop that buys, sells, and services bicycles. In January, the owner of the building you now lease tells you that she has found a buyer for the property and plans to sell it in six months. Using the six-step problem-solving model, develop a plan for how to proceed.

Review

CHAPTER SUMMARY

Communication Skills

1. Communication skills include the ability to write effective business letters and memorandums. There are certain basic rules you should follow while writing letters or memos.
2. Communication skills also include the ability to speak well on the telephone and face to face.
3. Listening is a key communication skill for entrepreneurs. It is often more important than speaking.
4. All good business communication is clear, positive, and persuasive. It should ask for a clear result, and be persuasive in getting that result.

Math Skills

5. Basic computational skills, including addition, subtraction, multiplication, and division, are necessary for business.
6. Taking averages, calculating percentages, and determining growth rates are everyday business activities.
7. Sales transactions are a part of all businesses. Managing a cash drawer is also an important responsibility.
8. Interest rates on loans are also important to understand as an entrepreneur.

Problem-Solving Skills

9. Many entrepreneurs use a problem-solving model to help them solve problems in a logical manner. The model consists of six steps: defining the problem, gathering information, identifying various solutions, evaluating alternatives and selecting the best option, taking action, and evaluating the action taken.
10. Group problem-solving techniques include brainstorming and consensus building.
11. Brainstorming consists of generating a large number of fresh ideas from a group of people. Consensus building involves trying to get all sides to agree on a solution to a problem.

What Do You Know Now?

Read *Build a Business* again. Then answer the questions a second time. How have your responses changed?

VOCABULARY BUILDER

Choose the term that best fits the definition on the right. Write your answers on a separate sheet of paper.

1. The percent that is the basis for interest earned or paid.
2. A memo from one person in a company to another
3. An agreement among a group of people
4. An amount added to the cost price to determine the sales price
5. A creative group problem-solving technique that involves generating a large number of fresh ideas
6. Amount of money borrowed in a loan
7. An amount deducted from the retail price to determine the sales price
8. Number of years for which a loan is extended
9. A short written form of business communication that has a set format
10. An amount charged for borrowing money

a. brainstorming
b. consensus
c. discount
d. interest
e. interoffice memo
f. markdown
g. markup
h. memorandum
i. principal
j. rate of interest
k. term

REVIEW YOUR KNOWLEDGE

11. Which form of written communication is best suited to communicating with customers and suppliers? Which form is best suited to communicating with employees?

12. Why is it important to use a customer's name when you meet?

13. What four actions can you take to improve your listening skills?

14. What are four computational skills you will need to know to operate your business? Give an example application for each of these skills.

15. How do you calculate an average?

16. What is a disadvantage of credit card sales?

17. List at least three business applications for which percentages are used.

18. What are the six steps in the formal problem-solving model?

19. Why is brainstorming beneficial?

20. What does consensus building aim to do?

APPLY WHAT YOU LEARNED

21. You have just opened a car wash. Write a business letter to announce the opening. Next, write a letter to three people you have interviewed and wish to hire, offering them a specific position. Then write a memo to your new employees explaining the weekly work schedule you plan to follow.

22. You need to order supplies for your car wash and plan to interview suppliers by telephone. Make a list of questions to ask each supplier and the points you want to make in your conversation.

23. Monthly sales for your car wash for the first year were as shown.

Jan. $2,750	Apr. $2,890	Jul. $2,975	Oct. $3,350
Feb. $2,820	May $2,920	Aug. $3,025	Nov. $3,400
Mar. $2,875	Jun. $2,960	Sep. $3,130	Dec. $3,550

Calculate total sales and average monthly sales. Find the profit or loss for the year, assuming that total expenses were $21,250. Find the average monthly growth rate. If sales continue to grow at this rate, what will sales be for each month next year?

24. You begin the day with 100.00 in your cash drawer. At the end of the day, you have 258.50 in cash, 45.28 in checks, and $187.87 in credit card slips. You gave a refund of $20.00 to one customer. What were your receipts for the day?

25. To grow your car-wash business, you need to offer a new service to customers. In a group, brainstorm ideas for new services.

THINK CRITICALLY

26. How would you feel if a business letter was addressed to you but your name was misspelled? What would this error tell you about the person who sent the letter?

27. Why is a good telephone manner important for an entrepreneur? Why can listening be more important than talking?

28. Emily Newton delivers newspapers. She has a list of customers. What basic calculation will Emily use to determine how many newspapers she needs? Some people have requested that their papers not be delivered this week. What math skill will Emily use to determine the number of newspapers she now needs? How should Emily determine the total each customer owes at the end of the month?

29. For Emily's newspaper route, how would she calculate how fast sales have grown from the first year to the third year? How would she compute average monthly growth rate in the third year?

30. Emily wants to start making at least $500 per month to help finance her college education. Use the six-step problem-solving model to help Emily decide how to accomplish her goals.

31. COMMUNICATION You have a business designing web pages for companies that specialize in online sales. Several customers have not paid yet for services you provided. One customer's account is 30 days past due. Write a letter to this customer requesting payment.

32. MATH Marc Rago owns Art Deco, an art supply store. Last year sales of paper products totaled $45,750, sales of acrylic paints totaled $38,840, sales of oil paints totaled $25,670, and sales of paint brushes totaled $48,800. All other products sold were put in the "miscellaneous" category. Total sales were $215,000. What was the amount for miscellaneous sales? Total expenses for the year were $164,300. What was Marc's profit?

33. MATH You would like to buy the building you now lease. If you borrow $75,000 at an interest rate of 8 percent, how much interest would you pay total in the first year? In five years?

34. RESEARCH Find one example of an actual business letter and one example of an actual business memo. Write a paragraph for each, describing whether the document conforms to the rules given in this chapter, and if not, how it breaks them.

This Is Your Business Project

1. Write a letter to potential customers about the goods or services your business will provide. Plan on paper a telephone conversation you will use as a follow-up to the letter. Work with a classmate and do a mock phone conversation based on your plan.

2. Project your first year sales by month for each category of products or services you will offer. Calculate average monthly sales, total sales, and monthly growth rate. Research a cost price on one of your items and determine a selling price using a markup strategy. Project monthly sales units, and the amount of profit you will make.

3. Estimate how much money you need to start your business. Your local bank offers a loan with 7.5 percent interest over a six-year term. How much interest will you pay in the first year?

4. Think of a problem that may arise in your business. Use the six-step problem-solving model to deal with this problem. Brainstorm other solutions with classmates or family members.

Chapter 3

ENTREPRENEURS IN A MARKET ECONOMY

LESSONS

3.1 What is an Economy?

3.2 The Concept of Cost

3.3 Government in a Market Economy

BUILD A BUSINESS

Darrell's Digs

"Hey, Li!" Darrell called to his friend from across the aisle in the local mall.

Li waved and walked over to Darrell. "Hey yourself," she said. "What's up?"

"Well, it looks like I'm going to be able to open up my landscaping business soon," Darrell beamed. "I did some research last night to find out if I would be regulated by the government in any way. I have to buy a business license, and pay yearly taxes on my profits. Other than that, I'm good to go. Some businesses have to go through inspections and follow very strict rules, so I'm lucky."

"That's great!" Li exclaimed. "I know you've been looking forward to starting a landscape business for awhile. What are you going to name it again?"

"Darrell's Digs. I can't wait. I enjoy working with flowers and plants so much. I need to start determining how much to charge, though. I know that demand for a service will affect the price, so I have to figure out how much people will pay for certain services."

"Yeah, I'm sure people will pay more for you to plant some trees than for you to cut their grass."

"That's for sure. Digging a big hole for a big tree is a lot harder than mowing a lawn! I also have to consider all my costs when determining my prices."

"Like storage of your equipment and the amount of gasoline you use?"

"Exactly. The money I have to pay in expenses has to be considered in order to make a profit."

"And I guess you also have to factor in any employees you might hire as well, huh?"

"Sure will," said Darrell. "They'll help my business do things faster, but there are costs involved. I'd have to pay salaries, and possibly health insurance. But I probably won't need many employees to start off with."

"You know, Darrell," said Li, "I moved here from China a few years ago. The United States has a market economy, but China has a command economy. It's been an interesting experience, living in countries with two different economies. Each one has different ways of distributing goods and services. If your landscaping company operated in a country with a command economy, it would be run differently than one in a market economy. In a command economy, the government makes decisions. In a market economy, individuals are the ones making the decisions."

"That is pretty interesting," said Darrell.

What Do You Know?

1. Besides storage and gas, what other costs do you think Darrell will have in his landscaping business?
2. The government requires Darrell to purchase a license for his business. What other ways do you think the government has an effect on businesses?
3. How is a command economy different from a market economy?

What Is an Economy?

Different countries have different economic systems. These different systems affect how an item is produced, how it is distributed, and the demand for the item. An economic system even determines whether an item is available at all. You must always consider market structure, including supply, demand, and price, when starting a business. These factors all need to be considered if your business is to succeed.

MARKET AND COMMAND ECONOMIES

All economies produce goods and services. Goods are products, such as television sets, compact discs, or greeting cards. Service businesses include theme parks, restaurants, repair shops, and landscaping companies.

SCARCITY In every economy, there are limited resources to produce goods and services. However, individuals have unlimited needs and wants. This produces the basic economic problem of scarcity. Scarcity occurs when people's needs and wants are unlimited and the resources to produce the goods and services to meet those needs and wants are limited. For example, not everyone can own diamonds because there are too few diamonds to go around. If all goods and services were free, like air, everyone could consume everything.

Scarcity occurs in every economy. So what is it that makes economies different? Economies must choose a way to allocate, or distribute, the goods and services that are available to the people who need or want them. Different economies have different ways of choosing which needs are satisfied and how many resources are used to satisfy those needs. These different allocation processes are what create different economies.

COMMAND ECONOMY In a *command economy*, the government determines what, how, and for whom products and services are produced. Because the government is making the decisions, there is very little choice for consumers in what is available. The government sees no reason to have more than one type of the same item. This means individuals may not always be able to obtain exactly what they want. There will be shirts and pants, but there will not be many styles and colors to choose from.

MARKET ECONOMY Market economies are about personal choice. In a *market economy*, individuals decide what, how, and for whom to produce goods and services. Decisions about production and consumption are made by millions of people, each acting alone. Individual choice creates the market, so there are many items available that are very similar. If a good sells, it will remain on the market. If not, the good will not continue to be produced. There will be many styles of shirts to appeal to every taste. But a manufacturer will not continue to produce a shirt that no one buys.

Individual choice also exists in how items are produced. A furniture maker always has choices for manufacturing her goods. In addition, products and services are always available to everyone who has the means to pay for them.

 **CHECKPOINT** How does a market economy differ from a command economy?

Entrepreneurial Timeline

| 1600 | 1700 | 1800 | 1900 |

Making Money in Colonial America

Entrepreneurs usually want to make a profit. For colonial America, the profit lay overseas. There were more people buying goods in Britain than in the colonies because America was largely unpopulated. Traveling between the colonies was slow. In 1723, it took four days to journey the 100 miles from Philadelphia to New York! However, ocean transportation wasn't much better. It took two months to cross the Atlantic Ocean. Pirates and storms sometimes kept ships from even reaching Britain. But the risks were always worth the potential profit from selling goods in the large British market.

Because of these conditions, American business in the first part of the 18th century was informal and slow paced. When money was not available, entrepreneurs traded their wares and services for the goods they needed. Bills of exchange were used in place of currency. It was also not unusual for business transactions to occur in taverns, coffee houses, and even in the streets.

If a market economy is based on personal choice, why does there always seem to be just enough of everything? In a market economy, individual consumers make decisions about what to buy, and businesses make decisions about what to produce. Consumers are motivated to buy goods and services that they need or want. Business owners are driven by the desire to earn profits. These two groups, consumers and producers, together determine the prices and quantities of goods and services produced.

To understand how this works, you need to understand two important forces: supply and demand. **Supply** is how much of a good or service a producer is willing to produce at different prices. Imagine that you are a supplier of lawn-mowing services. Let's say that at a rate of $10 an hour, you are willing to spend eight hours a week mowing lawns. If your neighbors are willing to pay just $1 an hour, you might decide not to bother mowing lawns at all. If, however, the going rate for lawn mowing rose to $50 an hour, you would probably increase the number of lawns you would mow. You might even try to round up friends to help you mow even more lawns.

As the price of lawn-mowing services rises, suppliers are willing to produce more. The quantity of lawn-mowing services supplied rises as the price for mowing a lawn increases, as shown on the supply curve graph.

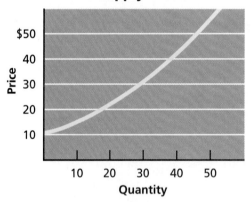

Supply Curve

Suppliers are willing to supply more of a product or service at a higher price.

Now let's look at the demand side of the market economy. **Demand** is an individual's need or desire for a product or service at a given price. Let's say that you are interested in having your lawn mowed. At a rate of $10 an hour, you figure it is worth having your lawn mowed every two weeks. If, however, the rate fell to just $5 an hour, you might be willing to have your lawn mowed every week.

As the price of the service or product decreases, consumers are willing to purchase more of the product or service. Demand rises as the price falls, as shown on the demand curve graph.

Demand Curve

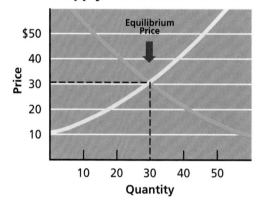

Individuals are willing to consume more of a product or service at a lower price.

WHEN SUPPLY AND DEMAND MEET How do the forces of supply and demand work together to determine price in a market economy? The point at which the supply and demand curves meet is what is known as the **equilibrium price and quantity.** This is the price at which supply equals demand.

Supply and Demand Curves

The point at which the supply and demand curves intersect indicates the equilibrium price and quantity. In the diagram on the left, the equilibrium price will be $30 a unit, and 30 units will be produced.

Above the equilibrium price, fewer people are interested in buying lawn-mowing services than in selling them. In this part of the diagram, suppliers will not be able to sell as much of their services as they would like because they have priced their services too high. Below the equilibrium price, the price is too low. Consumers would be very happy to purchase lots of the service at these prices, but suppliers are not willing to produce enough to meet their demand. Only at the equilibrium price does the amount consumers want to buy exactly equal the amount producers want to supply.

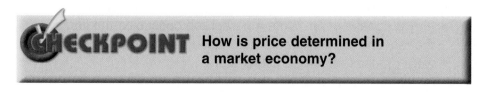

CHECKPOINT How is price determined in a market economy?

Point your browser to

http://www.ideas-in-action.swep.com

Complete the activity for Chapter 3.

MARKET STRUCTURE AND PRICES

In a competitive market, many suppliers compete for business, and buyers shop around for the best deal they can find. In this kind of market, prices are said to be determined competitively.

Not all markets are fully competitive. In some sectors of the economy, there is little or no competition. AMTRAK is the only train line serving certain routes in the United States. Although it competes with other means of transportation, in many areas of the country AMTRAK does not face direct competition from other train lines.

When a company controls all of a market, it has a **monopoly**. A company that has a monopoly is able to charge more than a company that has to compete with other companies. In a competitive market, a company cannot charge prices that are much higher than its competitors. Consumers will simply switch to the lower-priced good or service. With a monopoly, consumers have nowhere else to go. They will continue to buy a product or service, even if the producer raises prices.

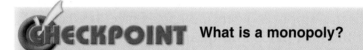 **CHECKPOINT** What is a monopoly?

THINK CRITICALLY

1. Have you ever wanted something, had the money to buy it, but couldn't find the item? Why couldn't you find it?

2. Think of an item you purchase often. If the price is similar at several stores, do you always buy at the same store? Why or why not?

3. How high would the price have to go for your favorite soft drink in order for you not to buy it anymore? Why?

MAKE CONNECTIONS

4. MATH Media Store A sells 100 CDs a day at $16.95 each. Media Store B wants to bring in more revenue a day than Store A does. It also wants to sell at a lower price. How many CDs will Store B have to sell in a day at $14.95 in order to surpass Store A's revenue by $99.00?

5. COMMUNICATION Ask three friends to name an item they purchase often. Write a paragraph describing the items, the reasons the items were purchased, and reasons the items were purchased at a particular store.

The Concept of Cost

To determine how much profit they are earning, entrepreneurs need to know how much it costs to produce their goods or services. To do so, they must consider all the resources that go into producing the good or service to determine a price to charge.

The Jewel Box, a small company that produces handmade jewelry, requires office space, materials, labor, management, and other costs to make goods. All of these resources go into making a piece of jewelry, and all of them must be taken into account when figuring out the price to charge. A company that prices its product based only on the materials involved in producing it will lose money and go out of business very quickly.

FIXED AND VARIABLE COSTS

Every business has fixed costs and variable costs. **Fixed costs** are costs that must be paid regardless of how much of a good or service is produced. Fixed costs are also called sunk costs. **Variable costs** are costs that go up and down depending on the quantity of the good or service produced.

To understand the difference between fixed and variable costs,

consider The Bread and Bagel Shop, a small business owned by entrepreneur Michael Miller. Whether or not customers buy his baked goods, Michael pays the same monthly rent, the same insurance fees, and the same interest on the loans taken out to finance his business. These are Michael's fixed costs. He must pay them even if The Bread and Bagel Shop makes no sales.

The store also has variable costs, including the expense of buying flour, sugar, and coffee. These expenses rise directly with the number of items sold. The more cups of coffee, bagels, and donuts the company sells, the more resources it must buy to make more goods. In contrast, when fewer loaves of bread are purchased by customers, Michael does not pay for more flour to make more bread.

Understanding the difference between fixed and variable costs is important. A business with many fixed costs is a higher risk than a business with mostly variable costs because fixed costs will be incurred regardless of sales. If sales turn out to be much lower than expected, the business will be stuck with many bills to pay and little revenue.

CHECKPOINT What is the difference between a fixed and a variable cost?

MARGINAL BENEFIT AND MARGINAL COST

Entrepreneurs make business decisions based on the concepts of marginal benefit and marginal cost. **Marginal benefit** measures the advantages of producing one additional unit of a good or service. **Marginal cost** measures the disadvantages of producing one additional unit of a good or service.

Michael Miller of The Bread and Bagel Shop wants to increase his sales. Michael thinks about keeping the store open two extra hours every day. He estimates that during the last two hours of every day, he will sell an additional 150 baked goods and 30 cups of coffee, bringing in additional revenues of $100 a night. This $100 represents the marginal benefit from keeping the store open an extra two hours a day.

Should Michael stay open two extra hours each day? To figure out if staying open

later makes economic sense, Michael needs to figure out the marginal cost of staying open later. He will need to purchase additional ingredients to produce another 150 baked goods and 30 cups of coffee. He will have to pay overtime wages to at least two employees. He will also use more electricity. Adding up these costs, Michael estimates that staying open two extra hours will cost him $125 a day. Because the marginal cost of staying open ($125) exceeds the marginal benefit ($100), Michael decides not to change the store's hours.

**CHECKPOINT** How do entrepreneurs use the concepts of marginal benefit and marginal cost?

OPPORTUNITY COST

Another type of cost you should think about is opportunity cost. **Opportunity cost** is the cost of choosing one opportunity or investment over another. For example, you want to start your own business. But you have been offered a job that pays $28,000 a year. In addition to the salary, you will receive two weeks paid vacation, and your company will pay your medical insurance. If you add in these benefits, which you estimate are worth $3,000 a year, the total of $31,000 represents the opportunity cost of starting your own business. It is the amount you could have earned by choosing a different path.

Business people use the concept of opportunity cost to make business decisions. Jamie Cooper, for example, has $2,500 in extra cash that she wants to put back into her cake decorating business. Jamie

can invest the money in an advertising campaign, or she could invest the money in new equipment. If Jamie decides to use the money for advertising, she will not be able to purchase new equipment. The opportunity cost of the advertising campaign, therefore, will be the value of the new equipment. Like all entrepreneurs, Jamie will have to choose between various investment options.

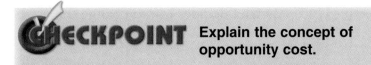

CHECKPOINT Explain the concept of opportunity cost.

THINK CRITICALLY

1. Opportunity cost can affect you personally. Name an item you've wanted to purchase but haven't because you wanted another item more. Name something you've wanted to do but couldn't because you chose to do something else instead.

2. Name three fixed costs in your life. How do you prepare to pay them? Name three variable costs that you have. How can variable costs be like opportunity costs?

MAKE CONNECTIONS

3. **MATH** A new home-based entrepreneur, Laura Perez, subscribed to a long-distance telephone service that charged $0.36 a minute. Laura is very busy and makes many calls. She was shocked when her first bill showed 454 minutes and a total fee of $163.44. Laura shopped around and found a competing service offering $0.11 a minute. How much would she have saved on her first bill if she had been using the second service?

4. **COMMUNICATION** Interview someone you know who has a small business. Explain marginal cost and marginal benefit. Ask the business owner about her or his experiences with these concepts. Write a paragraph describing the business owner's experiences.

5. **PROBLEM SOLVING** Suppose you have a home-based business making candles. You currently sell your candles through a local craft shop. However, you are considering opening a shop to sell your candles yourself. Apply the problem solving model you learned in Chapter 2 to this situation. What are all the costs involved in opening your own shop?

Lesson 3.3

Government in a Market Economy

GOALS

EXPLAIN the government's effect on what is produced.

RECOGNIZE the different roles the government plays in a market economy.

I f companies and individual consumers make decisions about production and consumption in market economies, what role does the government play? How do its actions affect entrepreneurs?

GOVERNMENT'S EFFECT ON WHAT IS PRODUCED

Although the U.S. economy is made up of private companies, the government has an effect on what is produced in three important ways.

PURCHASES First, the government purchases huge amounts of goods and services. For example, the aerospace industry is almost entirely dependent on government purchases. The National Aeronautic and Space Agency (NASA) is the sole purchaser of various devices produced by aerospace companies. Private companies also supply the government with everything from pens to office-cleaning supplies.

TAXES Second, the government taxes certain goods and services. Most states charge sales tax on retail sales, and most charge extra taxes on certain items, such as cigarettes, gasoline, and alcoholic beverages. These taxes reduce consumption of these products, reducing producers' revenues.

SUBSIDIES Finally, the government provides subsidies, or payments, to producers of certain kinds of goods. Agricultural products are commonly subsidized. The government also pays subsidies to companies that locate their businesses in certain inner-city neighborhoods, known as enterprise zones. Entrepreneurs whose businesses can operate in such areas may be able to benefit from these subsidies.

 **CHECKPOINT** How are entrepreneurs affected by taxes and subsidies?

ROLES OF THE GOVERNMENT

In a market economy the government plays different roles. The government may serve as a regulator, as a provider of public good, as a provider of social programs, and as a redistributor of income.

The Government as a Regulator

A market economy is based on private companies producing goods and services in order to earn profits. Sometimes, however, this desire to earn profits motivates business owners to engage in practices that put consumers in danger.

INSPECTION To protect consumers, the government regulates certain businesses. The U.S. Department of Agriculture (USDA), for example, inspects meat and poultry plants to ensure that appropriate hygienic measures are being observed. The U.S. Occupational Health and Safety Administration (OSHA) inspects factories to ensure that conditions are safe for workers.

LICENSES The government also regulates by requiring some businesses to obtain licenses. Barbers and beauticians, for instance, must fulfill certain training requirements, and they must be licensed by the state in which they work. Entrepreneurs entering fields requiring licenses must pass examinations and pay licensing fees before they can start their businesses.

 **CHECKPOINT** How does the government ensure that products are safe for consumers?

The Government as a Provider of Public Good

For most products, the benefits of ownership apply only to the owner of the product. Your next-door neighbor, for example, gets no benefits from your microwave oven, just as you get no benefits from your neighbor's central heating. A **public good** is a good from which everyone receives benefits, not just the individual consuming the good. Vaccinations against communicable diseases are a public good, because everyone benefits from the fact that other people are vaccinated. The country's armed forces are a public good, because everyone benefits from the national security they provide. Because the country as a whole benefits from these kinds of goods and services, the government has a role to play in providing them.

Many entrepreneurs benefit from the fact that the government provides public goods. Engineering firms consult on the building of highways, for example, and construction companies build schools.

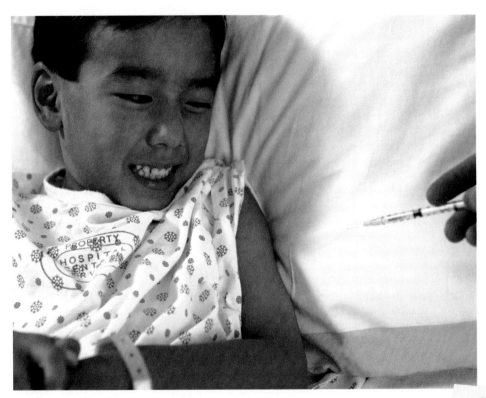

The Government as a Provider of Social Programs

The government provides a number of social programs for people. Social security, welfare, medical research, and aid for dependent children and the aged are but a few of the many social programs the government offers. The benefit of these programs lies in the fact that people who require help receive it. Plus, the cost of providing these programs is spread among millions of taxpayers, which greatly reduces the cost to any one person. Although there is much debate over how well social programs work, there is still a net

In Class Activity

As a class, brainstorm a large list of public goods. Give reasons why the government is justified in providing each good. Does the benefit to society outweigh the cost of providing the good?

benefit to society. A large sum of money is spent on cancer and other medical research each year. Many children and elderly persons are well taken care of and do not need to rely on private charity for survival.

The Government as a Redistributor of Income

The government further affects the economy by redistributing income. People with higher incomes pay more in taxes than people with lower incomes. Lower income individuals then benefit from social programs designed to help them in their situation. In this way, income is more evenly distributed among members of a society.

This redistribution of income affects entrepreneurs because the percentage of income that must be paid in taxes increases as earnings increase. Thus, an entrepreneur who earns very little might pay only

What Went Wrong

Misjudging the Customer
The Case of the Failed Ice Cream Shop
Business: The Cold Cow, Las Vegas, Nevada * Open for business: 8 months

Don wasn't happy selling office equipment in Kansas. For years he dreamed of starting his own business. His wife, Carol, encouraged the dream. She hoped it would allow them to escape the harsh winters of the Midwest. Together, they researched lots of business ideas and franchise opportunities. They negotiated a franchise agreement with "Cold Cow," a chain of ice cream stores based in Kansas. The company had a good reputation, a quality product, and a great marketing hook. People would come from miles around to see custom flavors hand-mixed right before their eyes.

They chose Las Vegas as the site for their business. The population was nearing two million and growing. Twenty-nine million tourists visited each year! The only other chain in the city, Baskin-Robbins 31-flavors, was doing quite well in several locations. They located in a new mini-mall about five minutes from "The Strip," using the Cold Cow signage and decor. They advertised using proven copy and promotions in newspapers and on radio. They also distributed introductory price-off coupon-flyers all over town.

In less than eight months the business was bankrupt. What went wrong? Don and Carol overestimated demand, their customer base. For starters, the 29 million tourists are only traffic for the hotels and casino shops and don't travel off "The Strip" much at all. Second, in the West, mini-malls only serve the residents living within a three- to four-mile area. Third, newspaper and radio advertising is expensive and mostly wasted unless you have several locations. The last straw for Don and Carol was that most of the nearby residents, those who were in fact their realistic customer-base, always used the "price-off" coupons.

Think Critically
1. What mistakes did Don and Carol make in estimating demand for an ice cream shop in Las Vegas?
2. How did the use of "price-off" coupons affect their ability to make a profit?

15 percent in income tax, while one who earns a great deal might pay 40 percent in taxes.

However, it is widely agreed that redistributing income is a positive action. Feelings of excessive inequality can arise in those who feel there is nothing they can do about their economic situation. They may have a very low level of education, or they may actually be unable to work. Hostile emotions and even riots can result from these feelings of inequality. By redistributing income, the government reduces the chance of social problems due to low income.

 **CHECKPOINT** **Give three examples of public goods and explain why the government might want to provide them.**

"YOU CAN SAY THAT AGAIN!

I only hope that we never lose sight of one thing—that it was all started by a mouse.

—Walt Disney of Walt Disney Studios"

THINK CRITICALLY

1. NASA is the sole purchaser of many items from the aerospace industry. What is another industry that benefits almost exclusively from government purchases?

2. What are some public goods that affect you? What public good would affect an entrepreneur whose job is to research information for other businesses?

3. Why is redistribution of income a benefit to society? Do you agree that income should be redistributed? Why or why not?

MAKE CONNECTIONS

4. MATH Entrepreneurs might pay from 15 to 40 percent in income tax. If a small town florist takes in $630 a week, how much must be set aside to pay the 15 percent tax? The 40 percent tax?

5. COMMUNICATION Interview two small business owners in your area. Ask the owners whether they are influenced by government regulations. Present your findings to your class.

CHAPTER SUMMARY

What Is an Economy?

1. In a command economy, the government determines what, how, and for whom products and services are produced.
2. In a market economy, individuals decide what, how, and for whom products and services are produced.
3. Supply is how much of a good or service a producer will make at different prices.
4. Demand is an individual's need or desire for a product or service at a given price.
5. When supply and demand meet, supply equals demand. This point is referred to as the equilibrium price.
6. In competitive markets, prices are similar for like products. Companies cannot charge prices that are much higher than their competitors.

The Concept *of* Cost

7. Fixed costs exist regardless of how much of a good or service is produced.
8. Variable costs go up and down depending on the quantity of the good or service produced.
9. A business with a high percentage of fixed costs may not always earn enough profit to cover its expenses.
10. Marginal benefits are the advantages of producing one additional unit of a good or service.
11. Marginal costs are the disadvantages of producing one more unit of a good or service.
12. Marginal benefits and marginal costs should be considered to determine whether an idea is financially feasible.

Government in a Market Economy

13. The government plays many roles in a market economy. To protect consumers, the government regulates private companies.
14. Providing public goods, such as vaccinations and national defense, is also a role of the government. Public goods benefit everyone, not just the individual receiving the good.
15. The government also provides social programs. Income is commonly redistributed by the government so lower income individuals receive benefits.

What Do You Know Now?

Read *Build a Business* again. Then answer the questions a second time. How have your responses changed?

VOCABULARY BUILDER

Choose the term that best fits the definition.
Write your answers on a separate sheet of paper.

1. The point at which the supply and demand curves meet
2. A measurement of the disadvantages of producing one additional unit of a good or service
3. A good from which everyone receives benefits, not just the individual consuming the good
4. How much of a good or service a producer is willing to produce at different prices
5. Costs that must be paid regardless of how much of a good or service is produced

a. demand
b. equilibrium price and quantity
c. fixed costs
d. marginal benefit
e. marginal cost
f. monopoly
g. opportunity cost
h. public good
i. supply
j. variable costs

6. A measurement of the advantages of producing one additional unit of a good or service
7. An individual's need or desire for a product or service at a given price
8. The cost of choosing one opportunity or investment over another
9. Costs that go up and down depending on the quantity of the good or service produced
10. One company controls the entire market

REVIEW YOUR KNOWLEDGE

11. How are decisions made in a market economy?
12. How do supply and demand work together in a market economy?
13. What happens to price when there is a monopoly?
14. What type of cost is incurred regardless of how much of a good or service is produced?
15. How do the concepts of marginal benefit and marginal cost help entrepreneurs make decisions?

16. Why should you consider the opportunity cost of becoming an entrepreneur?

17. In what three ways does the government affect production of goods and services in the U.S. economy?

18. What are the other roles the government plays in a market economy?

19. Name three examples of public goods. Why do they benefit everyone?

APPLY WHAT YOU LEARNED

20. You plan to start a pet-sitting/dog-walking business. Analyze the possible demand for such a service by brainstorming answers to the following questions: Who is likely to hire a pet sitter? Who is likely to hire a dog walker? Besides caring for the pets, what other services could such a business perform?

21. You are planning to start a day-care business for children. What government regulations might impact your business? How might you obtain further information about these regulations?

THINK CRITICALLY

22. If the price of a product is set below the equilibrium price, what happens to demand? What happens to supply?

23. Markets for new products often are monopolies. Why do you think this is so? Can you think of examples of markets for new products (past or present) that are monopolies?

24. What do you think the fixed costs and the variable costs would be for a movie-rental business?

25. You are planning to start a business as a street vendor selling soft pretzels. What government regulations will be imposed on your business? How will each of these regulations affect your business?

MAKE CONNECTIONS

26. **MATH** You have a business baking and selling chocolate chip cookies using your favorite recipe. Go to the store and price the ingredients you need to make the cookies. Then calculate the cost for ingredients for baking 120 cookies if each batch makes 40 cookies. Are these fixed costs or variable costs?

27. **COMMUNICATION** Use newspapers, magazines, the Internet, and other tools to find a business that has a monopoly in a particular market area, as AMTRAK does. Write a one-page report about the company, keeping the following questions in mind: What is the product? Does the company have a patent on the product? When was the product introduced to the market?

28. **RESEARCH** Identify and research economies in the process of converting from a command to market economy. What event or events led to the conversion? What involvement, if any, do U.S. companies have in these countries' economies? Discuss your findings with the class.

29. **RESEARCH** Using information from your local Chamber of Commerce, find out whether it is necessary to purchase a vendors' license in order to operate a retail business in your area. If so, how much does it cost? Is it necessary to renew the license? If so, how often? What is the procedure for applying for such a license?

This Is Your Business Project

1. Draw a supply and demand graph for at least one good or service your business will provide. Then use the graph to determine the price to charge for that good or service.

2. Determine the fixed and variable costs for your business. Estimate how much money you will need to cover these costs. Make a chart showing these expenses. How much money must you make each month to cover these expenses? Do you need to adjust your original price for your business to make a profit?

3. Consider adding another product or service to your business. What are the marginal costs and benefits of adding this new product or service? Is it a good or bad idea to add the item?

4. Brainstorm and write down all the ways that you think the government may affect your business. Will your business be regulated? Taxed? Subsidized?

Chapter 4

SELECT A TYPE OF OWNERSHIP

LESSONS

4.1 Run an Existing Business

4.2 Own a Franchise or Start a Business

4.3 Choose the Legal Form of Your Business

BUILD A BUSINESS

The Pastry Shop

On graduation day from the culinary arts institute, Natalie and Crystal realized they had many decisions to make if their dream of opening their own bakery was going to happen. Crystal said to Natalie, "We need to sit down and talk about our future."

"Yes," Natalie replied, "we need to get going if we are going to make our bakery rise."

"Real funny," Crystal replied sarcastically. "So, where should we locate?"

"There's an ad in the paper advertising an existing bakery for sale," Natalie said. "That way maybe we could purchase the equipment and supplies to get us started right away. Plus, customers who go to the bakery now would still come after we bought it."

"Is that the one owned by the Holcombe family? I remember seeing the FOR SALE sign when I was over there last week. Mrs. Holcombe and her daughter were fighting about something. No one was waiting on the customers and everyone was getting upset," Crystal said.

"It sounds like they have some problems. Sometimes working with your family is a good thing. After all, the Holcombes have owned that bakery for 20 years. But it must be causing the family some problems," Natalie concluded.

"If we bought their existing bakery, we would have to do something to change people's opinions about the service. And who knows what other problems we might find!"

"We could always start our own bakery from scratch," Natalie said.

"There you go again!" Crystal said. "But that could be hard, too. Not only would we have to find a place to have our bakery, but we'll also have to buy everything we need to get started and build up a customer base."

"There's one other option for our business. We could buy a franchise," Natalie said.

"A franchise, what is that?" Crystal asked.

"A franchise is the legal right to sell someone else's products. We could buy a franchise for Mrs. Fields' Cookies and then open a Mrs. Fields' cookie shop."

"Well, that would help us with lots of our decisions. We would know what we were selling and have somewhere to buy all of our supplies," Crystal concluded. "But would we get to make our own confections if we were a franchise?"

"That depends on the franchise agreement," Natalie said.

"Decisions, decisions, what shall we do?" moaned Crystal.

"Speaking of decisions, we also have to decide if we're going to be a partnership. There may be some advantages to incorporating our business, you know."

"There's also something to be said for being the only owner. I wouldn't have to listen to your little witty comments any more. Just kidding!" laughed Crystal.

What Do You Know?

1. What are some advantages of purchasing an existing business?
2. What are the differences between operating a family business or a franchise?
3. Why should the legal form of a business be considered?

Run *an* *Existing* Business

When most people consider going into business for themselves, they think about starting a new business. But there are two other ways of becoming an entrepreneur: purchasing an existing business or entering a family business.

PURCHASE AN EXISTING BUSINESS

Owners of businesses sell their businesses for a variety of reasons. These can include insufficient sales or profits, worry about new competition, fear of new economic conditions, retirement, a dispute between partners, the death or illness of a partner, and the owner's desire to do something different.

There are many ways to find out which businesses are for sale. You may find advertisements in the classified section of the local newspaper. You might decide to use a business broker. A **business broker** is a person who sells businesses for a living. People in your industry might know of businesses for sale. You may also find businesses for sale through other sources, including landlords and leasing agents, lawyers and bankers, management consultants, the Small Business Administration, Chamber of Commerce offices, and bankruptcy announcements.

Advantages of Buying an Existing Business

There are many advantages of buying an existing business.

1. *The existing business already has customers, suppliers, and procedures.* The business may also have built up goodwill, or customer loyalty. Of course, the new owner may want to change some of the policies and procedures established by the former owner. But fine-tuning systems that are already in place is likely to be much easier than creating systems from scratch.
2. *The seller of a business may train a new owner.* Experienced employees may be available to help the new owner learn about the company.
3. *There are prior records of revenues, expenses, and profits.* This means that financial planning will be easier and more reliable than it would be for a completely new business.

4. ***Financial arrangements can be easier.*** The seller of the business may accept an initial partial payment and allow the rest to be paid off in monthly installments. This can reduce or eliminate the need for bank financing. If bank financing is needed, getting it may be easier since banks are more likely to lend to an established business.

Disadvantages of Buying an Existing Business

Buying an existing business sounds like an easy way to become an entrepreneur. However, buying a business can be risky.

1. ***Many businesses are for sale because they are not making a profit.*** Owners frequently try to sell businesses that are not financially viable.
2. ***Serious problems may be inherited.*** Businesses can have poor reputations with customers, trouble with suppliers, or be poorly located.
3. ***Capital is required.*** Many entrepreneurs just do not have the money to purchase a business. Starting a small business of their own may be their only option.

CHECKPOINT What are some of the advantages and disadvantages of buying an existing business?

STEPS TO PURCHASE A BUSINESS

Buying a business is a complicated process that requires a lot of thought. If you are considering buying a business, you will want to follow these steps:

1. ***Write specific objectives about the kind of business you want to buy, and identify businesses for sale that meet your objectives.*** This will help you find the right business for what you want to do.
2. ***Meet with business sellers or brokers to investigate specific opportunities.*** Ask about the history of the business, the reason for its sale, its financial performance, and the price the owner is asking for the business.
3. ***Visit during business hours to observe the company in action.*** Inspect the facility closely to make sure that it meets your needs.
4. ***Ask the owner to provide you with a complete financial accounting of operations for at least the past three years.*** Analyzing these reports will help you see how much profit you can make and how much you will probably be paying out in expenses.
5. ***Ask for important information in written form.*** Get a list of all assets to be transferred to the new owner, a statement about

Observe the business you are thinking about buying during business hours.

any past or pending legal action against the business, a copy of the business lease or mortgage, and a list of all the suppliers. Have an accountant and a lawyer help you review all of the material. Be suspicious if the owner refuses to provide all of the information you request.

6. ***Determine how you would finance the business.*** Contact lending institutions, and ask the seller if he or she would be willing to finance part or all of the purchase. This topic will be discussed in Chapter 7.

7. ***Get expert help to determine a price to offer for the business.*** An accountant or a **valuator,** an expert on determining the value of a business, can help. Present the offer in writing to the seller. If an agreement is reached, have a lawyer draw up a sales contract.

CHECKPOINT   What steps should you take when purchasing a business?

ENTER A FAMILY BUSINESS

The United States economy is dominated by family businesses. According to some estimates, as many as 90 percent of all businesses, including the vast majority of small- and medium-sized companies, are owned by families. Even many large companies, such as the Ford Motor Company, continue to be owned largely by people who are related to the company founder.

Advantages of a Family Business

Entrepreneurs who work for their family businesses enjoy the pride and sense of mission that comes with being part of a family enterprise. They also enjoy the fact that their businesses remain in the family for at least one more generation. Some enjoy working with relatives. They also like knowing that their efforts are benefiting others whom they care about.

Josh Morgan runs Morgan's, a restaurant that has been in his family for three generations. In his grandfather's time, Morgan's was a simple coffee shop, catering largely to people in the neighborhood. Later, thanks to changes

made by Josh's mother, Mary, Morgan's became a fashionable lunch spot for people from all over town. When Mary retired two years ago, Josh took over. He carried on some Morgan traditions and implemented some new ideas, such as a gourmet take-out department. Josh takes great pride in seeing how the restaurant has evolved since his grandfather's time. He also enjoys the thought that one day his grandchildren may hang pictures of him on the walls of the restaurant that will then belong to them.

Disadvantages of a Family Business

Family businesses have several drawbacks. Senior management positions are often held by family members, regardless of their ability. This sometimes means that poor business decisions are made. It also makes it difficult to retain good employees who are not members of the family. Family politics often enter into business decision making.

What Went Wrong

Partnership Woes
With a Friend Like This....

Business: SP Communications * Open for business 1 year

Stan and Peter met while working at a video production company. Stan was in charge of editorial and production. Peter ran the sales force. Stan decided to begin his own company and invited Peter to join him. SP Communications seemed like a perfect partnership. Peter would handle sales and administration, while Stan managed clients and directed production.

Things seemed to be going well, especially when they landed a major project. But Peter wanted a "creative" job too. He spent most of his time producing videos rather than looking for new business. Stan's loyalty to Peter made him blind to many things that were obvious to others. Because of their friendship, he trusted that Peter was taking care of his side of the business.

As it turned out, Peter wasn't very good at the tasks he took on. He made mistakes that reduced expected profits. He wasn't making new sales contacts, which was supposed to be the main part of his job. If that weren't enough, the feeling that he was letting his friend down made

Peter feel even worse. Peter began to avoid talking to Stan. He stopped coming into the office. Finally, he stopped returning phone calls.

By the time Stan realized what was happening to the business, it was too late. There weren't any new sales. What Stan thought were profits were the result of Peter not paying their bills. Stan was left with more than $150,000 in unpaid bills and other debts. A tearful message on the answering machine from Peter sheepishly announced, "I'm moving out to California for a while. Sorry it didn't work out." It took Stan three years to dig out of the financial mess, and get his new company, Strategy First, up and running successfully.

Think Critically
1. How might Stan and Peter have avoided the problems that led to the end of their partnership?
2. Why is this situation a good example of the difficulty in maintaining partnerships between friends?

Plus, the distinction between business life and private life is blurred in family-owned businesses. As a result, business problems end up affecting family life as well.

Entrepreneurs who do join their family business must be prepared to make compromises. Unlike individuals who start or buy their own companies, people who work for their families lack the freedom to make all decisions themselves. They may also be unable to set policies and procedures the way they would like to.

 **CHECKPOINT** What are some of the advantages and disadvantages of entering a family business?

THINK CRITICALLY

1. When you purchase an existing business, why is it important to know the owner's reason for selling?

2. Your family owns a successful business that distributes flowers from around the world to local florists. Both your parents work full time in the business. They have offered you a position in the company after you graduate from college. Will you accept their offer? Why or why not?

MAKE CONNECTIONS

3. PROBLEM SOLVING You purchased a company that makes and sells fine chocolates. You have a staff of 20 employees. As the new owner, you have noticed a lot of wasted product. You believe that some of the processes in use should be more efficient. Use the six-step problem-solving model as a guide for planning a meeting you will have with your employees to discuss this issue.

4. COMMUNICATION Interview someone who owns a family business. Find out how long the business has been in operation and how many family members are employed in the business. Ask the owner what the advantages and disadvantages are of owning a family business. Compare this list to the advantages and disadvantages discussed in the text. Write a report on your findings.

Own a *Franchise* or *Start* a Business

Purchasing a franchise is another route by which you can become an entrepreneur. Jiffy Lube stations are franchises. So are many McDonald's restaurants. These retail outlets are owned by private entrepreneurs who operate them as their own businesses.

FRANCHISE OWNERSHIP

A **franchise** is a legal agreement that gives an individual the right to market a company's products or services in a particular area. A *franchisee* is the person who purchases a franchise agreement. A *franchisor* is the person or company who offers a franchise for purchase.

More than 500,000 people in the United States own franchises, and the number is growing. Franchising opportunities are available in virtually every field, from motels to pet stores to video outlets. *The Franchise Opportunities Handbook,* a publication of the U.S. Department of Commerce, lists more than 1,400 franchise opportunities by category. It also provides information about costs and capital requirements. Sources for finding out about franchise opportunities include the following:

1. *A Consumer Guide to Buying a Franchise,* published by the Federal Trade Commission
2. Books on franchising available at your public library
3. *The Wall Street Journal*
4. Magazines such as *Forbes, Barron's, Business Start-Ups,* and *Entrepreneur*

Operating Costs of a Franchise

If you decide to purchase a franchise, you will have to pay an initial franchise fee, start-up costs, royalty fees, and advertising fees. You may also be asked to pay for nationwide advertising of the franchise. The **initial franchise fee** is the fee the franchise owner pays in return for the right to run the franchise. The fee can run anywhere

Entrepreneurial Timeline

1925   1950   1975   2000

Stop the Presses!

John H. Johnson, creator of *Ebony* magazine, became one of the first African Americans to run and operate a very large business. While working as publisher of a company newsletter, Johnson imagined creating a general interest magazine aimed at his ethnic community. In 1942, he used his mother's furniture as collateral and borrowed $500 to organize the Johnson Publishing Company. The resulting magazine, the first publication of its kind, was called the *Negro Digest*. With high subscription sales and friends asking for the magazine at newsstands, circulation topped 50,000 copies in the first year.

Johnson went on to create other African-American-related magazines, including *Ebony*, his best seller at over 2 million copies circulated each month. Johnson is also involved in radio, television broadcasting, and cable television. Through print, radio, and television, Johnson reaches over 60 percent of the adult black population. He is considered the most powerful black businessman today, and his company grosses more than $140 million every year.

from a few thousand to a few hundred thousand dollars. It is usually nonrefundable. **Start-up costs** are the costs associated with beginning a business. They include the costs of renting a facility, equipping the outlet, and purchasing inventory. **Royalty fees** are weekly or monthly payments made by the owner of the franchise to the seller of the franchise. These payments usually are a percentage of your franchise's income. **Advertising fees** are fees paid to support television, magazine, or other advertising of the franchise as a whole.

Jim Saurbrey purchased a Mr. Rooter franchise, a company that provides plumbing services. In return for the right to use the Mr. Rooter name and logo, Jim paid a franchise fee of $17,500. In addition to this fee, Jim spent $30,000 renting office space, leasing vehicles, and purchasing equipment.

During its first year of operation, Jim's franchise earned $36,000 in profits. He returned 4 percent of those earnings, or $1,440, to Mr. Rooter in royalty fees. During Jim's second year in business, his company earned $51,000. That year he paid $2,040 in royalty fees.

 **CHECKPOINT** What are the costs involved in purchasing and operating a franchise?

Advantages of Owning a Franchise

There are four main advantages to owning a franchise.

1. *An entrepreneur is provided with an established product or service.* This allows entrepreneurs to compete with giant companies.

2. *Franchisors offer management, technical, and other assistance.* This can be onsite training or classes, aid with starting the new business and handling daily operations, and tips on crisis management. Some franchisors even offer help on everything from site selection and building design to equipment purchase and recipes. Most also maintain toll-free telephone numbers that franchisees can call for advice.

3. *Equipment and supplies can be less expensive.* Because franchises are parts of large chains, they are able to purchase in huge quantities. Some of the savings they enjoy as bulk purchasers are passed on to the franchisee.

4. *A guarantee of consistency attracts customers.* Because a franchise contract mandates a certain level of quality, consumers know that they can walk into a franchise anywhere in the country and receive the same product or service. The cheeseburger sold at a Wendy's in Long Beach, California, will be very similar to the cheeseburger sold in Towson, Maryland. The quality of a room at a Ramada Inn in New Jersey will be much like the quality of a Ramada room in Oregon.

If you begin a franchise, the franchisor may offer training to get you started.

Disadvantages of Owning a Franchise

Although franchising sounds like a great idea, there are four main disadvantages that you need to consider.

1. *Franchises can cost a lot of money and cut down on profits.* The initial capital needed to purchase a franchise business often is high. Also, some of the profits you own as a franchise owner are returned to the franchisor as royalty fees.

2. *Owners of franchises have less freedom to make decisions than other entrepreneurs.* Many of the business decisions that entrepreneurs generally make themselves have already been made for franchisees. Franchisees must offer only certain products or services, and they must charge prices set by the franchisor. Many

YOU CAN SAY THAT AGAIN!

"The harder they say [expanding my business] will be, the more interested I am."

—*Maria Elena Ibanez, founder of International High Technology, international distributor of computers*

entrepreneurs object to this type of control because it inhibits the freedom they sought as independent business owners.

3. ***Franchisees are dependent on the performance of other franchises in the chain.*** A franchisee can benefit from the successes of other franchisees. But if other franchisees run sloppy operations, customer opinions of the chain will decline. As a result, customers may stop going to a franchise, even if a particular store maintains high standards.

4. ***The franchisor can terminate the franchise agreement.*** If the franchisee fails to pay royalty payments or to meet other conditions, the investment in the franchise can be lost. Similarly, when the franchise expires, the franchisor can choose not to renew the agreement.

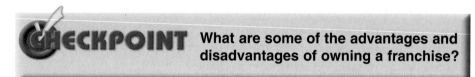

CHECKPOINT What are some of the advantages and disadvantages of owning a franchise?

Evaluating a Franchise

There are many things to consider when purchasing a franchise. These are questions you should ask to evaluate a particular franchise.

1. What is the projected demand for the franchised product or service in the area I want to locate in? Will I be guaranteed an exclusive territory for the duration of the franchise term, or can the franchisor sell additional franchises in the territory?

2. What are the costs and royalty fees associated with the franchise?

3. How profitable have other franchises in the area been? What do other franchisees think of the franchisor?

FRANCHISES REQUIRING SMALL INVESTMENTS

Franchise	Description	Franchise Fee	Start-Up Costs	Royalty Fee
Jani-King	Commercial cleaning service	$6,500–33,000	$1,900 and up	10%
Merle Norman Cosmetics	Cosmetic studio	$7,500–71,900	$35,000–135,000	5%
Merry Maids	Residential cleaning	$13,500–21,500	$11,350–19,850	5%–7%
Duraclean	Carpet and furniture restoration	$41,900	$3,500–26,100	2%–8%
Mr. Rooter	Plumbing, sewer, and drain cleaning	$17,500	$19,100–67,800	3%–6%
Computertots	Computer enrichment programs	$15,000–29,900	$7,700–12,500	6%
Unishippers Association	Discounted overnight air express service	$15,000–70,000	$22,800–61,000	12%–6.5%

Source: *Business Start-Ups,* May 1998

4. How long has the franchisor been in business? How profitable is the franchisor?
5. What services does the franchisor provide? Will the franchisor help me with marketing, merchandising, and site selection?
6. Are the benefits provided by the franchisor worth the loss of independence and the cost of purchasing the franchise?
7. What happens if I want to cancel the franchise agreement?

NET WORTH

Point your browser to

http://www.ideas-in-action.swep.com

Complete the activity for Chapter 4.

Some franchisors make false or misleading claims about their franchises. To make sure that you are not being cheated or misinformed, carefully study the documents the franchisor gives you. Be suspicious of any company that will not back up its claims with written financial statements. Also beware of high-pressure sales tactics. A franchisor that tries to get you to sign a franchise agreement right away is probably not offering you a good business opportunity. Buying a franchise is a big decision. Never allow yourself to be pressured into making the decision too quickly.

Franchise agreements are complicated legal documents. Because they can be difficult to understand, you should never sign one without consulting an attorney. Let your attorney know what promises were made to you orally. Then ask your attorney to confirm that the same promises appear in the contract.

CHECKPOINT **What are some of the questions you should ask when evaluating a franchise opportunity?**

STARTING YOUR OWN BUSINESS

For one reason or another, joining a family business or operating a franchise may not be possible for you, or it might not be right for you. This means that to be an entrepreneur, you will establish a business of your own. You need to consider the many advantages and disadvantages of starting your own business.

Advantages of Starting Your Own Business

Entrepreneurs who start their own business get to make decisions about everything from where to locate the business to how many employees to hire to what prices to charge. They are completely independent and decide their own destinies. Many entrepreneurs find enormous satisfaction in starting their own businesses. Many are attracted to the challenge of creating something entirely new. They also get a great feeling of triumph when their business turns a profit.

David Srivastava started his mail-order business, In a Jam, from his home. David started out selling dried fruit, which he sold through the mail. After a year and a half of disappointing sales, David began offering preserves and jams, products he felt had greater sales potential.

He also put more effort into packaging, and he designed the labels for the jars himself. His instincts proved correct: Eight years after starting out alone in his basement, David now has accounts with several large retail stores, and his company has 14 full-time employees.

CHECKPOINT Why do many entrepreneurs prefer to start new businesses rather than purchase existing businesses or franchises?

Disadvantages of Starting Your Own Business

There are many risks to consider when you start your own business. You must estimate demand for your product or service. There is no certainty that customers will purchase what you offer. Entrepreneurs who join family businesses, buy an existing business, or buy franchises do not have this uncertainty because it is already known that customers will buy the product or service.

Entrepreneurs who start their own business also must make decisions that other types of entrepreneurs need not make. What product or service to offer, the location, what employees to hire, and many other decisions must be made. The results of what may seem to be good decisions may not always be positive.

Lucy Donnelly realized how difficult it is to start a new business from scratch when she opened up a kitchen accessories store. Lucy had considered purchasing a store franchise but had ruled it out because of the high franchise fee.

Lucy's problems began when she realized that her customers did not consider her location to be convenient. As a result, fewer customers shopped in the store

In Class Activity

In small groups, debate the pros and cons of starting a business from scratch for each of the following areas: restaurant, retail gift shop, manufacturer's representative for industrial products.

than Lucy had projected. Contacting suppliers was more difficult than Lucy anticipated, and many of them proved unreliable. The high-priced items Lucy purchased in the hope of increasing profits did not sell well.

 **CHECKPOINT** Why is it more difficult to start a new business than to take over an existing business or purchase a franchise?

THINK CRITICALLY

1. What extra expenses could you expect to pay when operating a franchise as compared to operating a non-franchised company? Could you save money in expenses by operating a franchise? If so, how?

2. Do you think starting a business from scratch would be more challenging than buying an existing business or franchise? Why or why not? Write a paragraph to explain your answer.

3. In your opinion, what would be the greatest advantage of starting a new business? What would be its greatest disadvantage? Do you think the advantages outweigh the disadvantages? Why or why not?

MAKE CONNECTIONS

4. **RESEARCH** Identify a franchise that interests you. Research the franchise, and then evaluate the opportunity using the seven questions given in this lesson. Write a short report on your findings. At the end of your report, tell whether you think this franchise is a good opportunity.

5. **MATH** John and Molly Gonzales want to save enough money so that in five years they can purchase a cleaning service franchise. How much will they need to save each year if the franchise fee is $19,500 and start-up costs are $15,200? (Do not consider interest earned on savings when calculating your answer.) If the company earns $34,700 in profits the first year, and the royalty fee is 6 percent, how much will the Gonzales' first royalty payment be?

6. **PROBLEM SOLVING** Christopher wants to open a dance studio but wonders whether a demand exists for his new business idea. Use the six-step problem-solving model to help Christopher make a decision.

GOALS

EVALUATE the
different legal forms
for a business.

Choose the
Legal Form
of Your
Business

O nce you decide to start your own business, you must decide
what type of ownership the business will have. There are
three main types of ownership arrangements to choose from.

TYPES OF BUSINESS ARRANGEMENTS

A business that is owned exclusively by one person is a **sole
proprietorship.** A business owned by two or more people is a
partnership. A business with the legal rights of a person and which
may be owned by many people is a **corporation.** In addition, some
entrepreneurs set up their companies as *S corporations,* which are a
special kind of corporation.

Sole Proprietorship

Sole proprietorships enable one person to be in control of all business aspects. Sole proprietorships may be very small businesses with
just a few employees, or they may be large businesses with hundreds
of employees. The government exercises very little control over sole
proprietorships, so such businesses can be established and run very
simply. Accurate tax records and certain employment laws must be
met, but these are usually the only forms of government regulation
on a sole proprietorship. For this reason, the sole proprietorship is far
and away the most common form of ownership in the United States.

DISADVANTAGES It can be difficult
to raise money for a sole proprietorship. You are the only person con-
tributing money. Also, owners of sole
proprietorships face a risk that owners
of partnerships or corporations do
not. If a sole proprietorship fails and
debts remain, the entrepreneur's private assets may be taken to pay what
is owed.

Rachel Gibson learned this lesson
the hard way. Last year, her clothing

store went out of business, leaving $42,000 in debt. Because Rachel had set the business up as a sole proprietorship, she had to sell some of her personal assets, including her car, to pay off this amount.

 **CHECKPOINT** Why are sole proprietorships the most common form of business ownership?

Partnership

Many entrepreneurs prefer to go into business with one or more partners so that they have someone with whom to share decision-making and management responsibilities. Running a business as a partnership means that you will not have to come up with all of the capital alone. It also means that any losses the business incurs will be shared by all of the partners. Like sole proprietorships, partnerships face very little government regulation.

DISADVANTAGES Some entrepreneurs do not like partnerships because they do not want to share responsibilities and profits with other people. They fear being held legally liable for the errors of their partners. Partnerships can also lead to disagreements and can end bitterly.

PARTNERSHIP AGREEMENT When two or more entrepreneurs go into business together, they generally sign a *partnership agreement.* The purpose of the partnership agreement is to set down in writing the rights and responsibilities of each of the owners. It identifies the following:

1. name of the business or partnership
2. names of the partners
3. type and value of the investment each partner contributes
4. managerial responsibilities to be handled by each partner
5. accounting methods to be used
6. rights of each partner to review and/or audit accounting documents
7. division of profits and losses among the partners
8. salaries to be withdrawn by the partners
9. duration of the partnership
10. conditions under which the partnership can be dissolved
11. distribution of assets upon dissolution of the partnership
12. procedure for dealing with the death of a partner

 **CHECKPOINT** What are some of the advantages and disadvantages of a partnership?

GENERAL PARTNERSHIP AGREEMENT FORMING
"SUNNY SIDE UP"

By agreement made this 21st day of September, 20--, we, Ana Ortiz, Keesha Gentry, and Thomas Chase, the undersigned, all of Palm Harbor, Florida, hereby join in general partnership to conduct a food service business and mutually agree to the following terms:

1. That the partnership shall be called "Sunny Side Up" and have its principal place of business at 2013 Sand Drive, Palm Harbor, Florida, at which address books containing the full and accurate records of partnership transactions shall be kept and be accessible to any partner at any reasonable time.

2. That the partnership shall continue in operation for an indefinite time until terminated by 90 days' notice provided by one or more of the partners and indicating his, her, or their desire to withdraw. Upon such notice an accounting shall be conducted and a division of the partnership assets made unless a partner wishes to acquire the whole business by paying a price determined by an arbitrator whose selection shall be agreed to by all three partners. Said price shall include goodwill, and the paying of same shall entitle the payor to continue the partnership business under the same name.

3. That each partner shall contribute to the partnership: $22,000 for initial working capital and the supplies and equipment.

4. That in return for the capital contribution in item 3, each partner shall receive an undivided one-third interest in the partnership and its properties.

5. That a fund of $75,000 be set up and retained from the profits of the partnership business as a reserve fund. It being agreed that this fund shall be constituted on not less than 15 percent of the monthly profits until said amount has been accumulated.

6. That the profits of the business shall be divided equally between the partners, that the losses shall be attributed according to the subsequent agreement, and that a determination of said profits and losses shall be made and profit shares paid to each partner on a monthly basis.

7. That the partnership account shall be kept in the First Florida Bank and that all withdrawals from same shall be by check bearing the signature of at least one of the partners.

8. That each partner shall devote his or her full efforts to the partnership business and shall not engage in another business without the other partners' permission.

9. That no partner shall cause to issue any commercial paper or shall enter into any agreements representing the partnership outside the normal conduct of the food service business without notice to the remaining partners and the consent of at least one other partner and further that all managerial and personnel decisions not covered by another section of this agreement shall be made with the assent of at least two of the partners.

IN AGREEMENT HERETO, WE ARE

Ana Ortiz   Keesha Gentry   Thomas Chase

_Ana Ortiz_____   _Keesha Gentry_____   _Thomas Chase_____

Corporation

Unlike a sole proprietorship or a partnership, a corporation is treated independently of its owners. Since a corporation has the legal rights of a person, the corporation, not the owners, pays taxes, enters into contracts, and may be held liable for negligence.

Ownership of a corporation is in the form of shares of stock. A **share of stock** is a unit of ownership in a corporation. People who own stock in the corporation are called *shareholders,* or *stockholders.*

Jim Munroe set up his company, Munroe Office Supply, as a corporation. He created 100 shares of stock worth $1,000 each. Jim then issued 15 shares to each of three outside investors, which means they gave $45,000 total to be shareholders in his company. Jim kept the remaining 55 shares himself. This means that Jim owns 55 percent of his company, while outside investors own a total of 45 percent of the company. The individual or group that owns the most shares maintains control of the company.

Every corporation has a **board of directors,** a group of people who meet several times a year to make important decisions affecting the company. The board of directors is responsible for electing the corporation's senior officers, determining their salaries, and setting the corporation's rules for conducting business. The board of directors also decides how much the corporation should pay out in dividends. **Dividends** are distributions of profits to shareholders by corporations. The company's officers, not the board of directors, are responsible for the day-to-day management of the corporation.

DISADVANTAGES Setting up a corporation is more complicated than setting up a sole proprietorship or a partnership. To incorporate a business means to set a business up as a corporation. To **incorporate,** you will need the assistance of a lawyer, who will help you file articles of incorporation with the state official responsible for chartering, or registering, corporations. Because of this, establishing a corporation can be costly. A business must be careful when it decides to incorporate itself. Articles of incorporation must be written which fully detail the purpose of the business. If the articles are not written well, the corporation's activities can be limited.

Corporations are subject to much more government regulation than are sole proprietorships or partnerships. Much more paperwork is involved in running a corporation.

Another drawback of incorporation is that income is taxed twice. A corporation pays taxes on its income, and shareholders pay taxes on the dividends they receive from the corporation. This means that the corporation's profits are taxed as corporate income and again as individual income.

WHY INCORPORATE? If the corporate form of ownership is complicated and costly, why do entrepreneurs set up corporations? Liability is the main reason. **Liability** is the amount owed to others. The shareholders' liability

In Class Activity

As a class, make a chart of the three legal forms of business ownership. List the advantages and disadvantages for each.

is limited to the amount of money each shareholder invested in the company when he or she purchased stock.

Munroe's Office Supply has gone bankrupt, leaving $150,000 in debt. Each shareholder only loses the amount he or she invested in the corporation, so the outside people who invested $45,000 would lose their investment. Jim would also lose his investment of $55,000. If Jim set up his business as a sole proprietorship, he would have been liable for the $150,000. If the business had been set up as a partnership between Jim and his friends, all four partners would have been liable for the $150,000 debt.

Incorporation allows businesses to raise money through selling more stock. Lenders are also more willing to lend money to corporations than to sole proprietorships or partnerships. Finally, because shareholders do not affect the management of a corporation, the main shareholder of the company can change through the buying and selling of stock without disrupting the day-to-day business.

 **CHECKPOINT** **What is the main benefit of setting up your business as a corporation?**

S Corporation

Small corporations can elect to be treated as an S corporation. An **S corporation** is a corporation organized under subchapter S of the Internal Revenue Code whose income is taxed as a partnership. Unlike regular corporations, an S corporation is not taxed as a business. The individual shareholders are taxed on the profits they earn. Many companies establish themselves as S corporations because they lose money in the early years. Any losses suffered by S corporations can be used to offset other sources of taxable income.

Steve Miller works full time at a large company where he earns $38,000 a year. He also runs Forever Yours, a wedding consultant business. Like many new businesses, Forever Yours lost money in its first year when its expenses exceeded its revenues by $12,000. Since Steve had set his company  up as an S corporation, he was able to reduce his taxable income by $12,000. His taxable income for the year was thus $26,000 (the $38,000 salary less the $12,000 he lost on his business).

 **CHECKPOINT** **Why might a business become an S Corporation?**

CHARACTERISTICS OF THE LEGAL FORMS OF BUSINESS

Feature	Sole Proprietorship	Partnership	Corporation	S Corporation
Simple to start	✓	✓		
Decisions made by one person	✓			
Low initial cost		✓		
Limited liability			✓	✓
Limited government regulation	✓	✓		
Ability to raise capital			✓	✓
Double taxation of profits			✓	

THINK CRITICALLY

1. Which do you think is more risky: a sole proprietorship or a partnership? Why?

2. What would be the advantages and disadvantages of forming a partnership with a friend? Would you consider forming a business this way? Why or why not?

3. Why do you think the government regulates corporations more closely than it does sole proprietorships or partnerships?

MAKE CONNECTIONS

4. COMMUNICATION With a partner, write a skit about two people who wish to form a partnership. Decide on a business to enter and the duties each person will perform in the business. In the skit, the partners should negotiate the terms of the partnership agreement.

5. MATH Caren McHugh opened Best Foot Forward, a shoe store catering to women. To raise money, she organized as a corporation. She created 500 shares of stock, each worth $75. Caren holds 260 of the shares for herself. She sells the rest in even amounts to six investors. How many shares does each investor own? If Best Foot Forward fails and leaves $65,000 in debt, for how much would each investor be liable?

Chapter 4
Review

CHAPTER SUMMARY

Run *an Existing* Business

1. An existing business has an established customer base and relationships with suppliers. The seller may train you in how to run the business. Existing businesses also have records of profits made in the past.
2. Be careful when buying an existing business. It may not be making a profit, or other problems may be involved. A large amount of capital usually is needed to purchase an existing business.
3. There are seven important steps to follow when deciding to purchase an existing business.
4. Joining a family businesses has advantages, such as pride in the business and enjoyment in working with relatives. But family politics can negatively affect the business, and business problems can end up affecting family life.

Own a *Franchise* or *Start* a Business

5. Costs involved in owning a franchise involve an initial franchise fee, start-up costs, royalty fees, and possibly advertising fees.
6. Purchasing a franchise provides an established product or service for you to sell. Franchises are also recognized by customers. You may be able to purchase supplies at a low cost. But franchise ownership can be expensive. It also does not allow much room for independent decision making.
7. Many people create an entirely new business. There are risks, because there is no guaranteed demand for your product or service. You must also make all the decisions on every aspect of your business.

Choose the *Legal* Form of Your Business

8. Businesses can be set up as sole proprietorships, as partnerships, or as corporations. There are advantages and disadvantages to each legal form that should be considered when you decide how to set up your business.
9. An S corporation is a special kind of corporation where only the shareholders are taxed on earnings, not the business itself.

What Do You Know Now?

Read *Build a Business* again. Then answer the questions a second time. How have your responses changed?

VOCABULARY BUILDER

Choose the term that best fits the definition on the left. Write your answers on a separate sheet of paper.

1. Weekly or monthly payments made by the owner of the franchise to the seller of the franchise
2. A business owned exclusively by one person
3. Group of people who meet several times a year to make important decisions affecting the company
4. A unit of ownership in a corporation
5. A person who sells businesses for a living
6. Fee the franchise owner pays in return for the right to run the franchise
7. A business owned by two or more people
8. Distributions of profits to shareholders by corporations
9. A legal agreement that gives an individual the right to market a company's products or services in a particular area
10. A business with the legal rights of a person and which may be owned by many people
11. To set a business up as a corporation
12. Costs associated with beginning a business
13. The amount owed to others

a. advertising fees
b. board of directors
c. business broker
d. corporation
e. dividends
f. franchise
g. incorporate
h. initial franchise fee
i. liability
j. partnership
k. royalty fees
l. sole proprietorship
m. start-up costs
n. share of stock
o. S corporation
p. valuator

REVIEW YOUR KNOWLEDGE

14. What are the advantages of buying an existing business? What are the disadvantages?

15. What are some of the compromises that must be made by an entrepreneur who joins the family business?

16. Where can an entrepreneur obtain information about purchasing and operating a franchise?

17. Why should an entrepreneur consult with an attorney prior to signing a franchise agreement?

18. What kinds of decisions need to be made when starting a new business?

19. What are the risks in starting your own business?

20. Why do owners of sole proprietorships face more risks than owners of partnerships or corporations?

21. What is the purpose of the partnership agreement?

22. What decisions are made by a corporation's board of directors?

23. What is the benefit of an S corporation?

APPLY WHAT YOU LEARNED

24. You decide to start a business selling CDs over the Internet. What type of ownership will your business have (sole proprietorship, partnership, corporation)? Why did you choose this form?

25. You are meeting with the owner of an ice cream shop you would like to purchase. What specific questions are you going to ask her? What documents do you want to see? How will you evaluate whether or not to purchase this business?

26. Your family owns a successful restaurant. You are trying to convince them to open another restaurant in a different part of town. What information will you present to convince them to adopt your idea?

THINK CRITICALLY

27. The existing business you have purchased has trouble with suppliers. The previous owner did not pay them in a timely manner and many of them refuse to ship goods to you on credit. What actions would you take to improve this situation?

28. Franchisors often offer training and technical assistance. Why do you think they provide these services?

29. What are the risks involved in starting a new business? Can you think of ways to overcome these risks?

30. There are three forms of ownership for businesses. List two real companies that fit into each category. Why do you think these businesses were set up in these forms?

MAKE CONNECTIONS

31. **MATH** Manuel Vazquez owns 65 percent of the 200 shares of stock in a car dealership that is worth $24,000,000. There are 5 other stockholders, each owning an equal share. The dealership has recently lost a lawsuit and must pay damages of $1,200,000. What is Manuel's liability? What is the liability of each of the other stockholders?

32. **MATH** You have purchased a car wash franchise. The franchise fee was $25,000. You must return 6 percent of your earnings in royalty fees. During your first year, you spent $10,000 on equipment; $4,300 on operating costs (water and electricity); and $10,700 to your part-time

employee. Your first year total revenues were $120,000. Calculate the total expenditures for the first year. What was your profit? What will profits be in your second year if total revenues and costs remain the same? (Note: You do not need any new equipment.)

33. **COMMUNICATION** You are the owner of a coffee-shop franchise. The franchise agreement specifies that the franchisee must submit all advertising plans for approval. Write a memo to the franchisor outlining your plan to market the franchise's new bagels.

34. **RESEARCH** Use the newspaper, Internet, magazines, and other materials to research business opportunities. Find a business for sale that interests you. Find out information about purchasing it. Include franchise fees, royalties, projected earnings, and operating costs. Do you think this would be a good investment? Why or why not?

35. **COMMUNICATION** You want to buy a clothing boutique. Write a letter to the owner of the store expressing your interest and requesting the necessary information you need to make a decision.

This Is Your Business Project

1. To expand your business, you have decided to purchase similar businesses in your area. List the businesses in your area that compete with you. Write down the reasons you would or would not consider buying each company.
2. Find franchise opportunities available in your business field. Investigate one of these opportunities and gather information about it, such as franchise fees, royalties, projected earnings, operating costs.
3. Consider franchising your business to others. Write an advertisement offering to sell franchises to prospective business owners.
4. You have a friend who is interested in being your business partner. Write the partnership agreement for the two of you.
5. Make a list of all the advantages and disadvantages of becoming an S corporation. Determine how much stock to sell and the value of each share.

Chapter 5

DEVELOP
A BUSINESS PLAN

LESSONS

5.1 Why Do You Need A Business Plan?

5.2 What Goes into a Business Plan?

5.3 Create an Effective Business Plan

BUILD A BUSINESS

The Importance of a Plan

Consuela looked up from her accounting homework as her dad walked into the living room. "Hey, Dad," Consuela said, "what does it mean when someone says 'they did not plan to fail, they failed to plan'?"

"Where did you hear that?" Pablo asked.

"I saw a GOING OUT OF BUSINESS sign in the window of one of the stores in the mall today. I heard a man say it when he walked by."

"Well, Consuela," Pablo replied, "when people open businesses, they never plan to fail. But the majority of businesses that open do not make it. The main reason for this is because they did not plan properly. Chances are they knew how to do something really well, but they did not know much about business."

"You have your own business, Dad, and you're successful. So I guess you're a pretty good planner!"

"I may be now, Consuela. It wasn't the first time I went into business, though. I was looking for a job in the building supply industry and made money in the meantime doing home repairs and remodeling, mostly for family and friends. I thought I was only going to work for myself for a few months, so I didn't have a formal written business plan. I figured I didn't need one. But I stayed so busy that before I knew it, I was running my own business."

"That's cool, Dad," Consuela said. "But I thought you just said businesses have to plan or they fail. How did you stay in business?"

"I kept doing repairs for friends and family, and soon there was no one left who needed my services. No one else I knew needed any work done. I needed to advertise to keep my business going, and there was some equipment that I needed to buy to expand my remodeling business. But the bank would not give me a loan because I could not show them anything in writing about my business. They wanted to know where my business was headed and how much profit and expenses I could expect to have each year. To tell you the truth, I hadn't thought much about all that stuff before then. I'm sure the loan officer at the bank didn't think much of me or my business. But he was polite when I was turned down for a loan."

"So you didn't stay in business. But you own your own company now. What happened next, Dad?"

"After I closed my business, I found a job working for a construction company for a few years," Pablo replied. "While I did, I started doing some research about the home remodeling market and worked on a business plan. The next time I went to the bank, they knew I really meant business."

What Do You Know?

1. What kind of plans do you think someone should make before opening a business?
2. Where could you go to research a business idea?
3. Why is it important to have a written business plan?

Why Do *You* Need a Business *Plan?*

Now that you know the details of your business, you need to put everything down on paper. Writing out these details will help you visualize all the aspects of your business. It will also help you convince banks and other people to invest in your business idea.

THE BUSINESS PLAN

A **business plan** is a written document that describes all the steps necessary in opening and operating a successful business. It:

- describes what your business will produce, how you will produce it, and who will buy your product or service
- explains who will run your business and who will supply it with goods
- states how your business will win over customers from competitors and what your business will do to keep customers
- provides detailed financial information that shows how your business will succeed in earning a profit

Writing a business plan is one of the most difficult and important things you will do as an entrepreneur. Writing a solid business plan is critical because the plan can make or break your business.

Purpose of a Business Plan

The business plan serves three important purposes.

1. *A business plan explains the idea behind your business and spells out how your product or service will be produced and sold.* To convince investors that your business idea is solid, you

will need a completely new product or service, or one that is better or less expensive than products or services that already exist. You will need to identify who your target customer is and show how your company will be able to obtain and keep customers.

2. *A business plan sets specific objectives and describes how your business expects to achieve them.* A good business plan includes sales projections for the short term (the first year), the medium term (two to five years after start-up), and the long term (five years in the future). It describes what products and services will be introduced over the next five years and sets forth future business plans, such as expansion of the business.

3. *A business plan describes the backgrounds and experience of the people who will be running the business.* Banks and other lenders make financing decisions based on how much they think a company can meet its objectives. If you give good information on the background and experience of the people who will be running your company, the bank or investor will be more likely to invest money in your business.

In Class Activity

In small groups, brainstorm the ideal backgrounds and experiences of people who could run these new businesses: roofing company, software developer, convenience store, accounting firm.

CHECKPOINT What are the three main purposes of a business plan?

Importance of a Business Plan

Every new business must have a business plan. The business plan is important for several reasons.

1. *A business plan makes you think about all aspects of your business.* Stan Meyer began a graphic design business from his home. He spent many hours thinking about the business and thought he was ready to start it until he sat down to write his business plan. He had not

made sales and profit projections. He had also not thought about the possibility that he might need to hire staff if the business grew too large for him to handle alone. Drafting a business plan helped Stan gain even more confidence in his business idea.

It showed him that building a successful business based on his concept would be possible. Working on his business plan also helped Stan think through business strategies, recognize limits, and identify problems he might encounter.

2. *A business plan may help you secure financing for your business.* As you will learn in Chapter 7, lenders require a business plan before they will consider financing a business. Without a business plan you will not be able to obtain a business loan.

3. *A business plan helps you communicate your ideas to others.* By the time you write your business plan, you will have given a lot of thought to the business you want to establish. You will also believe that your business will succeed. If you communicate your ideas well on paper, you will convince the reader that your business will succeed. This can help you get a loan from a bank. It also may convince suppliers to extend credit to your company.

4. *A business plan can serve as a tool for managing your business.* Once your business is up and running, you can use

Entrepreneurial Timeline

| 1600 | 1700 | 1800 | 1900 |

British Business in the 18th and 19th Centuries

Great Britain was an unpredictable place for businesses in the 1700s and 1800s. During these years, Britain had a segmented market. This meant that British businesses sold to many regional and overseas markets, and all of these markets wanted different types of goods. No two regions wanted exactly the same item. It was difficult for businesses to make a profit under these conditions. To have a better chance of succeeding in business, entrepreneurs had to be extremely specialized in their production. A large quantity of the same item was never produced all at once, because all of the goods manufactured would not be sold quickly.

To try to ensure their success, these small specialized companies often completed each other's work. One company would spin cotton, while another wove it into fabric. Then yet another company actually sold the completed material to merchants and customers. Because of the need for specialization, British entrepreneurial businesses were based on family ties and good friends. This made labor, capital, business information, and market knowledge available to those who needed it. Entrepreneurs had cousins who were willing to work for them, aunts and uncles who could provide loans, and grandparents who could give them business advice!

the business plan in your decision making. Adam Rothwell regularly uses his business plan to help manage his company, Suburban Pools. Adam's plan laid out his vision of how the company would grow over time. By following the strategies he described in his plan, he has increased sales by offering new products and by targeting a larger area.

 **Why do entrepreneurs need to write business plans?**

THINK CRITICALLY

1. Why do you think the quality of the business plan is so critical to an entrepreneur's success?

2. Melinda Rosati wants to purchase her uncle's barber shop. Because it is an ongoing business, Melinda doesn't think she needs to write a business plan. Do you agree or disagree with Melinda's opinion? Why or why not?

3. Putting your business plan in writing helps you communicate your ideas to others. Do you think discussing your business plan out loud in a meeting can also help get your ideas across? Why or why not?

MAKE CONNECTIONS

4. **PROBLEM SOLVING** André Kitaevich uses the business plan he wrote to help him run day-to-day operations in his jewelry store. On what specific issues might André consult his plan?

5. **COMMUNICATION** You are starting a business in the home healthcare field. Write a paragraph explaining the idea behind the business. Be sure to spell out how you plan to market its services.

What Goes *into* a Business Plan?

Not all business plans are alike. A business plan for a sole proprietorship business based in a home differs from a business plan for a large corporation with offices in many cities. But, all business plans serve the purposes described in Lesson 5.1. Because all business plans have the same purposes, they all have the same seven basic elements.

SEVEN BASIC ELEMENTS OF A BUSINESS PLAN

Although business plans differ, all should include some basic information in the following areas:

1. history and background of your idea
2. goals and objectives for your company
3. products or services you will offer
4. form of ownership
5. management and staffing
6. marketing
7. current and projected financial statements

History and Background

Something must have sparked the idea for your business. Describing how you came up with your idea can help lenders, investors, and others understand how your business will operate.

Nora Ellis and Samantha Richards are qualified child-care workers who have worked together at a day-care center for many years. The center frequently turned away children because it did not have the room or the staff to take care of more toddlers. Nora and Samantha realized they could make a profit running their own day-care center and decided to open a center of their own. Their business plan explained that there was a high demand for quality day-care services in the area and that they were well positioned to meet this need.

Goals and Objectives

Your business plan should outline your short-term, medium-term, and long-term goals. This section describes your vision of where you want your company to be in the future. Some entrepreneurs are very clear about what they want to do with their businesses. Others know their short-term goals, but have not thought farther ahead. Nora and Samantha knew what their short-term and medium-term goals were. In the first year of business, they want to get financing that would allow them to lease or buy a facility, equip the facility, and staff eight employees. In their second and third years of business, they want to invest in more equipment and possibly expand their facility to accommodate more children. They had not thought through what their objectives were for the long term, though. Writing a business plan forced them to think about these goals, such as whether they want to remain a one-location day-care center or expand into a regional chain of centers.

Products or Services

This part of your business plan should describe the products or services your company plans to produce and sell. You should explain how these products or services differ from those already on the market. Highlight any unique features of your products or services, and explain the benefits customers will receive by purchasing from your company.

INDUSTRY This section of your business plan should describe the industry you will operate in. Things you should include in this section are:

- external factors affecting your business, such as high competition or a lack of certain suppliers
- growth potential of the industry
- economic trends of the industry
- technology trends that may affect the industry
- forecasts for industry growth

To find this information, you will need to perform research. Government documents, articles and books on industry leaders, the Internet, or other reliable sources are good places to start. Be sure to name all of these sources in your plan. Citing sources makes a business plan more convincing.

Downtown areas are good locations for many businesses.

LOCATION The product or service section of your business plan should also describe the location of your business. Lenders want to know exactly where your business will be because the location of a business is often a critical factor in its success.

Writing the products or services section of the business plan was easy for Nora and Samantha because they had a clear idea what they wanted to do. In the Industry section of their plan, they included population data for their area. This information showed that demand for their service could grow over time. They also cited government sources reporting that the demand for day-care services is expected to grow steadily as more and more women with young children join the labor force. For the Location section of the business plan, Nora and Samantha put down in writing that they planned to start the business in a prime location, in the heart of a community where most families have young children and both parents work outside the home.

Form of Ownership

In your business, you should have a section detailing your form of ownership. Provide information relevant to your form of business, such as who your partners are and how many shareholders you have. This section of the business plan is important because each legal form of business has an effect on how the business works and makes profits. If you use your business plan to obtain financing, the lender will be interested in this information.

Management and Staffing

The people who manage your company are critical to its success. The best business plan won't make your company succeed if it is carried out by people who are not capable. The Management and Staffing section of the business plan should show that you and the people who will be working for you have the experience, maturity, and common sense to manage your business well.

Nora and Samantha have master's degrees in early childhood education. Together, they have more than 35 years of experience in day care, including 15 years in management. To show readers of their business plan that they are well qualified to run a center, they included copies of their resumes and letters of reference from satisfied parents.

Marketing

In your business plan, you will also include information on marketing your business. You will explain who your prospective customers are, how large the market is for your product or service, and how you plan to enter that market. (Developing a marketing plan is examined in Chapter 9.) It should also explain how you plan to deal with competition.

You should list your company's advantages over the competition. These advantages can include:

- performance
- quality
- price
- promotion

- reliability
- distribution
- public image or reputation

Nora and Samantha's prospective customers are the 1,000 to 1,500 children between the ages of 2 and 5 who live in their area. Nora and Samantha determine that 90 percent of the families would be able to afford their center. To enter the market, Nora and Samantha will advertise in the local newspapers. They will send out fliers to families in their target market. They also will offer two months of care at a discounted rate for new customers.

Current and Projected Financial Statements

The financial section of your plan consists of three elements.

1. *Identification of risks.* Prospective lenders and investors will want to know what risks your business faces and how you plan to deal with them. Do not be afraid to list potential problems. Lenders know that every business faces risks. They will be reassured to see that you have clearly thought through the potential problems and will not be caught by surprise without a plan for dealing with them. Examples of risks that you could include are competitors cutting prices, costs exceeding projections, and demand for your product or service declining over time.

2. *Financial statements.* A new business must include projected financial statements in its business plan. An existing business must include current as well as projected statements. A financial statement based on projected revenues and expenses is called a *pro forma financial statement.* Each of the statements that you will need to prepare is described in Chapter 7.

3. *Funding request and return on investment.* You also need to indicate how much you need to borrow and how you plan to use the money. You should give investors an idea of how much money they could expect to earn on their investment in your business. You should also include how much money you are investing in the business.

Nora and Samantha know that their main risk is the possibility that parents will perceive their center as unsafe. Nora and Samantha have prepared a pamphlet entitled "Safety and Your Child." They plan to use this as part of their marketing package. They included a copy of their pamphlet in the appendix to their business plan.

Nora and Samantha have also included projected financial statements for their business, which show how much money and profit they expect to earn. They require $140,000 to start their business. Together they are contributing $85,000 of their own money. This means they need a bank to loan them $55,000. They include this information in their plan as well.

Did You Know?

The Small Business Administration (SBA) commonly gives loans to small companies. In the late 1990s, the number of SBA loans to women owners more than tripled. Loans to minority borrowers nearly tripled.

CHECKPOINT List the elements of a business plan and explain why each is important.

All business plans should include the seven basic elements. Some businesses need to provide additional information in their business plans. A business that has licensing requirements, or must meet legal restrictions and regulations, would include a legal issues section in its business plan. To identify any special sections that you should include, ask yourself what you would want to know about a business before you would lend it money.

As part of their business plan, Nora and Samantha devote a special section to health and safety issues. They describe their procedures for dealing with allergies, illnesses, and injuries. They also outline their plans for dealing with emergencies, such as burst water pipes or fires.

CHECKPOINT Why should some businesses include additional information in their business plans?

THINK CRITICALLY

1. Some elements of the business plan require outside source information. If your business manufactures cardboard boxes, what specific sources might you need to consult?

2. Why should you include management and staffing issues in your business plan?

3. A group of investors is planning to open a new amusement park. What special elements will need to be included in their business plan?

MAKE CONNECTIONS

4. MATH You plan to start a corporation. You have $67,500 in savings, but need $165,000 total to begin your business. How much money will you need from investors? What will be your percentage of ownership? If you have four outside investors, how much will each investor need to invest? What percentage will each investor own?

5. COMMUNICATION Write out what you think the short-term, medium-term, and long-term goals would be for a person who has just purchased an ice cream parlor.

Create an Effective Business *Plan*

Your business plan needs to convince readers that you have come up with a practical business idea. To do this, you must include information and data from objective sources to show that your idea is founded on solid evidence.

Researching and writing a business plan takes time, lots of time. In fact, most entrepreneurs spend 50 to 100 hours developing their business plans. The process requires patience, research, thought, and a great deal of writing and editing.

RESEARCH THE BUSINESS PLAN

Pulling together the information you will need to write your business plan involves researching all aspects of your business, from leasing space to what you will charge for your product or service to dealing with competitors. Researching all the parts of your business will teach you a great deal about running a business and may provide you with specific ideas for starting up your company.

Print Resources

Information for your business plan can come from many sources. Your public library will have many books on entrepreneurship. In addition, books on marketing, financing, hiring and managing a staff, purchasing a business, and operating a franchise can be helpful. The library will also have books devoted specifically to writing a business plan. Some books will have sample business plans. These books should provide you with valuable information on running your own business.

Magazines may also prove helpful, especially magazines devoted to small business ownership and to the industry you will be competing in. Ask your librarian to help you find magazines that contain information that may be relevant to your business plan.

Government documents, including publications issued by the Small Business Administration (SBA) and other federal agencies, may provide you with useful information. The SBA district office nearest you will have many publications that can help you complete your business plan.

Online Resources

Much of the information you can find in print resources is also available on the Internet. The SBA web site contains much of the same information that the SBA provides in print. Many magazine articles, and even some books, can be found on the Internet. In addition, there are many sites specifically for entrepreneurs and small businesses that may give you detailed information.

People Resources

People from many organizations can help you with your business plan. Counselors from Small Business Development Centers provide free one-on-one assistance in developing a business plan. They also provide inexpensive workshops on topics that may help you develop your plan.

Another source of valuable assistance is the Service Corps of Retired Executives (SCORE). There are more than 12,000 retired executives working with SCORE who volunteer their time to help younger entrepreneurs. They provide free confidential advice that could be helpful to you as you prepare your business plan. You

What Went Wrong

Business Plan Woes
Pop Goes the Planning
Business: POP-UP Graphics, Inc., Towson, Maryland * Open for business: 3 months

While working as a salesperson for a custom exhibit display company, Tim Tomlinson found a unique product not currently being marketed in the United States. It was a lightweight, portable, full-color display that could be set up and dismantled quickly. A company in Sweden was the manufacturer of this display. Tim thought it was ideal for trade shows and conventions.

Tim decided to become a distributor of the special displays. He drew up a sales and marketing plan for establishing a network of dealers across the United States. The Swedish company gave Tim exclusive U.S. sales rights and an inventory credit of $100,000 for his new company, POP-UP Graphics. Tim obtained a business loan, rented an office/warehouse, and hired staff. Tim went on a sales trip and signed deals for the cus-

tom displays up and down the East Coast. Within 60 days he had 27 dealers and $140,000 in sales.

But POP-UP Graphics fell down. Tim was doing a great job selling, but there was no overall business plan, no credit policies in place, and no customer service program. When he came in off the road, Tim found that his inventory was gone, orders were confused, and customers were furious. Tim contacted his former employer, who agreed to hire him back.

Think Critically
1. Why do you think the Swedish company gave Tim exclusive U.S. sales and an inventory credit for POP-UP Graphics?
2. How would a business plan have helped POP-UP Graphics succeed?

can set up a meeting with a SCORE volunteer, or you can work with a SCORE volunteer over the Internet.

Additional Resources

Many Internet sites provide information on writing business plans, including several sites that take you through the business plan step-by-step. You can even ask questions on some sites.

Your local Chamber of Commerce and Small Business Development Centers have information on trends affecting local businesses. **Trade associations** are organizations that promote certain types of businesses. These associations can be valuable sources of information as well.

To research your business plan, you should visit your local library.

Some entrepreneurs hire experts to help them. Professional business consultants can be found in directories available at your library or on the Internet.

Nora and Samantha, the two people who began their own child care business, began their business plan by taking books out of the library. They also read information they received from the Small Business Administration on child care facilities. Once they had an outline prepared, they met with a counselor from their local Small Business Development Center. The counselor helped them prepare their pro forma financial statements.

CHECKPOINT What resources are available to help you develop your business plan?

PUT YOUR BUSINESS PLAN TOGETHER

Your business plan is your best opportunity to let other people know what you want to do with your company. It gives you the chance to convince them that your idea is sound and that you have the talent and resources to make your idea a successful business venture.

To make the best of this opportunity, you will want to create an attractive document that is neat, well-organized, and inviting to read. Handwritten business plans are not acceptable. All business plans must be word processed and printed on standard-sized white paper. In addition, your business plan should follow a standard format.

Introductory Elements

Every business plan should begin with a cover letter, a cover sheet, a table of contents, a statement of purpose, and an executive summary. These elements help set the tone for the body of your business plan.

COVER LETTER A **cover letter** is a letter that explains or provides more information about a document or set of documents. The cover letter for your business plan should include your name, the name of your business, and your address and telephone number. It should briefly describe your business and its potential for success. It also needs to tell the reader how much capital you need.

THE MT. WASHINGTON

Children's

CENTER

5813 NORTH AVENUE, BALTIMORE, MARYLAND 21205

(410) 555-4445

April 11, 20—

Ms. Jane Stewart
Vice President
First National Bank
E. 35th Street
Baltimore, Maryland 21212

Dear Ms. Stewart:

Enclosed please find a copy of the business plan for the Mt. Washington Children's Center, a proposed new day-care center in northwest Baltimore that will serve approximately 50 young children. We believe that the acute shortage of high-quality day care in this part of the city will allow us to generate significant revenues for the center and that we will be earning a profit within a year of opening.

To establish the kind of center we envision, we plan to put up $85,000 of our own capital. We will need additional financing of $55,000. As you will note from our pro forma financial statements, we plan to repay the loan within five years.

Please let us know if there is any additional information you would like to receive. We look forward to hearing from you.

Sincerely yours,

Nora Ellis
Nora Ellis

Samantha Richards
Samantha Richards

COVER SHEET Your business plan should have a cover sheet that indicates the name of your company, the date, the owner of the company, the title of the owner, and the address and phone number of the company.

TABLE OF CONTENTS A *table of contents* is a listing of the material included in a publication. It shows the reader what each page covers. This textbook has a table of contents in the front. It is important that your table of contents be accurate, so make sure the sections are in the correct order and check that the page numbers shown in the table of contents are correct.

In Class Activity

In small groups, set short-, medium-, and long-term goals for one of the following new businesses: automobile service station, take-out restaurant, web site developer.

STATEMENT OF PURPOSE The statement of purpose very briefly describes why you are asking for a loan and what you plan to do with the money if you receive it. It should be no more than one or two paragraphs.

STATEMENT OF PURPOSE

The Mt. Washington Children's Center will operate as a private day-care center serving approximately 50 children in northwest Baltimore. The Center will offer excellent supervision in a clean, safe, and intellectually stimulating environment.

The project is requesting $55,000 in financing. This money will be used to:

- rent and remodel 4,000 square feet of indoor space
- prepare 18,000 square feet of outdoor space for use as a playground
- purchase equipment such as swings, jungle gyms, sand-boxes, and supplies
- pay salaries of eight employees until sufficient cash flow is generated to allow operating expenses to be covered

---

EXECUTIVE SUMMARY An executive summary is a short restatement of a report. It should capture the interest of its readers and make them want to read more. If the executive summary is unconvincing, a lender may decide not to read your entire business plan. This makes a strong executive summary critical to the success of your business.

The executive summary should be no longer than one or two pages, and it should be written in a clear, simple style. Your executive summary should:

- describe your business concept and communicate what is unique about your idea
- include your projections for sales, costs, and profits
- identify your needs (inventory, land, building, equipment, etc.)
- state the amount you are interested in borrowing

Although the executive summary appears before the business plan, it should be written after the business plan has been completed. To write the executive summary, go through the business plan and find the most important and persuasive points you have made. Then draft an outline of an executive summary based on these points.

E X E C U T I V E   S U M M A R Y

The Mt. Washington Children's Center (MWCC) will be established as a partnership in Baltimore, Maryland. It will be owned and operated by Nora Ellis and Samantha Richards, highly respected child-care professionals with more than 35 years of experience in the field. Three experienced teachers and three teacher aides will supervise approximately 50 boys and girls between the ages of 2 and 5. In addition, a receptionist/bookkeeper and a cleaning/maintenance person will be hired.

MWCC is being established in response to the shortage of high-quality child care in northwest Baltimore. Only two small day-care centers now serve a population of 45,000 upper-middle-class professionals. In 75 percent of these households, both parents work outside the home. The accessible location of the Center will make it an extremely attractive day-care option for parents in the area. When completed, its facilities, which will include four large outdoor play structures and eight personal computers, will represent state-of-the-art day care. Its staff will comprise the finest day-care professionals in Baltimore, led by a management team that is recognized throughout the region.

Market research indicates that the MWCC could expect to fill 90 to 100 percent of its student positions immediately upon opening and that the center would be profitable as early as the third year of operation. Expansion could begin in the third year. To finance the start-up of the company, its owners are seeking $55,000 in financing, which they would expect to repay within five years.

Once you have created a draft of your executive summary, ask people who do and don't understand your business to read the summary. If readers do not come away with a clear sense of what you plan to do and why you will succeed in doing it, your executive summary needs more work.

Nora and Samantha circulated their plan among several of their friends and colleagues. One day-care professional suggested mentioning that the center would be equipped with video monitors that allow supervision at all times. Another reader said that Nora and Samantha needed to add that they planned to invest $85,000 of their own money.

Main Body of Your Plan

The main body of your plan should include the seven elements described in Lesson 5.2. Also be sure to include any additional elements you think are necessary.

Lenders do not have time to read business plans that are long or hard to understand. This means that your plan should be short and to the point. Don't include unnecessary or irrelevant information. Use simple language that will give your readers a clear idea of what you want to do and how you plan to do it. Where possible, use charts and tables to illustrate your point.

Appendix

The appendix is the part of the business plan that includes any supporting evidence that was not included in the body of the report. Documents that might be included in the appendix include your resume, personal financial statements, income tax returns, copies of any large sales contracts you have already negotiated, letters of recommendation, or legal documents.

 **CHECKPOINT** **What is the purpose of each part of a business plan?**

THINK CRITICALLY

1. Why do you think it would be helpful to speak with people resources before you write your business plan? Can you think of other people besides those mentioned in the chapter who might be good resources?

2. Why is it possible to write an executive summary only after you have written your business plan? Why might the executive summary be more important than the body of the plan?

MAKE CONNECTIONS

3. COMMUNICATION Write a statement of purpose for a business plan a group of investors opening a new amusement park will need.

4. MATH If you intend to finance 20% of the total $174,500 you need to start a business, how much money would you be responsible for?

CHAPTER SUMMARY

Why Do *You* Need a Business *Plan?*

1. A business plan is a written document that describes what your business will produce, how you will produce it, and who will buy your product or service.
2. A business plan discusses issues such as who will run your business, how you will retain customers, and how your business will earn a profit.
3. Writing a business plan will help you to think about all aspects of your business, to secure financing, to communicate your ideas, and to manage your business.

What Goes *into* a Business Plan?

4. Business plans should include basic information in the following areas: history and background of your business idea, goals and objectives, products or services, form of ownership, management and staffing, marketing, and financial statements.
5. Some business plans should also include information on licensing requirements, legal issues, and other items relevant to a specific business.

Create an Effective Business *Plan*

6. Research your business plan through printed resources, people resources, and online resources. Books, magazines, and other printed resources can be good reference materials for your business plan. Some organizations, including The Small Business Association, offer assistance in writing a business plan.
7. Your local Chamber of Commerce and Small Business Development Centers are good sources for researching your business plan. Trade associations also may have helpful information.
8. Your business plan should be neat, well organized, and should always be typed.
9. Your business plan should include the following elements: cover letter, cover sheet, table of contents, statement of purpose, executive summary, main body, and appendix.

What Do You Know Now?

Read *Build a Business* again. Then answer the questions a second time. How have your responses changed?

VOCABULARY BUILDER

Choose the term that best fits the definition on the left. Write your answers on a separate sheet of paper.

1. Organizations that promote certain types of businesses
2. A written document that describes all the steps necessary in opening and operating a successful business
3. Financial statements based on projected revenues and expenses
4. A letter that explains or provides more information about a document or set of documents

   a. **business plan**
   b. **cover letter**
   c. **pro forma financial statements**
   d. **trade associations**

REVIEW YOUR KNOWLEDGE

5. Who is a business plan written for?
6. Why is writing a business plan so important?
7. What three purposes does a business plan fulfill?
8. How can a business plan help you run your business?

9. List the seven elements of a business plan.

10. Why should entrepreneurs identify short-term, medium-term, and long-term goals?

11. Where can you find industry data you may need for your business plan?

12. Why is it important to identify the risks you face?

13. What factors would make additional elements in your business plan necessary?

14. Why do you need to do research to write a business plan?

15. Why should a business plan be typed and follow a standard format?

16. What should the cover letter of your business plan do?

17. Why is an executive summary important to a business plan?

18. What is the purpose of the appendix of your business plan?

APPLY WHAT YOU LEARNED

19. You want to open a retail auto parts store. Your business plan will be aimed at lenders and suppliers. Which elements of the business plan will be of most interest to them? What elements will require extensive research? What sources do you think will be most helpful?

20. You are planning to start an advertising agency. What research do you need to conduct in order to write your business plan? What sources will you consult to obtain this information? To whom will your business plan be directed?

THINK CRITICALLY

21. Writing a business plan is a fundamental part of starting your own company. Do you think entrepreneurs ever need to update their business plans? Why or why not?

22. How do you think a business plan for a home-based business differs from that of a large corporation? How would a business plan for a manufacturing business differ from that of a service business?

23. There is a great deal of free advice available on starting and running a small business. Why do you think the government provides so much information and free help to entrepreneurs?

24. COMMUNICATION You are preparing a business plan for a self-storage facility (U-Store It). You are requesting a loan to buy the property and storage lockers. Write the cover letter and statement of purpose sections to the bank loan officer.

25. MATH You are seeking a $500,000 interest-free loan to purchase and run a 75 unit self-storage rental facility. The loan has a ten-year term. Your business plan indicates that each unit will be rented for $100 per month. Are you a good risk? What aspects besides your pro forma financial statements will the loan officer consider?

26. RESEARCH Contact a local insurance agent and obtain information about property insurance. You may also find information in magazines or on the Internet. Write a business plan section devoted to insurance issues.

This Is Your Business Project

1. Describe how you came up with the idea for your business project. Explain why there is a market/need for your product or service. Interview five or more people about your product or service. How many of them would buy or subscribe? Did any of them make suggestions? Prepare a one-page report that fully describes your product or service and how it differs from what is currently available.

2. List your short-, medium-, and long-term goals. What steps do you need to take to achieve each of these goals? Do you foresee any obstacles in attaining them? What are they?

3. Contact the Small Business Administration or a SCORE volunteer and ask for information for your type of business. Use this information to write a paragraph about the industry in which you will be competing. What are the economic, technological, or growth trends in this industry? Is the location of your business a critical factor in its success? Why or why not?

4. Begin the financial section of your business plan by writing a report that identifies the risks your business faces. For each risk, explain how you will overcome the problem. Use examples from magazine articles and experienced business people in your field to show how other businesses have succeeded when faced with similar problems.

Chapter 6

IDENTIFY AND MEET A MARKET NEED

LESSONS

6.1 The Value of Market Research

6.2 How to Perform Market Research

6.3 Understand Your Competition

BUILD A BUSINESS

Cheryl's Day Spa

Cheryl had always dreamed of having her own day spa business. She enrolled in the cosmetology program in high school and completed her training at the local technical institute. When her training was complete, she started working for a spa in a large metropolitan area. After working there for over ten years, she decided it was time to start her own business. She told her friend Leanne about her idea.

"Cheryl, if you open your own spa, Sabrina, Manuel, and I are all interested in working for you," Leanne said to her a few days later.

"Gosh, that would be great!" Cheryl responded. "I know that most of my clients would probably follow me, but I wasn't sure that that would be enough to support a spa. I think the spa would appeal to women and men aged 23 to 50. They'd be people who are concerned about their appearance, are willing to pay extra for quality service, and have an average income of $35,000. I'd like to locate the salon in my community, but I'm just not sure there would be enough demand there."

"You probably need to do some research," Leanne advised.

"That's what I was thinking. I checked the web site of the Chamber of Commerce and found some statistics about the community. There is a population of over 500,000 and a median household income of $71,000, so the customer base is there. Now I just need to find out if they are interested in day spa services."

"Why don't you make a survey?" Leanne suggested.

"Great idea!" Cheryl exclaimed. "After the surveys are completed, I could tally the results and see what potential customers think."

"You know there's something else you need to think about," Leanne told Cheryl. "You need to see what spas are already in the area and what services they offer."

"That's right! I can't forget my competition! If there are enough spas already in the area, even if there is customer interest, there might not be enough customers to support a new salon. I may have to come up with something different to attract customers."

"You know what else you need to consider," Leanne added. "You need a plan to make sure your customers keep coming back. After all, what good is a business if there are no customers?"

What Do You Know?

1. Why do you think it's important for Cheryl to know exactly who her customers are?
2. What kinds of questions do you think Cheryl should ask on her survey to determine if people are interested in her spa?
3. What could Cheryl do to make sure customers come to her spa and not a competitor's spa?
4. What are some things Cheryl could do at her spa to establish customer loyalty?

The Value *of* Market Research

Entrepreneurs with exciting new ideas are sometimes so focused on their products or services that they forget about the customer. But coming up with a good idea for a business is not enough to guarantee that a business will succeed. Before establishing your new enterprise, you will have to determine who your primary customers are and whether these customers are willing to buy your product or service. Market research is the key to finding out all of this information.

WHAT IS A TARGET MARKET?

As an entrepreneur, you will need to estimate demand for your products or services by identifying your target customers. The **target market** is the individuals or companies that are interested in a particular product or service and are willing and able to pay for it. Identifying your target market helps you to reach the people you most want to sell to. Target customers are the customers you would most like to attract. A car dealer selling moderately priced minivans would target middle-class families with children. A car dealer that offers expensive sports cars might target single people with very good incomes.

Understand Your Customer

Customers are the people who buy the products and services companies offer. The customer is your most important asset. Without customers, companies cannot remain in business. Understanding people's wants and needs will allow you to identify business opportunities. The more you know about your customers, the better you will be at giving them what they need and want.

Businesses that identify their target markets are the businesses that succeed. This is why you need to define your target market. If you concentrate your selling efforts on a certain type of individual, you will be more likely to give that individual exactly what he

Customers are your most important asset.

wants. This will make customers happy, and they will continue to buy from your business. When you fully understand your customers, you are more likely to own a successful business.

DEMOGRAPHICS AND PSYCHOGRAPHICS Part of understanding your customers is knowing their demographics and psychographics. **Demographics** are data that describe a group of people in terms of their age, marital status, family size, ethnicity, gender, profession, education, and income. **Psychographics** are data that describe a group of people in terms of their tastes, opinions, personality traits, and lifestyle habits. Putting all of this information together can give you an idea of the size of your market and how many people would be willing and able to purchase your product or service.

Family size is a demographic that may be important to your business.

Identify Your Target Market

To identify the target market for your product or service, you will need to answer the following questions:

1. Who are my customers: individuals or companies?
2. If my customers are individuals, how old are they? How much money do they earn? Where do they live? How do they spend their time and money?
3. If my customers are companies, what industries are they in? Where are those industries located?
4. What needs or wants will my product or service satisfy?
5. How many potential customers live in the area in which I want to operate?
6. Where do these potential customers currently buy the products or services I want to sell them?
7. What price are they willing to pay for my products or services?
8. What can I do for my customers that other companies are not already doing for them?

In Class Activity

In small groups, brainstorm five products or services with large target markets consisting of individuals. For each product or service, tell what need or want is being met. Share your results with the class.

As an entrepreneur, you should put yourself in your customers' shoes before you start your business. You should also think about your customers every day. By continually evaluating your market you will be ready to respond to changes in neighborhoods, customers' needs and buying habits, products and services, and competitors.

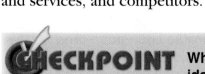 **CHECKPOINT** **What questions should you ask when identifying your target market?**

SAMPLE CUSTOMER PROFILE FOR A SPORTING GOODS STORE

- Individual 23 to 52 years of age
- Participates in sports
- Wants good-quality sports equipment
- Looks for good prices
- Lives in city of Blanchester
- Average Household Income: $42,000 per year

The Importance of a Customer Profile

A very useful part of analyzing your data is the creation of a customer profile. A **customer profile** is a description of the characteristics of the person or company that is likely to purchase a product or service. A customer profile can help you understand what you need to do to meet customer demand. The profile should include demographic data about the customer as well as relevant psychographic information about the customer's lifestyle and attitudes.

Market Segments

Market research can also be used to identify market segments. **Market segments** are groups of customers that share common characteristics. Segmenting, or dividing your target market into several small groups, can help you develop a product or service that will meet customer needs.

The process of market segmentation is important because most products and services only appeal to a small portion of the population. The leisure services market is a large market that includes many segments, such as outdoor adventurers, people who vacation frequently, couples who eat at restaurants, and more. Targeting the entire leisure market would not make sense. You would never be able to meet the needs of the entire market. Even the restaurant segment of the leisure services market has segments. Some people eat fast food on a regular basis, while others like a sit-down meal at a nice restaurant. There are people who like Italian food, and others who like seafood or Chinese food.

Understand the Competition

Knowing a lot about your competition also will help you define your target market. Businesses enter into areas where there is competition all the time. However, they have to identify some special customer need or want that is not being met. Customers may be happy with the products or services being offered, but they may be unhappy with the prices being charged. Customers might be dissatisfied with the quality of a product or service and might be willing to pay more for better quality. In either case, a customer need is going unmet by a competitor, indicating a possible opportunity for an entrepreneur.

**CHECKPOINT** Why is it important to have a customer profile and understand your competition when determining your target market?

For your business to succeed, you need to find out who your customers are, what they want or need, and how much they are willing to pay for your product or service. To collect this information about your customers, you will perform market research. **Market research** is a system for collecting, recording, and analyzing information about customers, competitors, goods, and services. You will draw on secondary data and primary data as you gather your information. Both types of research will help you identify ways in which you can meet customer needs.

Secondary Data

Entrepreneurs usually begin research of their target market by using secondary data. **Secondary data** is data found in already published sources. Information on population, family size, household income, economic trends, industry forecasts, and other information can be found in secondary data resources. Places to find secondary data include:

1. publications issued by government and community organizations, such as the U.S. Census, the Small Business Administration, and the Chamber of Commerce
2. books about specific industries
3. information on web sites for government and businesses
4. books about other entrepreneurs who set up similar businesses
5. specialized magazines and journals devoted to particular fields
6. newspaper articles and statistics

Kisha Nichols wanted to expand her family-owned chain of retail shoe stores. She decided to perform some secondary data research and visited the local Chamber of Commerce web site. The site provided her with demographics on population for her city and county, and industry forecasts for communities in her area. This information allowed Kisha to identify the largest markets as well as the markets expected to grow the most over the next ten years. She also found information in a book on the average income of retail shoe store owners in her state. Newspaper articles gave Kisha psychographic data on people's lifestyles in her area. Most worked in professional office settings, which meant they had a need for comfortable dress shoes. Studying secondary data gave Kisha a good idea of which community might provide the best prospects for one of her shoe stores.

Primary Data

Most market researchers also collect primary data. **Primary data** is information collected for the very first time to fit a specific purpose. A researcher collects primary data to help identify and understand the target market. There are a few different ways to collect primary data. The most common type of primary market research is a questionnaire, also called a survey. It is a list of questions you would like to ask your customers to find out demographic and psychographic information. A questionnaire can be presented by mail, over the phone, or in person. Information on how to put a survey together is provided in the next lesson.

Public places like parks are great areas to conduct market research using observation.

OBSERVATION Market research can also involve observation. If you are considering opening a juice bar in a shopping mall, you might want to see how many customers you could attract. You could go to the mall and count the number of people purchasing drinks at various food outlets. An entrepreneur interested in starting a motorcycle repair shop might count the number of motorcycles at a busy intersection.

FOCUS GROUPS Another way in which you could find out about the market is by conducting in-depth interviews with small numbers of people. A **focus group** is an interview with groups of target customers who provide valuable ideas on products or services. You can ask the same kinds of questions in a focus group that you would in a survey or questionnaire. The benefit of focus groups is that they allow for more in-depth discussion about a topic than a questionnaire does. Focus groups usually are led by a moderator, who asks questions

YOU CAN SAY THAT AGAIN!

"There is no perfect time to start your own company, so I [just] went ahead and did it."

—*Carlos Sol, owner of DelSol Inc. and winner of the Entrepreneur of the Year Award*

about buying habits, likes and dislikes, and interest in particular products and services. The focus group session is recorded so that the comments can be reviewed carefully after the session is over.

DISADVANTAGE OF PRIMARY DATA Primary data can provide the most up-to-date and useful information, but it can be time consuming and more expensive to conduct than secondary data. As an entrepreneur, you will need to determine how much secondary and primary market research data you need to collect.

 **CHECKPOINT** **What is the difference between primary and secondary market research data?**

THINK CRITICALLY

1. Why is it so important to determine who your target market is?

2. Why do entrepreneurs need to conduct market research?

3. You are thinking about opening a driving range and golf lesson center in your town. What type of secondary data should you consult? What type of primary data should you collect?

MAKE CONNECTIONS

4. MATH Marcel wants to open a car wash after graduating from high school. For several days, he observed the cars being washed at a competitor, and recorded the information below.

Day 1	Day 2	Day 3	Day 4	Day 5	Day 6
50 cars	45 cars	48 cars	26 cars	47 cars	55 cars

What is the average number of cars he counted each day? If his car wash were open five days a week, based on this data, how many cars might he expect to wash per year?

5. PROBLEM SOLVING Choose a market for a product or service sold to individuals. Use the six-step problem-solving model to identify a possible opportunity for an entrepreneur in that market.

6. COMMUNICATION Interview a business owner. Ask the owner the eight questions listed in the chapter for identifying a business's target market. Write a report based on what you find out about the owner's target market.

How to *Perform* Market Research

Primary data market research is time consuming and expensive. But it is extremely valuable. It will give you exactly what you want to know and uncover information you may not find in secondary data research.

FIVE STEPS OF PRIMARY MARKET RESEARCH

Primary data market research involves five steps.

1. Define the Question
2. Select a Research Method
3. Collect Data
4. Analyze Data
5. Draw Conclusions

1. Define the Question

In the first step in the market research process, you need to define exactly what it is that you are trying to find out. Maggie Blandin is thinking about starting a dog walking service. Before she invests in her business, Maggie would like to know how many dog owners live in the area, how many lack the time to walk their dogs themselves, and how much they might be willing to pay to have someone walk their dogs for them.

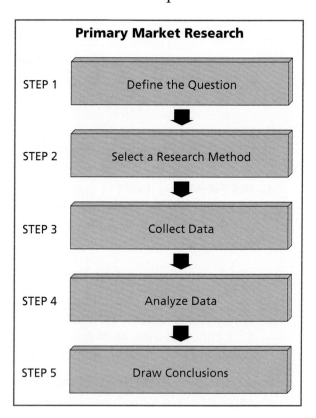

Primary Market Research

STEP 1 — Define the Question

STEP 2 — Select a Research Method

STEP 3 — Collect Data

STEP 4 — Analyze Data

STEP 5 — Draw Conclusions

2. Select a Research Method

Once you have defined the market research questions, you are ready to decide how you will go about answering them. Should you use a survey? Should you use an observation method? Is a focus group appropriate? What method you use will depend on what type of information you want to gather. For example, you can find out people's opinions in a survey or focus group, but not by observation. You should perform some secondary market research first to familiarize yourself with your market. You can then choose the best research method for the information you want to gather.

If you choose a survey, think carefully about how long it should be, what questions it should include, how it should be administered, and how many people you should survey. If you use observation to do your research, you need to determine where and when to get the best information. If a focus group is needed, you should think about what kind of customers to include and what questions to ask them.

Maggie decides that a survey is the best way for her to find answers about customer preferences for a dog walking service. Maggie thinks after she administers a survey, an observation method could give her more information on how many people in her area walk their own dogs.

 **CHECKPOINT** What are three ways you can collect primary data?

3. Collect Data

When you begin collecting data, you will first collect data from secondary data sources. Demographic and psychographic data, as well as information on economic trends and industry forecasts will help you determine what kind of primary data research to perform.

Maggie Blandin found that 60 percent of the households in her area owned one or more dogs, and that average annual household income was $75,000. Most households had one or more adults working in a professional field and putting in overtime each week. She also found that dog ownership was on the rise in her area. Based on this information, Maggie put together a survey that would help confirm household incomes and ask specific questions about the lifestyles, opinions, and choices of dog owners.

In Class Activity

In small groups, develop both demographic and psychographic profiles of your small group. Record the characteristics that group members have in common. Compare your group's results with those of other groups.

DESIGN A SURVEY Making a good questionnaire is very important. Questionnaires should be kept to a page in length when read over the phone or mailed to respondents. Longer questionnaires can be used if an interview is face to face. Questions should be clear and easy to answer, and only the most important questions should appear. If the response to a question serves no specific purpose, the question should not be used.

MARKET RESEARCH SURVEY

Thank you for participating in this market research survey. We appreciate your assistance in helping us identify the needs of pet owners in our community.

PLEASE CHECK THE BOX THAT BEST DESCRIBES YOUR SITUATION.

Age: UNDER 18 ❑ 19–30 ❑ 31–40 ❑ 41–50 ❑ 51–65 ❑ OVER 65 ❑

Gender: MALE ❑ FEMALE ❑

Annual Household Income:

LESS THAN $25,000 ❑ $25,001–$50,000 ❑ $50,001–$100,000 ❑ MORE THAN $100,000 ❑

Number of pets: 0 ❑ 1 ❑ 2 ❑ 3 ❑ 4 OR MORE ❑

Kinds of pets: DOG ❑ CAT ❑ FISH ❑ BIRD ❑ OTHER ❑ (PLEASE SPECIFY)

IF YOU OWN A DOG, PLEASE ANSWER ALL OF THE FOLLOWING QUESTIONS.

How often do you walk your dog?

EVERY DAY ❑ A FEW TIMES A WEEK ❑ ONLY ON THE WEEKENDS ❑ NEVER ❑

OTHER ❑ (PLEASE SPECIFY)

Who takes care of your dog when you are out of town?

KENNEL ❑ FRIEND ❑ NEIGHBOR ❑ OTHER ❑ (PLEASE SPECIFY)

Would you be willing to pay someone you trusted to take your dog for walks?

YES ❑ POSSIBLY ❑ NO ❑

How much would you be willing to pay to have your dog(s) walked for 30 minutes?

$10 ❑ $15 ❑ $20 ❑ $25 ❑ I WOULD NOT PAY TO HAVE MY DOG WALKED ❑

Would you be interested in having someone you trust take care of your pets while you are away?

YES ❑ POSSIBLY ❑ NO ❑

4. Analyze Data

Once you've collected all your data, you will need to interpret the information you have found. This analysis should be written down so you can refer to it later. Your customer profile, and the market segment you are targeting, should be considered when you analyze the data you've collected.

Through her secondary data market research, Maggie found that 2,500 dogs live in her area. In her primary data research, she found that 30 percent of dog owners in her area would pay $20 to have their dogs walked for 30 minutes. Many would pay to have them walked two or three times a week. This means she could easily have 750 dogs to walk each week.

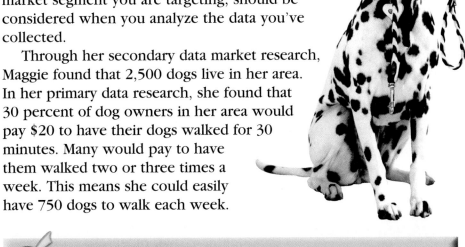

 **CHECKPOINT**   **What makes a good questionnaire?**

What Went Wrong

Competition
Price Wars
Business: Unicorp Technology, Silicon Valley, CA.

Unicorp was the first company in the computer industry to offer removable hard disk drives for personal computers. For years Unicorp had a unique position in the industry and had little direct competition. Eventually, the company was making $300 million in annual revenue.

Unicorp's first competition came from A-Tech Corporation, which offered a product similar in price and performance. A-Tech spent heavily on advertising and ran frequent reduced-price promotions. As a result, they took a lot of business from Unicorp. Unicorp decided to try to take back the market it had lost to A-Tech and launched a multi-million-dollar marketing campaign aimed at their target market.

The two companies went head to head, selling disk drives at lower and lower prices. However, consumers didn't need to buy a lot of hard drives, because the new drives held so much data. Only one company could win out, and it ended up being A-Tech. In less than two years, Unicorp lost $170 million and A-Tech bought them out for less than $10 million.

Think Critically
1. What was Unicorp's major disadvantage in competing with A-Tech?
2. What did each company fail to realize about its customers? How might the price war for removable cartridge hard drives have been avoided?

5. Draw Conclusions

Once you have analyzed and interpreted your data, you will need to determine how to use this information. This is when you will develop a plan of action based on the information you found in market research.

Maggie Blandin's market research has helped her conclude that her idea for a dog walking service is profitable. Her market research has identified people aged 31 to 50 who travel often, work long hours, and earn $50,000 to $100,000 a year as the target market for her business. She also now knows the amount of money people would be willing to pay for her service, and how much income she can expect to make.

In her first effort to get customers, Maggie plans to create a flier aimed at her target market, which she will distribute in neighborhoods and veterinarian offices. She also plans to distribute the flier downtown and in other business areas where many of her target market customers work.

 **CHECKPOINT** Describe the steps involved in conducting market research.

THINK CRITICALLY

1. Why is it important to define the questions you want your market research to answer?

2. Do you think primary data can become secondary data? Why or why not?

3. Why do you think short questionnaires are more effective than long ones? Why should you only include questions that serve a specific purpose?

MAKE CONNECTIONS

4. **PROBLEM SOLVING** Your family-owned business processes and sells orange juice to food distributors. In order to grow, the business needs to add to its product line. Apply the five market research steps to help determine an additional product your business could offer.

5. **COMMUNICATION** Write down four more questions Maggie could have included in her survey. Also write down why you think it would have benefited Maggie to ask these questions of her target market.

Identify *Your*
Competition

GOALS

DETERMINE your direct and indirect competition.

ANALYZE the strengths and weaknesses of competitors.

ESTABLISH strategies for maintaining customer loyalty.

Most new businesses face *competitors,* companies offering similar or identical products and services to the same group of target customers. As the owner of a new business, you will have to convince customers to buy from you and not your competitors. To do this, you must collect information about your competition.

DIRECT AND INDIRECT COMPETITION

Direct competition is competition from a business that makes most of its money selling the same or similar products or services as another business. **Indirect competition** is competition by a business that makes only a small amount of money selling the same or similar products or services as another business.

Find Your Direct Competition

Secondary data resources can give you information on your direct competition. Your direct competitors may be in the same geographic area as your business. The telephone directory will help you find the number and locations of competing businesses. Your local Chamber of Commerce will also have information on competitors in your business field. Observation methods can help you find your direct competitors. If you start a retail business, you can check out all of the malls, shopping centers, and retail outlets in your area.

For some businesses, direct competitors may be located far away. Carmen Quinterro publishes a travel newsletter on Ireland. Carmen's target customers live all over the United States. Her competitors include five other newsletters on Ireland, as well as several similar Internet sites. Carmen's competitors, located far from her home in Chicago, compete with Carmen for the same target customers.

Find Your Indirect Competition

Locating your indirect competition is more difficult than finding direct competitors. You should first think of all of the possible businesses that can compete with you indirectly. A large department store can stock some of the same products carried by a privately owned specialty shop. But the department store offers lots of other merchandise, and only makes a small amount of money on the items it sells that are the same as what the specialty shop offers. This makes the department store an indirect competitor to the specialty shop.

Competing with Large Businesses

Entrepreneurs may find it difficult to compete with large retailers for many reasons.

1. ***Large retailers usually are able to keep larger quantities of products in stock.*** They can purchase inventory in larger amounts because they have larger storage areas and more revenue to purchase inventory with.

2. ***Large retail chains don't rely on one single product line.*** If one product line does poorly, the store does not go out of business. Small businesses only have one product line and face risks because of that.

3. ***Large companies usually have more resources to devote to advertising.*** A larger company makes more revenue and can hire advertising professionals to create their advertising.

Small businesses only have one product line, such as groceries.

CHECKPOINT What is the difference between direct and indirect competition?

Entrepreneurial Timeline

1850   1875   1900   1925

Vegetables Are Good for You

Perhaps one of the most well-known women in the 1800s, and the first to own a widely successful company, was Lydia E. Pinkham. Like many women of her time, Lydia created her own medicines for her family. Because her husband could not find stable employment, she began to sell one of her remedies to make ends meet. Sold primarily as a women's health medicine, the first batch of "Lydia E. Pinkham's Vegetable Compound" was brewed on the basement stove. Lydia, her sons, and her father all pitched in on marketing efforts, which included writing, folding, and distributing a four-page brochure. A newspaper ad in *The Boston Herald* gave the first big boost to sales, so much so that Lydia began packaging other medicines as well. In 1881, Lydia's company was boasting $200,000 in sales each year. Lydia died in 1883, but her medicines can still be found today in some pharmaceutical and grocery stores.

STUDY INDIVIDUAL COMPETITORS

Point your browser to

http://www.ideas-in-action.swep.com

Complete the activity for Chapter 6.

Analyzing the strengths and weaknesses of your competition will help you figure out what you can do to get customers to buy from your business. Once you have determined who your direct and indirect competitors are, you will need to analyze each one by considering the following.

1. *Price.* What do they charge? Are your prices higher or lower?
2. *Location.* Where are your competitors located?
3. *Facility.* Is the building nice? Accessible? Appealing to customers?
4. *Strengths.* What does the competitor do that no one else does, or what do they do better than everyone else?
5. *Weaknesses.* What are some disadvantages of your competition?
6. *Strategy.* How will you attract customers to your business? How will you get customers to come to you instead of a competitor?

Looking at your competition in these key areas will help you find out what other companies are doing that is good or bad. It will also help you figure out the best ways to attract customers.

Interjit Singh wants to start a premiere car wash in an expensive suburb of Washington, D.C. He researches his direct and indirect competition. He finds that Royal Hand Wash is able to charge twice the price of the other competitors even though their location isn't the best. Royal Hand Wash guarantees non-scratch car washes and waxes done by people, not machines. Because Interjit's business will also offer car washes and waxes, and detailing done by hand, Royal Hand Wash is the direct competition. All other car wash businesses, including gas stations with automatic car wash machines, are his indirect competition.

 **CHECKPOINT** **What is the purpose of analyzing competitors?**

ANALYSIS OF COMPETITORS						
Competitor	Price	Location	Facility	Strength	Weakness	Strategy
Standard Gas	$6.00	Excellent	Good	Excellent location	Car wash not easily accessible	Target a different market
Lakeland Car Wash	$5.50	Fair	Good	Low price	Location	Target a different market
Ray's Car Wash	$5.00	Good	Fair	Low price	Facility	Target a different market
Royal Hand Wash	$11.50	Fair	Excellent	Excellent facility	Location	Offer lower prices, better service, more convenient location

Getting customers to buy products or services from you and not your competition is only one step in running a successful business. You must also make sure your customers remain loyal to you.

Listen and Respond to Feedback

Jason's business suffered when he did not listen to customers.

To keep customers, you will need to continually ask your customers questions about your company and respond to the answers they give. Companies that ignore customer concerns will not stay in business long.

Different companies stay in touch with their customers' needs in different ways. A cosmetics manufacturer may call customers the day after they receive a makeover to ask if they are happy with the products they purchased. Other companies have a customer feedback box where customers can put complaints or positive comments about the business. You can also design a survey for your customers to complete.

Jason Rose's business, the Metropolitan Athletic Club, closed because of his failure to respond to customer feedback. Club members had repeatedly complained about the lack of cleanliness of the locker rooms and the lack of available weight machines during peak hours. Jason ignored his customers' complaints, believing that the excellent location and low monthly fee would ensure his success.

Jason learned from his mistake, however. When he opened his next athletic club, he immediately tried to find out what customers wanted by conducting a market research study. His study revealed, among other things, that he should offer more aerobics classes and put high-speed hair dryers in the locker rooms. Due to his focus on customer satisfaction, Jason's club is doing very well and attracting new members all the time.

In Class Activity

With a partner, choose a successful business in your area. Then choose three competing businesses. Analyze each business in terms of the six factors listed in this lesson. Then make a chart listing the results of your analysis.

Other Strategies for Maintaining Loyalty

To maintain customer loyalty, businesses use many strategies. The main purpose of these strategies is to keep customers happy and keep them coming back to your business. Some of the most basic strategies include:

- Superior service
- More convenient hours than other businesses
- Easy return policies
- Store-specific credit cards

- Personal notes or cards for birthdays or a thank you for their business
- Frequent buyer programs

Kathleen McGuire, the owner of Flower Markets, encourages shoppers to buy all of their flowers from her by issuing them a frequent buyer card, which she stamps every time a purchase of $10.00 or more is made. Once the card has been stamped ten times, customers can redeem the card for a free carnation bouquet.

 **What are some strategies for maintaining customer loyalty?**

THINK CRITICALLY

1. Why should entrepreneurs analyze both direct and indirect competitors?

2. Name ten different ways you could attract customers to a retail business.

3. Why can customer feedback be considered a type of market research? Is this market research more or less valuable than research you conduct? Explain your answer.

MAKE CONNECTIONS

4. **COMMUNICATION** Devise a plan to maintain customer loyalty for a hair salon. Create an advertisement to let your customers know about this plan.

5. **COMMUNICATION** Shontel Washington just opened an art gallery. He would like feedback from the people who visit the gallery. Write a short questionnaire that would help Shontel learn more about his customers' feelings toward his business.

Chapter 6
Review

CHAPTER SUMMARY

The Value *of* Market Research

1. Understanding your customers is one of the most important aspects of running a business.
2. To identify your target market, you need to ask yourself many questions, such as "who are my customers?" and "what needs or wants will my product or service satisfy?"
3. You should also develop a customer profile and decide which segment of the market to target.
4. Market research is important to business because it helps you find out what your customers need and want. It also helps you understand your competition.
5. Secondary data is the information you find in published sources.
6. Primary data is information collected for the very first time to fit a specific purpose. Primary data can include questionnaires, focus groups, and interviews.

How to *Perform* Market Research

7. The five steps of market research are: define the question, select a research method, collect data, analyze data, and draw conclusions.
8. When developing a questionnaire, make it short, easy to read, and easy to understand. Also make sure all questions have a purpose.

Identify *Your* Competition

9. All businesses have both direct and indirect competition.
10. As an entrepreneur, you need to research who all your competitors are and figure out what your strategies are for dealing with each competing company.
11. There are many ways to maintain customer loyalty. You should ask for and respond to customer feedback. Offering frequent-buyer discounts and superior service also promote customer loyalty.

What Do You Know Now?

Read *Build a Business* again. Then answer the questions a second time. How have your responses changed?

VOCABULARY BUILDER

Choose the term that best fits the definition.
Write your answers on a separate sheet of paper.

1. A system for collecting, recording, and analyzing information about customers, competitors, goods, and services
2. An interview with groups of target customers who provide valuable ideas on products or services
3. Data that describe a group of people in terms of their age, marital status, family size, ethnicity, gender, profession, education, and income
4. The individuals or companies that are interested in a particular product or service and are willing and able to pay for it
5. Data found in already published sources
6. Information collected for the very first time to fit a specific purpose
7. Competition from a business that makes most of its money selling the same or similar products or services as another business
8. Data that describe a group of people in terms of their tastes, opinions, personality traits, and lifestyle habits
9. A description of the characteristics of the person or company that is likely to purchase a product or service
10. The people who buy the products and services companies offer

a. **customer profile**
b. **customers**
c. **demographics**
d. **direct competition**
e. **focus group**
f. **indirect competition**
g. **market research**
h. **market segments**
i. **primary data**
j. **psychographics**
k. **secondary data**
l. **target market**

REVIEW YOUR KNOWLEDGE

11. Why are customers so important to a business?

12. Why is it important to understand your competition?

13. What sources contain secondary data market research?

14. Describe the three types of primary data market research.

15. What is the purpose of conducting market research?

16. What are the five steps involved in conducting market research?

17. Why is it important to identify your direct and indirect competition?

18. What are some of the reasons entrepreneurs find it difficult to compete with large retailers?

19. When analyzing your competition, which key areas should you consider?

20. Why is it important to listen to your customers?

21. What are some of the strategies for maintaining customer loyalty?

APPLY WHAT YOU LEARNED

22. You want to start a word processing company that targets high school students who want someone else to key their term papers. Design a survey that would help you determine if there is a market for your company. Determine the best way to administer the survey.

23. Have 30 classmates not in this class fill out the survey. Analyze the results and put them in written form.

24. You are thinking about opening a lawn-service business. Working with a small group of classmates, develop a customer profile for your business.

25. For your lawn-service business, make a list of competitors in your market. Analyze each using the six factors listed in the text. Create a strategy for dealing with your competitors.

THINK CRITICALLY

26. What resources are available at your public library that could help you identify a target market in your community? How would you access relevant information on the Internet?

27. When is secondary market research data likely to be more useful than primary data?

28. What kind of demographic and psychographic information might you be interested in as part of a customer profile? What research method could be used to obtain such information?

29. Do you think that different strategies are needed to attract customers from direct competitors as opposed to indirect competitors? Why or why not?

MAKE CONNECTIONS

30. MATH If $300,000 worth of pizzas are sold in your town each year, and you captured 22 percent of the market, how much revenue would you earn a year?

31. MATH You have collected primary data research that says three-quarters of the people in your town would switch dry cleaners if they could save 50 percent on their dry cleaning. If the average resident in your town spends $7.00 a week on dry cleaning and the town has 5,000 residents, how much revenue could you expect to earn a year by opening a discount dry cleaner?

32. **COMMUNICATION** Set up an interview with a local entrepreneur to find out what running a business is really like. Before conducting the interview, draw up a list of questions. Present what you learn in the interview to the class.

33. **COMMUNICATION** Call your local Chamber of Commerce and ask them for information that would help Maggie, the owner of Doggone for a Walk, if she were to open her business in your town or city. Don't forget information on demographics and psychographics. Also ask for statistics on dog ownership in your area.

34. **RESEARCH** Use the Statistical Abstract of the United States to find out how many small businesses operated in the United States in 1975, 1985, and 1995. This research tool will be available at your local library.

35. **RESEARCH** Use the Internet to find the names of four companies that might be able to help you conduct market research. Record information such as how long the company has been in business, and what kinds of market research the business does. Write down your findings and compare them with the findings of other students.

This Is Your Business Project

1. Identify the target market for your business. Use secondary data sources that could help you assess demand for your product or service.
2. Using the secondary research you find, develop a customer profile for your business. Figure out which market segment of your industry you are targeting. Be specific.
3. Conduct primary data research for your business. Use the five step method described in the chapter. Develop a questionnaire that will give you the information you need. Give it to at least 30 people in your target market to fill out. Analyze your results, and determine what course of action you will take.
4. Determine who your competitors are, both direct and indirect. Analyze each competitor in terms of price, location, facility, strength, and weakness. Determine a strategy for dealing with each competitor.
5. Write down your strategies for maintaining customer loyalty, and describe why you think each one will work.

Chapter 7

FINANCE, PROTECT, AND INSURE YOUR BUSINESS

LESSONS

7.1 Put Together a Financial Plan

7.2 Obtain Financing for Your Business

7.3 Theft Proof Your Business

7.4 Insure Your Business

BUILD A BUSINESS

One Day at a Time

"Aaagh! I'm never going to have enough money," David moaned to Erica.

"What's wrong?" Erica asked.

"Well, I want to start a calendar production business. Everyone wants calendars for their lockers, and they like to put pictures in their lockers. So I decided that my business would custom design locker calendars with a person's own pictures. I've got a great name. I'm going to call it 'One Day at a Time'."

"Sounds like a great idea!" exclaimed Erica. "So what's the problem with money?"

"Before I can make any calendars I have to buy the things I need to make the calendars. And to get these things, I must have money."

"Why don't you go to the bank and get a loan?" Erica suggested.

"I've tried that. They told me I'd need someone to sign the loan with me. My parents said if I am going to do this, I have to do it all by myself. I made a list of all the things I need and how much they cost and I'm going to need about $3,000 to start my business."

"How much do you think you'll make once you get started, David?"

"I've done some figuring on that because the bank wanted to know. If I sell 5 calendars a week at $15 a calendar, then I should bring in about $300 a month."

"David, I bet during December and June you could sell more than that. People are always looking for gifts in December and in June you could make calendars targeted to the graduating seniors. They could have memory calendars to take to college."

"Great idea, Erica! I need to sit down and determine how much I will make and how much I will spend over the next year. If I have some idea of how long it will take to recover my start-up costs and I know when I'll start making a profit, it might be easier to get someone to invest in the business."

"You know, David, I might be interested in investing in the business and some of our other friends probably would, too. And I bet one of your other relatives would help you."

"Erica, that is another great idea! I don't know what I would do without you. I've got to get to a phone. I need to talk to Gran!"

"But David, have you given any thought to whether you need insurance? You may not need it right away, if you will be working out of your parents' house. But what about down the road? And what if someone pays for their calendar with a bad check? Do you know how you will protect yourself from things like that?"

"Erica, I'm beginning to think I should make you my partner!"

What Do You Know?

1. What things do you think David will need to start his business?
2. If David's projected income isn't as high as he likes, what can he do to increase his income?
3. What do you think people would want to know before they invest in David's business?
4. What kinds of insurance or theft protection do you think are available to businesses?

Put Together a *Financial* Plan

All businesses need money to survive. However, many entrepreneurs lack the money they need to start up and run a business. In fact, lack of money is one of the main reasons that small businesses fail. How can entrepreneurs with solid business ideas get the financing they need to start and run a business?

PREPARE FINANCIAL STATEMENTS

Before you can approach a lender or investor about financing your business, you will have to prepare financial statements. These statements include a list of start-up costs, a cash flow statement, an income statement, a balance sheet, and a personal financial statement. These statements allow potential lenders and investors to figure out if your business is viable. They also help lenders determine whether the financing you are requesting is reasonable.

The first four financial statements are estimates based on how you think your business will perform in its first year. Financial statements based on projections are known as **pro forma financial statements.** The personal financial statement you submit consists of actual figures listing your personal assets and liabilities.

Start-Up Costs

One of the pro forma financial statements is a list of start-up costs. **Start-up costs** are the one-time-only expenses that are paid to establish a business. Common start-up costs include:

- equipment and supplies, such as cash registers, computers, telephones, fax machines
- furniture and fixtures, such as desks and chairs
- vehicles, including delivery trucks and other automobiles
- remodeling, such as electrical and plumbing expenses
- legal and accounting fees
- licensing fees

Start-up costs should be considered when you are figuring out how much money you need to start your business. Most entrepreneurs have to borrow the money needed to cover start-up costs.

Felicia Walters plans to start a lighting fixture store. To help her determine how much money she will need to borrow, she calculates her start-up costs. She must include her estimate of start-up costs with the other documents she provides lenders.

Cash Flow Statement

A *cash flow statement* describes how much cash comes in and goes out of a business over a period of time. The amount of cash coming in is your *revenue.* The amount of cash going out is your *expenses.* The cash flow statement is important because it will show how much money you have to pay your bills. To create a pro forma cash flow statement, you will need to estimate your monthly revenues and monthly operating expenses.

Felicia must put together pro forma financial statements in order to apply for financing.

FORECAST REVENUES To complete a pro forma cash flow statement, you must first forecast your revenues. When you forecast your amount of revenue, you need to analyze the demand for each of your products and services. You also need to know the prices you will charge for each item.

Felicia Walters estimates that during her first month of business she will sell 20 halogen bulbs, 12 fixtures, 6 outdoor light sets, and 3 floor lamps. To calculate her total revenues, she multiplies the quantity of each type of product she expects to sell by the price she has set for each item.

START-UP COSTS, WALTERS ELECTRIC	
Item	Estimated Cost
Equipment and supplies	
Computers (3 @ $1,500)	$4,500
Modem	175
Cash registers (2 @ $1,800)	3,600
Fax machine	400
Supplies	300
Subtotal	8,975
Furniture and fixtures	
Desks (4 @ $400)	1,600
Chairs (8 @ $75)	600
Subtotal	2,200
Vehicles	
Delivery truck	10,000
Automobile	8,000
Subtotal	18,000
Remodeling	
Drywall replacement	1,000
Electrical work	2,500
Paint	1,000
Carpet	3,000
Subtotal	7,500
Legal and accounting fees	3,000
TOTAL	$39,675

FORECASTED REVENUES, WALTERS ELECTRIC			JANUARY 20--
Type of item	Quantity sold	Average Price per item sold	Revenue
Halogen bulbs	20	$15	$300
Fixtures	12	200	2,400
Outdoor light sets	6	175	1,050
Floor lamps	3	150	450
TOTAL			**$4,200**

FORECAST OPERATING EXPENSES Expenses that are incurred by a business every month are called **operating expenses.** They may include cost of goods (what you pay manufacturers or wholesalers to get products and services to sell), rent, salaries, payroll taxes, office supplies, utilities (electricity, telephone, water), insurance, and advertising.

FORECASTED OPERATING EXPENSES WALTERS ELECTRIC, JANUARY 20--	
Type of expense	Amount
Cost of goods	$2,400
Rent	900
Utilities	100
Salaries	2,000
Advertising	800
Supplies	---
Insurance	75
Payroll taxes	175
Other	50
TOTAL	**$6,500**

In Class Activity

In small groups, list the kind and amount of start-up costs each of the following businesses would require: clothing boutique, insurance agency, and plumbing contractor. Which of the businesses would be the most expensive to start?

PREPARE THE CASH FLOW STATEMENT After making projections of revenues and expenses, you are ready to prepare your cash flow statement. You should create monthly pro forma cash flow statements for the first year of operation and annual statements for the second and third years to give your lender an accurate picture of your cash flow over time.

Like most business owners, Felicia knows that her operating expenses will exceed her revenues during the first few months of operation. Her cash flow will be negative because her sales will be low and some expenses will be high.

BEST AND WORST CASE Many entrepreneurs create two types of cash flow statements based on a worst-case scenario and a best-case scenario. To create a worst-case scenario cash flow statement, you should project lower revenues and higher expenses than you think you will really have. To create a best-case scenario, you should project the highest revenues and the lowest expenses your business is likely to have.

PRO FORMA CASH FLOW STATEMENT WALTERS ELECTRIC					JANUARY–JUNE 20--	
	Jan	Feb	Mar	Apr	May	June
Revenues	$4,200	$4,410	$4,410	$4,620	$5,775	$6,090
Operating expenses						
Cost of goods	2,400	2,520	2,520	2,640	3,300	3,480
Rent	900	900	900	900	900	900
Utilities	100	100	100	100	100	100
Salaries	2,000	2,000	2,000	2,000	2,000	2,000
Advertising	800	800	800	800	800	800
Supplies	----	15	30	50	50	50
Insurance	75	75	75	75	75	75
Payroll taxes	175	175	175	175	175	175
Other	50	50	50	50	50	50
Total expenses	6,500	6,635	6,650	6,790	7,450	7,630
CASH FLOW	−2,300	−2,225	−2,240	−2,170	−1,675	−1,560

A worst-case scenario cash flow statement will help you identify how much cash you will need if things go worse than expected. A best-case cash flow statement will show you how much cash you will have if your business does better than expected. Together, these scenarios will help show you and potential lenders how much cash your business is likely to generate in any situation.

CHECKPOINT What does a cash flow statement show? Why should you prepare both a best-case and a worst-case pro forma cash flow statement?

Income Statement

An *income statement* is a financial statement that indicates how much money a business earns or loses during a particular period. The income statement shows how much profit or loss was generated by the business. For this reason, it is also known as a *profit and loss statement.* Creating a pro forma income statement for a number of years will help lenders see the long-term growth of your business.

Most businesses choose a year as the period measured by an income statement. However, some businesses choose to generate an income statement more often to view their revenues and expenses. New businesses often view their income statements monthly in order to determine whether a profit is being made.

DIFFERENCE FROM A CASH FLOW STATEMENT The cash flow statement deals with actual cash coming in and going out. It shows when you actually make a payment on an invoice, or when you receive money due to you from a customer. In contrast, the income statement shows revenues you have not received and expenses you have not paid yet. It is a futuristic look at the financial stability of your business.

Suppose Walters Electric sells $5,000 worth of lighting in June. The company's

PRO FORMA INCOME STATEMENT WALTERS ELECTRIC, 20--		
Item	Year 2	Year 3
Revenues	$115,000	$125,000
Operating expenses		
Cost of goods	55,400	60,000
Rent	10,800	10,800
Utilities	1,230	1,260
Salaries	24,500	25,000
Payroll taxes	2,205	2,315
Advertising	1,200	1,200
Supplies	600	615
Insurance	900	900
Other	615	615
Total expenses	97,450	102,705
Income	17,550	22,295

monthly income statement would show income of $5,000. But Felicia may not actually have received $5,000 because:

- Customers may have asked to be billed. Felicia will not receive their payments until July or August.
- Some customers may never pay their bills.

Because not all business transactions are paid for immediately, the income statement and the cash flow statement usually will be different. Customers are not the only people who defer payments. Felicia may receive $1,500 worth of merchandise to sell, but wait 30 days to pay the invoice. The cash flow statement will show that Felicia has the $1,500 cash she has not yet paid to her supplier. In contrast, the income statement would show that Felicia has paid the $1,500.

 **CHECKPOINT** What does an income statement show? How does an income statement differ from a cash flow statement?

Balance Sheet

Another pro forma financial statement you should prepare is a balance sheet. A *balance sheet* shows the assets, liabilities, and capital of a business at a particular point in time. It lists what a business owns, what it owes, and how much it is worth at a particular point in time. The balance sheet is based on an equation called the *accounting equation*.

$$\text{Assets} = \text{Liabilities} + \text{Owner's Equity}$$

Assets are items of value owned by a business. They include items such as cash, equipment, and inventory. **Liabilities** are items that a business owes to others. They include loans and outstanding invoices. *Owner's equity* is the amount remaining after the value of all liabilities is subtracted from the value of all assets. It is commonly referred to as the *net worth* of the business.

This financial statement is called the balance sheet because the accounting equation must always be in balance. This means that the assets of a business always equal liabilities plus owner's equity. A business that has more assets than liabilities has positive net worth. A business that has more liabilities than assets has negative net worth.

Felicia Walters creates a pro forma balance sheet for her company to show how her business will be doing after a year. Felicia's pro forma balance sheet shows that total assets exceed total liabilities. This means the company will have a positive net worth after the first year.

Cash is one kind of asset.

PRO FORMA BALANCE SHEET			
WALTERS ELECTRIC		DECEMBER 31, 20--	
Assets		**Liabilities**	
Current assets		*Current liabilities*	
Cash	$1,000	Accounts payable $12,000	
Accounts receivable	8,000		
Less uncollectible accounts	−500	*Long-term liabilities*	
Inventory	14,000	Loans payable $17,900	
Total current assets	22,500	**Total liabilities $29,900**	
Fixed assets			
Equipment	8,975		
Less depreciation	−1,795		
Furniture	2,200		
Less depreciation	−220		
Vehicles	18,000		
Less depreciation	−3,600	NET WORTH	
Total fixed assets	23,560	**Felicia Walters $16,160**	
Total assets	**$46,060**	Total Liabilities and Net Worth $46,060	

TYPES OF ASSETS Businesses usually separate assets into fixed assets and current assets. *Fixed assets* are assets that will be used for many years. They include buildings, furniture, and computers. *Current assets* are cash, assets that can be converted into cash, and items that are used up in normal business operations. Assets that can be converted into cash are inventory. Assets that are used up in business operations are supplies.

Another special type of current asset is *accounts receivable.* Remember that not all customers pay for products or services at the time they receive them. Accounts receivable tracks payments due for products or services provided to customers.

TYPES OF LIABILITIES Businesses usually separate liabilities into long-term liabilities and current liabilities. *Long-term liabilities* are liabilities that are payable over several years. A bank loan is a type of long-term liability. *Current liabilities* are liabilities that are payable within a short amount of time, such as a utility bill.

A special kind of current liability is *accounts payable.* Accounts payable tracks the payments a business owes to a supplier. Remember that businesses can choose to pay later for merchandise they receive now. Because a business generally pays its debts within a few months, accounts payable is a current liability.

UNCOLLECTIBLE ACCOUNTS Felicia knows that some of her customers will fail to pay her for the merchandise they purchased. Felicia subtracts from her assets the money she believes she will not receive. The amount a company estimates it will not receive from customers is known as the *allowance for uncollectible accounts.* Companies should include an allowance for uncollectible accounts so that the balance sheet provides an accurate statement of the value of the assets.

DEPRECIATION Felicia knows that some of her equipment will lose value over time, much like a car loses its value year after year. Because her fixed assets are no longer worth the $29,175 she paid for them, she adjusts their value on the balance sheet to reflect their now lower worth. **Depreciation** is the lowering of the value of an asset to reflect its current value. Depreciating your assets makes sure that your balance sheet provides an accurate picture of the value of your assets.

 **CHECKPOINT** What does the balance sheet show? What are the two special adjustments commonly made on the balance sheet?

Personal Financial Statement

Banks are usually interested in the personal financial status of the people they lend money to. For this reason, you will have to prepare a statement of your personal finances if you apply for a

What Went Wrong

Financing
Things Change
Business: Marti-Gras Clothing, Westport, Connecticut

In two years Marty Bucatini grew Marti-Gras Clothing from a start-up to a $38 million business. At the same time, the stock market had become more interested in investing in small companies. Therefore, Marty expected that "going public" would be a good way to raise large sums of money for his new business plans.

Bucatini and his managers worked with every possible financing source, from friends and family, to banks and investors. Now they would base their plan on being able to raise millions from both the private and public markets.

Marti-Gras intended to sell stock in the company in a $30 million IPO (Initial Public Offering). Sales that year were well on their way to $58 million, and the business needed the capital

to support that volume level. What they didn't expect was how much time company managers would need to spend on the fund-raising effort.

Then, Bucatini's financial advisors told him the market no longer had any interest in new 'small-cap' IPOs. So the company had to go back to private sources for money. Nine months after the IPO that wasn't, Marti-Gras' board, out of cash and out of possibilities for raising cash, filed for bankruptcy.

Think Critically
1. How could Marty have better used his management team and resources?
2. What do you think was responsible for Marti-Gras' downfall?

bank loan. A personal financial statement is a balance sheet of your holdings. It shows your personal assets, liabilities, and net worth.

As part of the packet of materials Felicia prepares for lenders, she includes her personal financial statement. It is similar to a balance sheet, but it lists her private assets and liabilities. For her personal statement, her owner's equity is shown as Felicia's net worth. Her assets include cash, checking and savings accounts, mutual funds, and stocks. Her liabilities include a car loan, credit card debt, and college loans she must still pay off. Felicia has $40,000 in assets and $12,200 in liabilities. She assesses her net worth by subtracting all her liabilities from all her assets. She has a net worth of $27,800.

 **CHECKPOINT** **What does a personal financial statement show?**

THINK CRITICALLY

1. Why do you think banks require so much financial information when considering lending money? Why should you provide both worst- and best-case scenarios for your pro forma cash flow statement?

2. Why do you think most businesses prepare income statements on an annual basis? Why might it be helpful to an entrepreneur to view an income statement each month?

MAKE CONNECTIONS

3. MATH The estimated start-up costs for a web site developer who plans to operate out of a home office are as follows: computer hardware, $4,500; computer software, $1,560; telephone system, $850; office supplies, $585; furniture and fixtures, $4,575; legal and accounting fees, $2,450. What are the total start-up costs?

4. MATH The web site developer's total assets are $32,820 and owner's equity is $24,680. What are total liabilities? Use the accounting equation to figure out your answer.

5. COMMUNICATION Write up your personal financial statement. Consider savings or checking accounts you have, income from a job or allowance, fixed assets (cars), and liabilities (money you owe).

Obtain Financing for *Your* Business

There are many different ways to obtain the money you need to start your business. Loans are available through commercial banks. They are also available through the Small Business Administration and other government agencies. You can also obtain money from individuals in return for giving them part of your profits.

BANK LOANS

Most companies take out loans from banks. You obtain debt capital when you borrow from a bank. **Debt capital** is money loaned to a business with the understanding that the money will be repaid, with interest, in a certain time period. Companies borrow money from banks in a variety of ways.

Types of Bank Loans

Banks make two kinds of loans: secured and unsecured loans. *Secured loans* are loans backed by collateral. **Collateral** is property that the borrower forfeits if he or she defaults on the loan. Banks demand collateral so that they have some recourse if you fail to repay your loan. Suppose you take out a $25,000 business loan and that you use your home as collateral. If you fail to repay the loan, the bank has the right to take ownership of your home and sell it to collect the money you owe. Banks accept different forms of collateral, including real estate, savings accounts, life insurance policies, and stocks and bonds.

Houses are commonly used as collateral on loans.

Unsecured loans are loans that are not guaranteed with property. These loans are made only to the bank's most creditworthy customers. Unsecured loans are usually made for very specific purposes. They are usually paid back within a short period of time, often less than a year.

TYPES OF SECURED LOANS There are three kinds of secured loans: lines of credit, short-term loans, and long-term loans. *A line of credit*

is an agreement by a bank to lend up to a certain amount of money whenever the borrower needs it. Banks charge a fee for extending lines of credit to their customers, whether or not money is actually borrowed. In addition, they charge interest on borrowed funds. Most small businesses establish lines of credit, which help them make purchases as necessary.

A *short-term loan* is a loan made for a very specific purpose that is repaid within a year. Businesses use short-term loans to help with seasonal cash flow problems. A landscaping company might take out a short-term loan in December, when business is slow, and pay it back in July.

A *long-term loan* is a loan payable over a period longer than a year. Long-term loans are generally made to help a business make improvements that will boost profits. Nicole Brenner, the owner of Chez Nicole, a small neighborhood coffee shop, took out a $50,000, five-year loan to help her expand her business. She plans to use the money to increase the size of her shop by 20 percent. She will repay the loan with the extra money she will earn by serving more patrons in her expanded dining room.

In Class Activity

Work in pairs and choose a business. List five reasons this business might need a short-term loan and five reasons this business might need a long-term loan. Present your results to the class.

Reasons a Bank May Not Lend Money

Banks use various guidelines to determine borrowers who are a good risk. They reject applicants who do not meet their criteria. Some of the main reasons banks turn down loan applications include:

1. *The business is a start-up.* Banks are often reluctant to lend money to start-up businesses because new businesses have no record of repaying loans. They are more likely to default on their loans than companies that are already in business.
2. *Lack of a solid business plan.* Banks evaluate businesses based on their business plans. A company with a poorly written or poorly conceived business plan will not be able to obtain financing from a bank.
3. *Lack of adequate experience.* Banks want to be sure that the people setting up or running a business know what they are doing. This does not mean that you have to have owned a business before to qualify for a bank loan. It does mean that you have to show that you are familiar with the industry and have the management experience to run your own business.

4. ***Lack of confidence in the borrower.*** Even if your business plan looks solid and you have adequate experience, you may fail to qualify for financing if you make a bad impression on your banker. Make sure you dress and behave professionally. Show up on time for appointments and provide all information your banker requests.

5. ***Inadequate investment in the business.*** Banks are suspicious of entrepreneurs who do not invest their own money in their businesses, and they are unlikely to lend to them. This means that you will have to commit a significant amount of your own money if you are to receive financing from a bank.

Obtaining bank financing for a start-up business is difficult. It is not impossible, though, if you can show you are confident, well prepared, and that you will be able to repay the loan. Being aware of the reasons banks do not lend funds can help you overcome the five most common objections. For instance, you can wear a business suit to the bank and arrive on time to make a good impression.

 **CHECKPOINT** What are some of the reasons banks reject loan applications?

SMALL BUSINESS ADMINISTRATION LOANS

Sometimes banks do not feel comfortable lending money for one reason or another. If this is the case, you can turn to the Small Business Administration for help.

SBA Loan Assistance

The SBA is a federal government agency whose purpose is to help small businesses. In addition to providing management and technical advice to owners or prospective owners of small businesses, the SBA guarantees loans made by commercial banks. This means the SBA agrees to pay the bank loan if you cannot. This loan guarantee can help small businesses get bank financing because the SBA will guarantee up to 90 percent of a bank loan. If you default on the loan, the SBA will pay a certain percentage of the loan to the bank. This helps banks feel more comfortable about lending money.

In addition to guaranteeing loans, the SBA sometimes makes loans directly to small businesses. The SBA does not have much funding available to give direct loans, however. Most of the loan assistance the SBA provides is in the form of guaranteed loans.

When the SBA guarantees a bank loan, it asks that the money be used to buy fixed assets, or as working capital for the business.

Working capital is the money needed to meet the day-to-day needs of a business. Working capital loans are usually extended for five to seven years. Fixed asset loans are extended for longer periods of time.

 **CHECKPOINT** Describe the two types of loans given by the SBA.

Requirements of SBA Loans

The SBA is the largest source of financing to small businesses in the United States. It aids about one million Americans every year. To qualify for assistance from the SBA, your company must meet certain requirements.

1. *Your business must be considered a small business.* The definition of "small" depends on the industry. In some retail industries, for example, a company can have sales of $13.5 million and still be considered small. To find out if your company qualifies for assistance, contact the SBA office in your district.
2. *Your business must not be the leader in its field.* If, for example, you own the most popular restaurant in your town, you will not qualify for SBA financing.
3. *Your business must comply with all federal employment laws.* These laws are covered in more depth in Chapter 14.
4. *Your business cannot create or distribute ideas or opinions.* This means that newspapers, magazines, and academic schools are not eligible for SBA financing.
5. *You must have been unable to obtain financing from a commercial bank.*
6. *You must invest a reasonable amount of your own money in the venture.* Entrepreneurs usually cover 30 to 50 percent of the total cost to begin their businesses.
7. *You must provide adequate collateral.* If the assets of your business are insufficient, you will have to provide personal guarantees to secure financing.

If you meet these requirements, you can apply for a loan from the SBA. The SBA will review your business plan and decide whether or not to finance your business.

Applying for an SBA Loan

To apply for an SBA loan, you will have to provide the following information about your business:

- type of business
- date business started or is projected to start
- location of business
- product or service

The SBA is authorized to provide up to $3.5 million, in increments of up to $750,000, in the form of direct or guaranteed loans, to individual nonprofit, community-based lending and training organizations.

- plans for business
- geographic area business will serve
- competition
- customers
- suppliers
- management experience
- financial statements for all owners, including federal income tax return for previous year
- description of how you plan to repay the loan, supported by cash flow statements
- business financial data (three years of balance sheets and income statements for existing businesses, pro forma statements for new businesses)
- projections for at least one year

You may also be asked to provide the SBA with copies of lease agreements, franchise agreements, licenses, letters of reference, partnership agreements, or articles of incorporation.

Regardless of how you obtain your financing, you will have to do calculations and prepare financial statements.

 **CHECKPOINT**   **Name the requirements for obtaining an SBA loan.**

OTHER SOURCES OF LOANS

Besides the SBA, there are other government agencies that make debt capital loans.

1. ***Small Business Investment Companies.*** SBICs are licensed by the SBA to make loans to and invest capital with entrepreneurs.
2. ***Minority Enterprise Small Business Investment Companies.*** MESBICs are special kinds of SBICs that lend money to small businesses owned by members of ethnic minorities.
3. ***Department of Housing and Urban Development.*** HUD provides grants to cities to help improve impoverished areas. Cities use these grants to make loans to private developers, who must use the loans to finance projects in needy areas.
4. ***The Economic Development Administration.*** The EDA is a division of the U.S. Department of Commerce that lends money

to businesses that operate in and benefit economically distressed parts of the country. Borrowing from the EDA is similar to borrowing from the SBA, but the application is more complicated and the restrictions are tighter.

5. *State Governments.* Government assistance may also be available at the state level. Almost all states have economic development agencies and finance authorities that make or guarantee loans to small businesses.

6. *Local and Municipal Governments.* City, county, or municipal governments sometimes make small loans to local businesses. The loans are usually small, $10,000 or less.

Finance Your Business with Equity Capital

Another way to get financing for your business is through equity capital. **Equity capital** is money invested in a business in return for a share in the business's profits. Entrepreneurs may seek equity capital when they do not qualify for bank or SBA financing and are not able to fully finance their businesses out of their own savings. Equity capital can also supplement debt capital that has been obtained. You may provide much of the equity for your business yourself. You may also obtain equity through people you know or through venture capitalists.

PERSONAL FINANCING Many entrepreneurs use their personal savings to finance the start of their business. You can use personal finances to help get debt capital from a bank. If you invest your own money, the bank sees that you have faith that your business will succeed.

FRIENDS AND FAMILY Some entrepreneurs ask friends and family for the capital they need to start their business. Borrowing from friends or family members is not always a good idea. Before borrowing from people you know, consider how the loan may affect your relationship. You may decide that the risk of losing a friend if you are unable to pay back the borrowed funds is not worth taking.

If you do decide to borrow money from friends or family members, clearly warn them of the risks involved in lending money to a start-up business. Be sure both you and they understand exactly how much interest and principal you will pay each month. Also specify what your obligations are to pay back the loan if your business goes bankrupt.

NET WORTH

Point your browser to

http://www.ideas-in-action.swep.com

Complete the activity for Chapter 7.

One way of obtaining equity capital is borrowing from friends.

VENTURE CAPITALISTS Some privately owned companies sell stock through venture capitalists. **Venture capitalists** are individuals or companies that make a living investing in start-up companies. They carefully research opportunities that they believe will make them a lot of money. They are usually interested in companies that have the potential of earning hundreds of millions of dollars within a few years. Because of this, many small businesses would have trouble getting venture capitalists to invest in their company.

Carlos Cisneros wants to start up a small software company, but he needs money. Two of Carlos' friends invest $20,000 in the business. If Carlos' company fails, they will lose all of their money. If the company takes off, Carlos' friends could end up earning hundreds of thousands or even millions of dollars.

CHECKPOINT What are some of the ways entrepreneurs can get equity capital?

THINK CRITICALLY

1. Why is a secured loan easier to obtain than an unsecured loan?

2. Why do you think most SBA assistance is in the form of loan guarantees?

3. What criteria do you think the Department of Housing and Urban Development (HUD) uses to grant loans to cities?

MAKE CONNECTIONS

4. MATH Tisha Appleton obtained a $45,000 loan for her start-up business. The SBA guaranteed 75 percent of the loan. How much has the bank risked losing if Tisha's business fails?

5. COMMUNICATION Conduct a phone interview with a local banker to find out if the bank makes loans to small businesses with Small Business Administration backing. If it does, ask if the loans are typically for working capital or fixed assets. Write a one-page report on your findings.

Theft Proof
Your *Business*

A s an independent business person, you will face many risks. Some of the risks you face involve theft. Shoplifters or employees may steal your merchandise. Burglars may break into your business and steal your equipment. People may use stolen credit cards or write checks when they don't have money in their account. You can take steps to protect yourself against the different kinds of theft.

SHOPLIFTING

Shoplifting is the act of knowingly taking items from a business without paying. Customers shoplift millions of dollars in merchandise every year. The problem exists in virtually every type of retail business.

If you own a retail business, you will have to take steps to prevent or reduce shoplifting. Some of the things you can do include the following:

1. Instruct your employees to watch for customers who appear suspicious.
2. Hire security guards or off-duty police officers to patrol your store.
3. Post signs indicating that you prosecute shoplifters.
4. Ask customers to leave their bags behind the counter.
5. Install electronic devices, such as mounted video cameras, electronic merchandise tags, and point-of-exit sensors, that detect shoplifters.

 **CHECKPOINT** How can entrepreneurs protect their businesses from shoplifters?

EMPLOYEE THEFT

Most employees are hard-working and honest. But there are a few who will take things from your business, such as office supplies, fixed assets, and even money. These employees can devastate your business financially.

As an entrepreneur, you need to be aware of the possibility of employee theft. You need to take steps to prevent the problem from occurring. You also need to know how to detect the problem and to handle it once it is detected.

Some businesses, such as restaurants and retail stores, are more vulnerable to employee theft than others. If you own such a business, you may need to adopt the following procedures:

1. ***Prevent dishonest employees from joining your company.*** Screen job applicants very carefully. Consider using a company that specializes in verifying job applicants' educational backgrounds and searching their criminal records, driver's license reports, civil court records, and credit reports.

2. ***Install surveillance systems.*** Often the mere knowledge that they are being filmed by a video camera deters employees from stealing.

Office supplies may be stolen by employees.

Entrepreneurial Timeline

| 1960 | 1970 | 1980 | 1990 |

Airing Good Business Practices

When cable television first began in the 1970s, it provided remote places with network stations such as ABC, CBS, and NBC. No one thought of using it as an entertainment medium, except for Kay Koplovitz. After working for UA-Columbia Satellite Services for four years, she decided to leave the firm in 1977 to establish an independent cable network. She convinced her former employer that her idea was viable, and their partnership created the first advertiser-supported independent cable network, the USA Network. Kay has lots of other firsts, too. She was the first to negotiate cable rights to major league sports. With Kay at the helm, USA was the first cable network to obtain exclusive rights to a syndicated television series, and the first to secure an exclusive package of first-run movies with a major motion picture studio. The USA Network boasts over $400 million in sales each year. A pioneer and leader in the cable industry, Kay is considered one of the most powerful women in television.

3. **Establish a tough company policy regarding employee theft.** It should detail what the consequences of employee theft are. Make sure that all employees are aware of the policy.

4. **Be on the lookout.** Watch for cash discrepancies, missing merchandise or supplies, vehicles parked close to loading areas, and other signs that something may be wrong. Keep an eye on employees who seem to work at odd hours, perform their jobs poorly, or complain unreasonably. Make inquiries if an employee has an unexplained close relationship with a supplier or customer or has a personal lifestyle that seems inconsistent with his or her salary.

In Class Activity

In small groups, develop a profile of an employee who is likely to steal. Then brainstorm a list of suggestions regarding how an employer can take measures to avoid hiring this type of person.

CHECKPOINT How can you protect your business against employee theft?

OTHER TYPES OF THEFT

In addition to shoplifting and employee theft, all business owners must be aware of the possibility that their business could be robbed. They could also be the victims of credit card fraud or bounced checks.

Robbery

Almost all businesses are vulnerable to robberies. You can choose a safe location for your business to guard against being robbed. You can also install dead-bolt locks and burglar alarms. To limit losses in the event of a robbery, many businesses keep a minimum amount of cash in the cash register. Once more than a certain amount is received, the cash is transferred to a safe. Some businesses also use surveillance cameras, which deter prospective robbers from entering the business in the first place. Be aware that you may be robbed regardless of the number of preventative measures you take. It is simply a risk of being open for business.

Credit Card Fraud

Business owners lose millions of dollars every year because of stolen credit cards. If a purchase is made on a stolen credit card, a business may not be able to collect the money. To prevent stolen credit cards from being used to purchase goods, you can install an electronic credit authorizer. This machine checks to see if a credit card is valid. If the card has been reported stolen or if the cardholder has exceeded the credit limit, authorization will not be granted.

Bounced Checks

A *bounced check* is when a check is written and there are insufficient funds in the checking account to cover the amount of the check. Preventing losses from bad checks is more difficult. To minimize losses, you can establish a policy of accepting checks drawn on in-state banks only. You can also charge an additional fee if a customer writes a bad check to your business. Asking for identification, like a driver's license, can help you track down a person who writes you a bad check so you can collect money due to you. If bad checks are a serious problem in your area, you may decide not to accept checks at all.

 **CHECKPOINT** How can you help prevent robberies and bounced checks?

THINK CRITICALLY

1. What types of behavior do you think potential shoplifters might exhibit?

2. You own a pizza shop. You suspect that one of your delivery people is charging customers more than what they actually owe and keeping the difference. How would you handle this situation?

3. What is the downside to the decision of not accepting personal checks?

MAKE CONNECTIONS

4. **MATH** At closing time, the Old World Café's cash register totaled out at $884. The cash added up to $534, and the credit card slips equaled $237. How much of the day's proceeds are not accounted for? What reasons might explain the difference?

5. **PROBLEM SOLVING** Last year the Christmas season profits at Ray's Sporting Goods were reduced significantly because of shoplifting. In small groups, participate in a consensus building exercise to brainstorm ways to approach the problem this year.

Insure *Your* Business

GOALS

DETERMINE the different types of insurance you may need for your business.

PURCHASE insurance.

A s a business owner, you are at risk from more than just criminal activity. A fire could destroy your building. An accident could injure an employee. A burst water pipe could ruin your inventory. You can protect yourself against some financial losses by buying insurance.

TYPES OF INSURANCE

The most important types of insurance you will need for your business include property insurance, casualty insurance, life insurance, and workers' compensation insurance.

Property Insurance

Property insurance insures all business property against normal risks, including fire, robbery, and storm damage. Most businesses purchase all three kinds of property insurance. Insurance companies usually offer separate policies for buildings, vehicles, and other business property (such as cash, equipment, and inventory).

Property insurance does not cover floods or earthquakes. If your business is located in a part of the country that is prone to special kinds of natural disasters, you may want to purchase a separate insurance policy that covers those kinds of catastrophic events.

Casualty Insurance

Casualty insurance protects a business against lawsuits. It can protect you from having to pay damages if an accident occurs on your premises. It also can protect your business against lawsuits claiming that a defect in the product you manufactured or sold caused bodily injury to a customer.

YOU CAN SAY THAT AGAIN!

"Don't take any money out of the business for a while—put it back in, and don't get too far in debt."

—*Lillian Vernon founder and owner of the Lillian Vernon Corporation*

Life Insurance

Life insurance is insurance that is paid in the event that the holder of the policy dies. A business owner buys life insurance so that his or her heirs have enough money to continue the business.

Workers' Compensation

Workers' compensation consists of payments to workers who are injured on the job. All businesses are required by law to provide workers' compensation. Workers' compensation covers medical expenses incurred as a result of work-related injuries. It provides income benefits to workers who are unable to work as a result of their injuries.

Other Kinds of Insurance

Other types of insurance that you may want to purchase include flood, business interruption, crime, and renter's insurance. Depending on your business and its location, you may or may not decide to purchase these additional kinds of protection.

 **CHECKPOINT** List all the types of insurance you can purchase for your business.

BUY INSURANCE

Buying insurance can be complicated. How much is too much or too little insurance to have? A good insurance agent can help you make decisions about purchasing coverage.

Choose an Insurance Agent

Insurance is sold by agents who represent many different insurance companies. It is also sold by agents who work for a single company. Before selecting a particular company, talk to an agent who represents more than one insurer. Or ask representatives of several different companies to talk with you about their policies.

The market for insurance is competitive. This means that different agents will be eager to sell you insurance. To get the best price, contact a few agents and compare prices and policies. Then consider how you feel about the agents. Remember that the person who sells you your policy will be involved in processing your claim should you ever need to collect on your policy. It is therefore important to choose someone whom you trust. You may already have an agent you trust with your car insurance or other types of insurance you may have. That agent can be a starting point in your research.

In Class Activity

Choose a partner. One partner should role-play a person who has just obtained a loan to open a roller-skating rink. The other should role-play the insurance agent, who must educate the new business owner about the types of insurance available.

Determine How Much Coverage You Need

The first step in buying insurance is determining the kind of coverage you think you need. Make a list of the property you own. Identify your equipment, inventory, vehicles, and other significant items of value, and put a value next to each. Then think about the kinds of risk you would like to insure against. If, for example, your business is located near a river that floods, you may want to purchase flood insurance. If you live in a low-crime area, you may want to consider not insuring your business against break-ins. Understand, however, the implications of not having insurance if something should happen.

The next step is determining how much coverage you need. Be sure it covers any and all debts you may have incurred while starting your business. Li-Li Tang, owner of Computer Systems, has a $50,000 bank loan on her business, as well as two small loans for $5,000 each. She wants to get at least $60,000 worth of property insurance to cover these outstanding debts in the event of a problem.

Insurance agents earn commissions on the amount of coverage they sell. They therefore have an interest in selling you lots of coverage. To make sure you need the coverage your agent is suggesting, talk to other business owners in your area or counselors from SCORE or the SBA.

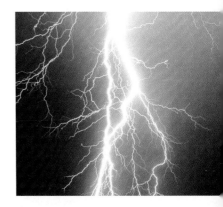

You may want your property insurance to cover damage from electrical storms.

 **CHECKPOINT** How can you determine how much insurance you need?

THINK CRITICALLY

1. Tim Stanton has just opened a surf shop on the beach in South Florida. He has purchased property insurance to insure his business against normal risks to his buildings, vehicles, and other business property. Against what additional risks should he consider insuring his business?

2. What issues should you consider in choosing an insurance agent?

MAKE CONNECTIONS

3. **MATH** Sylvia Bruemmer is an insurance agent who has just sold the following insurance policies to a business owner: property insurance, $100,000; casualty insurance, $50,000; and life insurance, $200,000. How much will Sylvia earn on each separate policy if she makes a 5% commission? What will be the total commission on all 3 policies?

4. **COMMUNICATION** You have just opened an insurance agency that specializes in insuring businesses. Write a sales letter to prospective customers introducing yourself and your services.

Chapter 7
Review

CHAPTER SUMMARY

Put Together a *Financial* Plan

1. Your financial plan will consist of five financial statements: start-up costs, a cash flow statement, an income statement, a balance sheet, and a personal financial statement. All of these statements except for the personal financial statement will be pro forma financial statements. They are estimates of how your business will perform.
2. A cash flow statement shows actual cash coming in and going out of a business over a period of time. A income statement shows revenue and expenses that may not yet have been received or paid out.
3. A balance sheet shows the assets, liabilities, and owner's equity of a business. As its name implies, the balance sheet must always remain in balance.

Obtain Financing for *Your* Business

4. A bank may help you finance your business with a secured or an unsecured loan.
5. To help new businesses that cannot obtain financing from commercial banks, the Small Business Administration offers loan guarantees. If your loan application has been rejected by a bank, you may be eligible to apply for an SBA loan.
6. Besides the SBA, there are other government agencies that may fund your business venture. You can also consider financing your business with equity.

Theft Proof Your *Business*

7. Once you have found financing, you will need to think about protecting your business from theft. Shoplifting and employee theft are just some of the risks business owners face.

Insure *Your* Business

8. There are many types of insurance you can purchase for your business. You will have to choose an insurance agent you trust who will sell you the right insurance in the right amounts.

What Do You Know Now?

Read *Build a Business* again. Then answer the questions a second time. How have your responses changed?

VOCABULARY BUILDER

Choose the term that best fits the definition.
Write your answers on a separate sheet of paper.

1. Expenses that are incurred by a business every month
2. Financial statements based on projections
3. The lowering of the value of an asset to reflect its current value
4. Items of value owned by a business
5. One-time-only expenses that are paid to establish a business
6. The act of knowingly taking items from a business without paying
7. Property that the borrower forfeits if he or she defaults on the loan
8. Money loaned to a business with the understanding that the money will be repaid, with interest, in a certain time period.
9. Money invested in a business in return for a share in the business's profits
10. Individuals or companies that make a living investing in start-up companies

a. assets
b. collateral
c. debt capital
d. depreciation
e. equity capital
f. liabilities
g. operating expenses
h. pro forma financial statements
i. shoplifting
j. start-up costs
k. venture capitalists

REVIEW YOUR KNOWLEDGE

11. What materials do you need to prepare for a potential lender or investor to assess whether your business appears viable?

12. How are start-up costs different from monthly operating expenses?

13. Why should you create a worst-case and best-case scenario cash flow statement?

14. What does an income statement show?

15. What is the accounting equation?

16. Why does an entrepreneur prepare a personal financial statement?

17. Why do banks demand collateral?

18. What requirements must you meet to quality for SBA assistance?

19. What are SBICs and what do they do?

20. Why would an entrepreneur seek equity capital?

21. What can you do to prevent shoplifting? Robberies?

22. What are some of the things that may indicate to a business owner that an employee is stealing?

23. How do you prevent losses from credit card fraud and bad checks?

24. Describe all the different types of insurance.

25. Why is buying insurance for your business important?

APPLY WHAT YOU LEARNED

26. You want to establish an amusement park. Make a list of the start-up costs. Forecast your monthly revenues and operating expenses. Create both a worst- and best-case scenario cash flow statement. Create a personal financial statement.

27. You have established that you will need to borrow money to start the amusement park. What type of financing will you seek? Why? Will you qualify for a bank loan or assistance from a government agency? What kinds of equity might you use to finance your business?

28. You will need to purchase insurance for the amusement park. List the major types of insurance and explain the reason why you need each.

THINK CRITICALLY

29. If you are not applying for business loans or attracting investors to your business, do you think you still need a financial plan? Why or why not? Why do you think an entrepreneur may hire an accountant to assist with the preparation of the financial plan for the business?

30. What is the advantage of a line of credit versus a short- or long-term loan? Do you think a line of credit would be more or less difficult to qualify for? Why?

31. Why do you think the SBA and other government agencies are willing to take a risk on an entrepreneur when a bank will not?

32. Businesses lose millions of dollars every year because of stolen credit cards and bounced checks. Why wouldn't a business owner protect him or herself by accepting only cash?

33. Do you think all business owners need insurance? Why or why not? What do you think are some of the reasons an entrepreneur would

not purchase insurance? Do you think insurance coverage is necessary to obtain financing for a business? Why or why not?

MAKE CONNECTIONS

34. **MATH** You own a music store that sells instruments and sheet music and provides services such as lessons and instrument repair. You owe $25,000 to instrument vendors and publishers. You have a ten-year bank loan of $50,000. Your bank account balance is $13,000; you own inventory worth $57,000; and you expect $2,000 in receivables. Fixed assets are $22,000. What are your total assets? What are your total liabilities? What is your owner's equity?

35. **COMMUNICATION** You are applying for an SBA loan for your music store. Write a letter to the SBA that provides all of the information about your business. Elaborate on your plans for your business and how you plan to use the money. How do you plan to repay the loan?

This Is Your Business Project

1. Prepare the following documents for your business: list of start-up costs; cash flow statement; income statement; balance sheet; and personal financial statement. What is your owner's equity?
2. Determine how much money, if any, you need to borrow to begin your business. Decide if you will obtain financing through a bank, the SBA, another government agency, or with equity capital. Write down why you think one or more of these ways to finance your business will work. Contact the SBA office to obtain information about financing. What information will they need to assist you? Does your company qualify for assistance from the SBA? Why or why not?
3. Establish the ways you will prevent shoplifting. Research how much it will cost you if you buy special equipment or hire a guard. Write the company policy regarding employee theft. Also write out how you will prevent robberies, credit card fraud, and bad checks.
4. Contact an insurance agent to obtain information on insuring your business. What types of insurance do you need? How much coverage should you buy?

Chapter 8
CHOOSE YOUR LOCATION AND SET UP FOR BUSINESS

LESSONS

8.1 Choose a Retail Business Location

8.2 Choose a Location for a Non-Retail Business

8.3 Obtain Space and Design the Physical Layout

8.4 Purchase Equipment, Supplies, and Inventory

BUILD A BUSINESS

Expanding and Moving

"Scott, how would you like to work for me?" Greg asked his younger brother. "It's time to expand my tee-shirt business."

"Sounds like a good idea," Scott responded. "Where are you going to locate?"

"I think we'll just work out of my apartment. I've got a phone and a computer. That's really all I need to get started. You can help me get customers, vendors, and maybe help out with the financial stuff."

"Count me in!" Scott exclaimed.

Everything went well for Scott and Greg during their first year partnering together. They made good profits, and they both enjoyed the business. One day, Scott started thinking about the future of his business and realized that he needed to talk to his brother.

"Hey, Greg, we need to hire an administrative assistant. There are more orders coming in than we can handle by ourselves. And since we're adding custom embroidery, we'll have even more customers. Because we're growing, we should relocate."

"Well, let's look in the want ads and see what's available. Where did you have in mind for an office?" Scott asked.

"It doesn't really matter where we locate. We always go to the customer. But one thing that would be helpful is if we got an office near the factory that prints our shirts. That way, we can take orders directly to the factory and answer any questions they might have."

"Greg, I think I've found just the spot for us. It's in an industrial park; the price is reasonable; and public transportation is available for our employees if they need it."

"Give them a call and let's get moving," Greg replied.

The two brothers visited the site and liked it. "How will we know this is really the right location for us?" asked Scott.

"Well, we should lay out the floor plan of the business, to make sure everything we need can be put in this building. You know, the iron-on department could go here. There's plenty of room by the front door for a reception area, too."

"And the factory right next door can supply us with most of the items we need produced. But I wonder if we should ask a few factories to tell us how much they would charge us for the work they do for us?"

"Hey, that's a good idea," said Greg. "Why don't you find a couple of vendors and ask them for price quotes?"

What Do You Know?

1. What were the advantages and disadvantages of having the business in Greg's apartment in the beginning?
2. If Greg and Scott decided to offer retail sales, would they need to consider different things in a location?
3. Why is it a good idea to look at several vendors when deciding who will supply your business?

Choose a *Retail* Business Location

Choosing a location for your business will be one of the most important decisions you will make as an entrepreneur. One type of business you may choose to open is a retail business. Choosing a bad location for your retail business could spell disaster. Choosing a good location can mean your business succeeds right from the start.

LOCATION POSSIBILITIES

Retail businesses can operate in many locations. The type of area you choose will depend on the kind of business you operate and the type of people in your community.

Downtown Areas

In some communities, downtown areas represent central location opportunities you may want to consider. Because offices and professional businesses are located in downtown areas, customers will be willing to shop at your business on their breaks or on their way to and from work. Downtown is also a central area in most cities and is accessible to many individuals. Rents vary widely from city to city, so you will need to do some research if you are thinking of using a downtown location.

Many downtown areas recently have lost business to neighborhood, community, and regional shopping centers. Crime, traffic, and lack of parking spaces and evening customers make downtown areas less appealing to some business owners.

Neighborhood Shopping Centers

Neighborhood shopping centers are small shopping centers that serve a certain neighborhood. Businesses such as supermarkets, dry cleaners, and drugstores usually are housed in these shopping centers. Such centers represent good locations for stores selling goods or services that people need to purchase frequently. Rent is usually low in these centers, which can make them ideal for small businesses.

Customers of neighborhood shopping centers are mainly residents of the surrounding area who shop at these centers because of their convenience. It could be a disadvantage if only customers in the immediate area come to your store, however.

Community Shopping Centers

Community shopping centers are designed to serve residents of many neighborhoods. Although rents are generally higher than in neighborhood shopping centers, they are usually still affordable. And stores in community shopping centers can earn higher profits. Community centers usually have one or two major tenants, known as anchor stores, and 10 or more smaller stores. Anchor stores include

- department stores (Dillard's, Macy's, Nordstrom's, JC Penney)
- discount stores (Wal-Mart, Kmart)
- large supermarkets (Kroger, Food Lion, Safeway)
- large drugstores (Drug Emporium, Rite Aid, CVS)

Anchor stores advertise heavily and attract customers from throughout the community. Other businesses typically benefit from this advertisement. Customers shop at the anchor store and then may browse and buy at a smaller store located in the shopping center.

 **CHECKPOINT** **What are the advantages of locating downtown? Locating in a community shopping center?**

Regional Shopping Centers

Regional shopping centers are designed to attract customers from an entire region. These large shopping areas usually have three or four anchor stores and more than 40 other stores. Many regional shopping centers are malls. If your business requires a large amount of walk-in traffic to be successful, you may want to locate in a regional shopping center. Rents at these centers are high, however, making it more difficult to earn profits. Also, the distance to the shop may be too great for some consumers. For convenience, they may decide to patronize businesses closer to their homes.

A downtown area might be a good location for your business.

Super-Regional Shopping Centers

Super-regional shopping centers are extremely large and house hundreds of stores. The largest of these centers are the West Edmonton Mall, in Edmonton, Canada, and the Mall of America, in Bloomington, Minnesota. Both have about 800 stores. Most tenants in these centers are large chain stores that can afford the very high rents charged. Also, if convenience is a factor for your business, customers may not be willing to travel a great distance to come to your store. Such centers usually are not recommended for new business owners.

Stand-Alone Stores

Stand-alone stores can be located just outside of shopping centers or far away from other businesses. These stores often depend on drive-by traffic. They must have plenty of parking, good signs, and effective lighting if they are to be successful.

Businesses locate in stand-alone locations because rent is often less expensive than it is elsewhere. Also, a competing business is less likely to be right next door. Advertising is often necessary to earn a profit as a stand-alone store because people must have a reason to come specifically to your business. Restaurants, auto dealers, and tire stores are often operated as stand-alone stores.

Warehouses

Some retail stores, such as appliance dealers or furniture sellers, operate in warehouses. Warehouses are generally one of the cheapest rental facilities because they do not have to look nice on the inside. Locating your business in a low-rent warehouse may allow you to

RETAIL BUSINESS LOCATION ADVANTAGES AND DISADVANTAGES		
Location	Advantages	Disadvantages
Downtown	• Central • Likely to attract business shoppers	• Parking problems • Distance from suburbs • Crime • Lack of evening shoppers
Neighborhood shopping center	• Supermarkets and other businesses bring in customers • Low rent	• Attracts only customers who live in area
Community shopping center	• Anchor stores bring in customers • Moderate rent	• Distance is too great when convenience is important
Regional shopping center	• Anchor stores bring in customers • Walk-in traffic • Attract customers from a large area	• Distance is too great when convenience is important • High rent
Super-regional shopping center	• Huge number of customers • Service a large area	• Very high rent • Competition from many companies • Distance is too great when convenience is important
Stand-alone store	• Rent can be lower • No competition next door	• No anchor store to attract customers • Extra expense of advertising
Warehouse	• Low rent • Can charge lower prices than competition	• No anchor store to attract customers • Requires heavy advertising • Customers may not be aware of your business

charge lower prices than your competitors. However, locating away from other retailers also can mean that most potential customers will not know where your business is. For this reason, businesses that operate out of warehouses generally advertise heavily.

 **CHECKPOINT** What are the main options for locating a retail business?

BEGIN SELECTION OF YOUR SITE

Given all the possible types of locations for retail businesses, how do you decide where to locate? One way of identifying your options is to buy a map of your area and mark the trade area. The **trade area** is the area from which you expect to attract customers. Indicate on the map all of the locations that might be appropriate for your business. Also indicate the location of all of your competitors. Using a different color marker or symbol, mark the locations of businesses that do not compete with yours but may attract the same kind of customer. If you want to open a poster store that will attract mostly teens, mark the locations of other stores that also appeal to this target market. Examples are trendy clothing stores and music stores.

Location Type and Availability

The next step is to identify which type of location is right for your business. Do you want to locate in a community shopping center? A stand-alone store? Downtown? Determining which type of location you want will help narrow your search.

After deciding on the type of location, you must determine what buildings of this type are available in your trade area. The classified section of your local paper will list available locations. You also can find locations simply by driving around your trade area. Signs advertising an available building will be hung in the front window or be on the front lawn of the building. Web sites and search engines also may be helpful in determining what

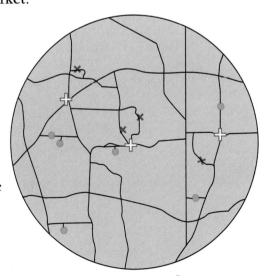

✖ = Competitors   ● = Businesses that attract same target market   ➕ = Proposed locations

In Class Activity

Make a list of at least 20 retail stores in your city. Classify each by location. Discuss whether any of these stores would do better business in a different location.

options are open to you. Mark each possible location you find on your trade area map.

QUESTIONS TO ASK After getting a list of possible locations, inspect each location to assess its appeal. Is the location safe? Is it attractive? Does it seem to attract the kind of customers your business will be targeting? Is it easy to reach? Is parking adequate? Do businesses in the vicinity seem to be thriving? After answering these questions you should have only one or two viable business locations.

Michele Kim is planning to open a fabric store. Convinced that there is a market for her product, Michele proceeds to identify the best location for her store. She rules out a downtown location because of the lack of parking and the fact that many shoppers are not willing to go downtown in the evenings. After thorough research, she settles on a community shopping center because of the low rent, the good parking, and the safety of the center at all hours.

CHECKPOINT What are some of the factors you should consider when selecting a specific site for your retail business?

THINK CRITICALLY

1. Why do you think rents are lower in neighborhood shopping centers than in community and regional centers?

2. When marking the trade area for your potential business, why should you indicate the locations of your competitors?

MAKE CONNECTIONS

3. PROBLEM SOLVING Using a map of your area, mark the potential trade area for a new furniture superstore. Then use the six-step problem-solving model to help determine at least two appropriate locations.

4. COMMUNICATION As a downtown business owner, you actively work to recruit other businesses to the area. Write a letter to the editor of your local newspaper about the advantages of locating a business downtown.

Choose a Location for a *Non-Retail* Business

GOALS

EXAMINE a location for a service business.

SELECT a location for an industrial business.

OPERATE your business from your home.

L ocation can be very important for non-retail businesses, which include service, wholesale, and manufacturing businesses. Owners of each type of non-retail business must face different considerations in choosing a location.

LOCATION FOR A SERVICE BUSINESS

For some service businesses, such as restaurants or hair salons, location is as important as it is for a retail business. Owners of these types of businesses will have to be very careful when choosing a location. Convenience is an important factor for many service businesses. Eileen Whitman runs a small company that repairs computers. Because most of her customers are businesses, Eileen chose a downtown location for her company. Being close to her customers means that in an emergency she can have computers she works on back in service the same day.

IS LOCATION ALWAYS IMPORTANT? Location is much less important for other types of service businesses. Customers never actually visit some service businesses, such as plumbing or carpet-cleaning companies. Locating these kinds of businesses in expensive areas does not make sense. Being close to customers may be important, however, because customers are more likely to call a company located nearby.

 **CHECKPOINT** How important is location for a service business?

LOCATION FOR AN INDUSTRIAL BUSINESS

Industrial businesses, such as manufacturing and wholesale companies, ship their products directly to their customers. This means customers rarely see these plants. Operating in an up-scale location that attracts lots of retail traffic is not necessary for an industrial business. Availability of good employees and low cost are the key factors in determining where an industrial business locates.

Non-retail businesses sometimes are located in industrial parks. **Industrial parks** are sections of land that can be used for industrial business locations. They are usually located where space is less expensive, away from housing developments and downtown areas. Communities sometimes subsidize rents in industrial parks in order to attract industrial businesses.

Tim Morrison's company specializes in sending bulk mail for large companies. His corporate customers send him mailing labels and copies of their catalogs, which he mails from his shop. All of Tim's contact with his customers takes place over the phone. There is no reason for him to locate his business in a prestigious part of town.

ENTERPRISE ZONES Industrial businesses may locate in enterprise zones. **Enterprise zones** are areas that suffer from lack of employment opportunities. Entrepreneurs who set up businesses in these areas may be eligible for favorable tax treatment based on the number of jobs their businesses create.

Some businesses may find the tax benefits offered by enterprise zones attractive. Others, however, may find that these benefits do not make up for the lack of an appropriate customer base or the increased risk of crime in these areas.

CHECKPOINT What are the main factors determining where to locate an industrial business?

OPERATE YOUR BUSINESS FROM HOME

Leasing or buying business property is expensive. To avoid such expenses, many entrepreneurs operate their businesses from their homes. You may decide that is a good option for you, too. However, zoning laws may govern whether or not you can put your business in your home. You will need to check the zoning laws in your area to be sure you are legally able to operate your business from your home.

Home-based businesses are ideal for small companies whose customers need not visit the premises. Rashid Zerbe runs a computer company from his New York apartment. Starting out with little more than a $1,500 computer, Rashid began a web site design firm that now employs five people. Tina Mills runs her one-person marketing consulting company from her home in Los Angeles, California. Tina's clients include large corporations, and all of her business is done over the phone.

OFFICE SPACE CONSIDERATIONS Most entrepreneurs who work from their homes set off a special room or area for their business. This part of the home is considered their office. It is generally out of bounds for chil-

In Class Activity

In small groups, brainstorm a list of rules an entrepreneur might make if he or she decides to work at home. When sharing your rules with the class, ask one person from your group to write your rules on the board.

dren and other family members. Limiting the office to business use is very important if the office will be deducted as a business expense, since the Internal Revenue Service (IRS) will not recognize a deduction for a room or area that is used for non-business as well as business purposes.

Advantages and Disadvantages

Working at home has a number of advantages. Rent, utility, insurance, maintenance, and other costs are reduced or eliminated. Some of the expenses that do occur may be subtracted as business expenses from income taxes. The time and expense of commuting are also eliminated when you run a business from your home.

Working at home has several disadvantages as well. Some people find it difficult to concentrate because of interruptions from family members or friends. Others find they miss the personal interactions that come with working outside the home. Yet others find that they spend more time working on their business than they really want because their business is located in their home.

**CHECKPOINT** What are some of the advantages of operating a business from your home?

THINK CRITICALLY

1. Name five types of service businesses for which location is important. Name five types of service businesses for which location is not important.

2. Why do you think businesses that locate in enterprise zones are eligible for favorable tax treatment?

3. Do you think advances in technology have played a part in some new business owners' decision to operate from their home? Why or why not?

MAKE CONNECTIONS

4. COMMUNICATION You plan to start a home-based business. Write a paragraph explaining how you will overcome the disadvantages of working at home.

5. RESEARCH Call your local Chamber of Commerce to find out where the nearest enterprise zone is. Ask if there are tax advantages for a business to locate there. Write down your findings in a short report.

GOALS

EVALUATE leasing versus buying space.

CONSIDER the costs and kinds of leases.

DESIGN the layout for different types of businesses.

Obtain Space and *Design* the Physical Layout

Once you choose a location for your business, you will have to lease or buy space. You will also have to design the physical layout, or floor plan, of your place of business.

LEASE OR BUY SPACE

Unless you operate your business out of your home, you will have to lease or buy business property. There are advantages to buying space. Owning property can be a tax advantage. Owning the building that houses your business gives you a tax deduction. And, a rent payment may be just as much as a loan payment for the purchase of a building.

Most entrepreneurs lack the money to purchase property for their businesses. Even entrepreneurs who can afford to purchase property generally prefer not to be locked into a particular location. Some leases require the owner of the building to pay certain expenses. For these reasons, most businesses lease space.

Entrepreneurs can buy or lease property.

Kinds of Commercial Leases

In a lease contract, there is a tenant and a landlord. The **tenant** is the person who pays rent to occupy space owned by someone else. The **landlord** is the person who owns and rents out buildings or space. There are three kinds of commercial leases.

1. A *gross lease* is when the tenant pays rent each month for the space occupied and the landlord covers all property expenses for that space. Expenses such as property taxes, insurance on the building, and building maintenance are paid by the landlord.
2. A *net lease* occurs when the landlord pays building insurance, and the tenant pays rent, taxes, and any other expenses.
3. With a *percentage lease,* the tenant pays rent each month, plus the landlord receives a percentage of the tenant's revenue each month.

Commercial lease agreements are usually long and complex. You should never sign one without consulting an attorney. Your attorney will review your lease to make sure that it covers all conditions and costs, including the basic rent, maintenance fees, utility costs, insurance costs, and other items.

Compare Different Locations

Once you have selected some possible locations for your business, you will need to compare the costs and benefits of leasing property at each. To do so, you will need to calculate how much rent you will be paying per customer.

Juan Martinez plans to open a music store. He looks for a location that is convenient, far from other music stores, and safe for customers. He finds two locations that meet his needs, one in a neighborhood shopping center and the other in the local downtown area.

CALCULATING RENT PER CUSTOMER To make a decision on which location he should select, Juan finds the amount of rent for each space, and the number of projected customers for each location. He puts this information in a table. Juan divides the amount of rent by the number of projected customers to determine the rent per customer.

What Went Wrong

Location
Right Space, Wrong Place

Business: Jimmy T's Rib House, Concord, California * In business, 6 months

Jim Teal opened Jimmy T's Rib House, and within the first ten months he was making profits. One day a commercial realtor advised Jim that a restaurant four times the size of his current space was on the market. The realtor said he could get Jim a good deal on the lease if he liked it.

Jim knew that the city where the location was had no other barbecue rib restaurant. He researched and verified the population numbers and demographics for the geographical area. It was in a good neighborhood, on a main road, just off the freeway. He even did a traffic-flow study, and the numbers were terrific. The "Grand Opening Week" went well. But then business began to fall off.

Yes, there was plenty of traffic, but Jimmy T's was on the wrong side of the street. Customers coming west from the freeway exit couldn't cross the center island, and there was a "No U-Turn" sign at the corner. When Jim tried to improve his visibility and signs to attract and direct more freeway traffic, he found that city regulations prevented it. After six months, Jim took his loss and moved back.

Think Critically
1. What questions about location should Jim have asked the realtor before assuming the lease?
2. Who else should Jim have questioned about the location?

COSTS AND BENEFITS OF TWO LOCATIONS		
	Downtown	**Shopping Center**
Rent per Month	$ 925	$1,100
Projected Customer Traffic per Month	8,500	12,000
Rent per Customer	$ 0.11	$ 0.09

From his calculations, Juan determines that he will be paying a lower rent per customer at the shopping center, although the total rent will be higher. Juan leases space at the shopping center.

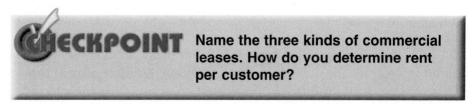

CHECKPOINT Name the three kinds of commercial leases. How do you determine rent per customer?

DESIGN THE LAYOUT OF YOUR BUSINESS

After you have leased or purchased a facility, you will need to design your layout, or floor plan. Your layout must include enough space for employees, customers, merchandise, and equipment. It must also have space for restrooms, stockrooms, storage and offices.

Create the Floor Plan

You will need to prepare a scale drawing of the layout. Graph paper will help you draw your layout to scale. To create a scale drawing, let 1 inch represent 1 foot of actual space. For example, a 4-foot-by-3-foot

Sample Floor Plan

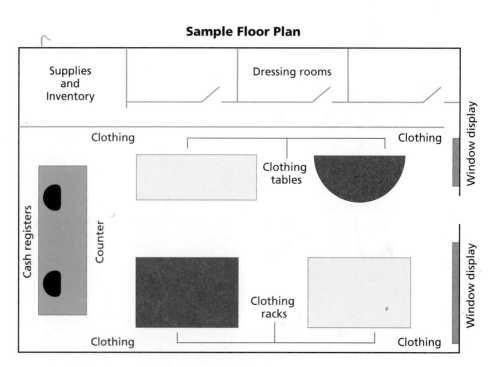

room is represented by a 4-inch-by-3-inch rectangle. Indicate the planned use of each area. Also indicate the location of furniture, display cabinets, shelves, fixtures, and equipment. Your drawing will help you identify potential problems in your layout. It will also help you communicate with the people who may do remodeling work.

Decide on a layout, an outside sign, and window displays that match your image. If you sell expensive jewelry, you will probably decide on a sophisticated outside sign and an elegant inside design that will appeal to your target customer. If you sell outdoor equipment, you will select a very different design for your store.

Layout of a Retail Business

For a retail business, appearance is very important. A store with inviting window displays and creatively displayed merchandise sends a positive message. A store with crowded aisles and piles of sale items does not. Some ways you can send a positive message about your store are:

The layout, lighting, and displays in your store should appeal to your target customer.

1. *Choose lighting that is appropriate for the kind of merchandise you sell.* Good lighting is important for any business where customers inspect merchandise closely. Avoid fluorescent lighting, which creates an unattractive glare.
2. *Think carefully about window displays.* Use them as a way to display new merchandise or seasonal items.
3. *Make the entrance inviting.* This will put customers at ease.
4. *Use common sense when organizing the merchandise in your store.* Customers should always easily find what they want. Inventory and supplies should also be well organized so that you can find things faster and serve your customers better.
5. *Leave at least four feet of aisle space.* This makes it easy to move around in your store.
6. *Create attractive in-store displays.* Customers are drawn to displayed merchandise.
7. *Use wall space wisely.* Use wall space that is too high to reach for displaying merchandise.
8. *Place the cash register in a central location* so that customers will not have to search for a cashier.

The goal of your layout should be twofold. It should attract customers to your store, and it should make their experience a pleasant one so that they return. Sending a positive message will attract people to come to your store again and again.

 **What should you do to create a positive message about your store?**

Layout of a Service Business

Service businesses can be divided into two categories:

- Service businesses where people come to the business location to receive a service (restaurants, hair salons, tax preparation services)
- Service businesses that travel to the customer's location and perform the service on-site (exterminators, plumbers, cleaning services)

The layout of the first type of service business should be considered just as carefully as that of a retail business. However, on-site service businesses are never visited by their customers, so an attractive layout is not important. Organization should be a major consideration of on-site service businesses so that supplies and other items are easy to find.

In Class Activity

In groups, choose one of the following businesses and design its layout: retail sporting goods store, copy shop, wholesale carpet distributor, custom paper manufacturer. Share your layouts with the rest of the class.

Layout of a Wholesale Business

Customers of wholesale businesses are concerned with price and quality, not physical appearance. For this reason, a wholesale business only needs to be well organized.

Wholesalers are constantly receiving and shipping large volumes of products. Things wholesale businesses can do to facilitate shipping and receiving are:

1. Locate in a one-story warehouse.
2. Keep merchandise close to the shipping dock. This minimizes the distance it will have to be moved when it is brought into and taken out of the warehouse.
3. Store popular items in accessible locations.
4. Be sure there are areas that can accommodate merchandise of all sizes.
5. Keep walkways free of merchandise so that employees can exit the building quickly in an emergency.
6. Store items safely. For instance, do not stack too many boxes on top of one another, as they may fall if they become unsteady.

Layout of a Manufacturing Business

For manufacturing businesses, efficiency, not attractiveness, is what counts. Other important considerations include the following:

1. Work teams should be situated close together.
2. Supervisors should be able to observe the people they supervise easily. They should sit near each other.
3. Exits should be clearly marked and easily accessible so that employees can quickly leave the plant in the event of an emergency.
4. Any hazardous materials should be stored safely.
5. Equipment and machinery should be positioned in a way that reduces the chance of an accident.

NET WORTH

Point your browser to

http://www.ideas-in-action.swep.com

Complete the activity for Chapter 8.

 **CHECKPOINT** **What factors are important in laying out a retail business? A service business?**

THINK CRITICALLY

1. What is the difference between a gross lease and a net lease? How does a percentage lease work?

2. Why are layout considerations for a service business that serves customers at the place of business similar to those for a retail store?

MAKE CONNECTIONS

3. **COMMUNICATION** Make a video of the layout of a local business, or use graph paper and a tape measure to show the layout on paper. (Be sure to obtain the permission of the owner before you perform this activity.) Share your information with the class, and explain whether you think the layout could be improved.

4. **MATH** Melanie Hsu is searching for locations for a retail auto parts store. She has two location choices. The first is in a community shopping center and leases for $2,500 per month. Another stand-alone location on the outskirts of town leases for $1,250 per month. The business should attract 14,000 customers per month at the community shopping center and 6,500 customers per month at the stand-alone location. What is the cost per shopper at each location?

Purchase
Equipment, Supplies, *and* Inventory

Every business needs equipment and supplies. Many businesses also need inventory. Machinery, cash registers, and furniture are types of equipment. Supplies include things like paper, pens, and pencils. Inventory is the items a business sells to customers. Without these things, a business cannot function correctly. If there is no inventory, what will you sell? If there is no paper, how will you send a letter? Suppliers or vendors can provide your business with everything you need to function.

OBTAIN EQUIPMENT AND SUPPLIES

To determine what equipment and supplies you need to start your business, make a list of what you think you will need. All businesses need standard items such as furniture, lamps, and office supplies.

Businesses also need special items specific to the type of business. For example, lawn-care companies and landscaping firms would need lawn fertilizer. Your list should include both standard items needed by all businesses and items specific to your particular business.

Once you have listed all of the items you need, indicate how much of each item you require. Be sure to list the minimum quantity you need right now, not the amount you might need if your business succeeds. Being overly optimistic could leave you with many bills that will be difficult to pay if your sales fall short of your projections.

CHECKPOINT Why do businesses have both standard and special equipment and supply needs?

Identify Suppliers

To fill the standard and special needs of your business, you will need to research vendors. **Vendors** are companies that sell products and services to businesses. Vendors are also called suppliers. Valuable sources of vendor information include the following:

- Telephone directory advertising section
- Trade magazines (specialized magazines devoted to a particular industry), which carry vendor advertising

STANDARD EQUIPMENT AND SUPPLY NEEDS FOR MOST BUSINESSES	
Type	**Items**
Furniture	Desks, chairs, bookcases, filing cabinets, tables, computer stands
Fixtures	Lamps, overhead lights
Office Equipment	Computers, modems, fax machines, telephones, photocopiers
Office Supplies	Stationery, pens and pencils, scissors, tape, staples, paper clips, binder clips, manila folders, calendars
Maintenance Supplies	Toilet paper, paper towels, cleaning supplies
Kitchen Supplies	Coffee maker, small refrigerator, coffee, tea

- Trade associations
- The Internet
- Other companies in your industry
- SBA and SCORE

Shira Silberg wants to open an assisted-living center for senior citizens. To find suppliers of furniture, linens, and many other items, Shira looks through copies of trade magazines for advertisements from companies that target the nursing-home industry. Shira also contacts nursing-home trade associations and locates vendor web sites for additional information. Finally, she contacts other assisted-living centers to find out which vendors they use.

Evaluate Proposals

Most of the items you will need to start your business will be available from a variety of vendors. So who should you buy from? Before you make a purchase, contact several vendors and ask them to quote you a price for the merchandise you are interested in purchasing. A *quote* is an estimate for how much you will pay for a merchandise or service. Also ask them about the quality of their merchandise, their financing terms, and the quantity discounts they offer. Once you have all the information you need, compare the various proposals. Choose the vendor that provides the best combination of products at a cost that fits your business.

Shira selects her suppliers by asking for proposals from the vendors that appeal to her the most. She then compares prices, service, quality of merchandise, and discount options. Shira knows that the lowest price is not always the best option because paying a little more can pay off in higher quality. She decides on a higher priced linen service because that service provides the best options for her company.

In Class Activity

In small groups, brainstorm a list of equipment and supplies you would need to open one of the following businesses: hardware store, greeting card shop, pet store, tree cutting service.

 **CHECKPOINT** How do you choose vendors for your business?

Entrepreneurial Timeline

| 1700 | 1720 | 1740 | 1760 |

An Electric Career (In More Ways than One)

You might remember Benjamin Franklin for being one of America's founding fathers or for flying a kite in a thunderstorm. But he was also an entrepreneur. In 1729, at the age of 23, he moved to Philadelphia to start a printing business. The problem was, lots of other people in the city were doing the same thing. How was Franklin to succeed? He decided he needed to open up a print shop that did something better. He created the *Pennsylvania Gazette,* a newspaper filled with entertaining stories and letters. Circulation went through the roof. He also printed *Poor Richard's Almanac.* It wasn't a creation of his own, but a European idea he modeled to fit America. The *Almanac* had everything from stories and poetry to weather forecasts and recipes. There was something for everyone to enjoy, and everyone did. In fact, the only book that sold more copies was the Bible. Franklin was a master at finding better ways to sell things and making money from his ideas.

PURCHASE INVENTORY

Retailing, wholesaling, and manufacturing businesses must purchase inventory before they can open for business. **Inventory** is the quantity of goods and materials on hand. For retail and wholesale businesses, inventory is merchandise purchased with the intent of reselling it to customers. For manufacturing businesses, inventory consists of the parts that go into producing the business's product as well as finished goods.

Purchase Inventory for a Start-Up Business

Determining the amount of inventory to keep in stock is difficult for all business owners. It is particularly difficult for owners of new businesses, who do not know what their level of sales will be.

Chris Keating wants to open an art supplies store. He wants to have enough inventory that his shelves look full. He also wants to be able to offer his customers a full line of art supplies. Not knowing how high or low his sales will be at first, Chris doesn't want to purchase too much inventory. He doesn't want to

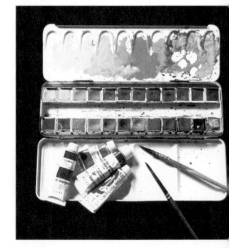

tie up his cash in inventory if he can't sell it quickly. Chris also is worried about finding room to store the inventory. Because of these concerns, Chris purchases just enough stock to fill his shelves.

Purchase Inventory for an Ongoing Business

Once your business is up and running, you will have a better idea of how much inventory you need. To make sure that you do not run out of stock unexpectedly, you can establish reorder points for each product you sell. The **reorder point** is a predetermined level of inventory when new stock must be purchased. How low you set the reorder point depends on how long it takes your supplier to get merchandise to you, how many units of the item you sell each month, and how important it is for you not to be out of stock.

Chris sells 150 erasers a month. Because he never wants to be out of stock, he sets his reorder point at 30. Every time his inventory of erasers falls at or below 30 units, he places an order to renew his stock.

 **CHECKPOINT** How do you determine the amount of inventory to keep in stock?

THINK CRITICALLY

1. Why is it important to obtain price quotes from several different vendors before purchasing business equipment and supplies?

2. Do you think that a retail store should always have its products physically available for customers to examine? Can you think of examples where customers do not purchase the actual products on display?

MAKE CONNECTIONS

3. COMMUNICATION You are a wholesale distributor of party supplies. A new store, Party Express, has asked you to submit a proposal for supplying its paper goods inventory. Write a letter to Party Express with your recommendations for the types and amounts of goods they should purchase. Include prices and information on financing terms.

4. COMMUNICATION Use the Internet, trade magazines, newspapers, and other sources to search for suppliers of house paint for professional painters. Write a short report on your findings.

Review

CHAPTER SUMMARY

Choose a *Retail* Business Location

1. Retail businesses can locate in downtown areas, in various kinds of shopping centers, or in stand-alone locations.
2. You will have to consider the advantages and disadvantages of each type of location to determine the best one for your business.
3. Selecting a trade area for your business is an essential part of choosing the right location.

Choose a Location for a *Non-Retail* Business

4. Location may or may not be important for a service business. If the service is performed away from the business location, where the business site is located is not important.
5. Industrial businesses need not locate in areas that are accessible to consumers. The choice of location for these kinds of businesses depends largely on price.
6. Some entrepreneurs work out of their homes. An advantage of working at home is that certain costs can be reduced or eliminated. A disadvantage is that interruptions during the day can make it hard to concentrate on work.

Obtain Space and *Design* the Physical Layout

7. To evaluate leases, you can compare the costs and expected benefits of various locations. Calculating the rent per customer can help you determine which location is most cost effective.
8. The layout of a business depends on the type of business. For retail businesses, the aim of a layout is to attract and keep customers. For wholesale businesses, the aim of a layout is to store inventory in the most efficient manner. For manufacturing businesses, the aim of a layout is to facilitate the production process.

Purchase Equipment, Supplies, *and* Inventory

9. Once you have determined your equipment and supply needs, you will need to evaluate a number of vendors.
10. The methods used to purchase inventory differ depending on whether the business is just beginning or has been established.

What Do You Know Now?

Read *Build a Business* again. Then answer the questions a second time. How have your responses changed?

VOCABULARY BUILDER

Choose the term that best fits the definition.
Write your answers on a separate sheet of paper.

1. Person who owns and rents out buildings or space
2. Areas that suffer from lack of employment opportunities
3. Companies that sell products and services to businesses
4. Person who pays rent to occupy space owned by someone else
5. The quantity of goods and materials on hand
6. Sections of land that can be used for industrial business locations
7. A predetermined level of inventory when new stock must be purchased

a. enterprise zones
b. industrial parks
c. inventory
d. landlord
e. reorder point
f. tenant
g. trade area
h. vendors

REVIEW YOUR KNOWLEDGE

8. What are all the types of areas for locating retail businesses?
9. How should you select a specific site to locate your retail business?
10. For which types of service businesses is location important?
11. What factors should owners of industrial businesses consider in choosing a location?
12. What are the advantages and disadvantages of operating a business from your home?
13. Why do most entrepreneurs lease space rather than buy?
14. How should you compare different leasing options for different locations?
15. What do you need to consider when designing the layout of your business?
16. Why does the layout of a business change depending on the type of business?
17. What standard equipment and supplies are needed by most start-up businesses?
18. How do you identify potential vendors?
19. How do you evaluate different vendors?
20. What is the purpose of a reorder point?

APPLY WHAT YOU LEARNED

21. You are planning to open a card and gift shop. Identify the trade area. What types of locations are available in your community? List the advantages and disadvantages of each. Are there competing gift shops in any of these locations? Are there other businesses that do not compete but attract the same kind of customer? Why do you think each of these businesses chose this particular location?

22. You are leasing space for your new restaurant and are negotiating the lease with the landlord. What are the advantages and disadvantages of each type of lease? What type of lease will you request? Why?

THINK CRITICALLY

23. Why does the location of a retail business play a role in its success? Can you think of successful retail businesses that are located in remote areas? Why do you think they are successful?

24. What tools are available to business owners to help their businesses succeed in less desirable locations? Do you think these tools are effective? Why or why not?

25. Why do service, wholesale, and manufacturing businesses face different considerations in choosing a location? What types of businesses should consider locating in an enterprise zone? Besides tax advantages, why do you think an enterprise zone is a good location?

26. How do the layout design considerations differ for retail, service, wholesale, and manufacturing businesses? Are there any common considerations? If so, what are they?

27. Why is it important to evaluate different vendor proposals? What information do you need from vendors? What do you think is a good way to evaluate the vendor's product and delivery reliability?

MAKE CONNECTIONS

28. RESEARCH Speak to the owners or managers of five local businesses. What do each of these business owners see as advantages and disadvantages of their locations? Are these businesses successful?

29. COMMUNICATION Design the layout of a clothing store. Create a scale drawing of the space and show the placement of all of the equipment. You may want to use pictures from catalogs or magazines to show the type of equipment you have selected. Present your plan to the class and explain why you think your layout will make your business successful.

30. RESEARCH Make a list of the major equipment you need to open a restaurant. Use library resources, the World Wide Web, and other research materials to locate three vendors of restaurant equipment and obtain pricing for the selected equipment. What are their financing terms? Do they offer quantity discounts? Which vendor will you select and why?

31. MATH You are choosing between a neighborhood shopping center and a stand-alone store for your shoe store. The monthly rent for the shopping center is $3,200; the rent for the stand-alone location is $2,500. The projected customer traffic at the shopping center is 6,500, and the traffic at the stand-alone location is 5,100. Which location will you choose and why?

This Is Your Business Project

1. Choose the location area that is best for your business. Why is it the best choice? Put your reasons on paper.

2. Using a local map, mark the trade area for your business. Mark the appropriate locations for your business and the locations of your competitors. Are there any businesses in the trade area that do not compete, but attract a similar type of customer? If so, mark those on the map. For each area, write an evaluation that outlines why this would or would not be a good place to locate your business.

3. Will you buy or lease space, or will you run your business from your home? Why? Write a short paper explaining why you've chosen this way to obtain the space for your business.

4. Design the physical layout of your business. Create a scale drawing of the space and show the placement of all of the furniture, fixtures, and equipment. Indicate the planned use of each area shown. How does this layout meet your goals?

5. Make a list of the equipment and supplies you will need to start your business. Using the telephone book, trade magazines, and the Internet, locate five vendors. Contact each vendor to obtain information about their products, pricing, financial terms, and product availability. How do they compare? Which vendor will you select? Why?

Chapter 9

MARKET
YOUR
BUSINESS

LESSONS

9.1 The Marketing Mix— Product, Distribution, Price

9.2 The Marketing Mix— Promotion

9.3 Set Marketing Goals

BUILD A BUSINESS

Mixing Up the School Store

About two months had passed since Tiffany and Mike first began the school store. They opened for an hour each day after school. They were disappointed when no more than five customers came in each day.

"You know, Mike," Tiffany said, "I think we need to take a look at our product mix. We chose a few items for the store that we thought our friends would buy. But it doesn't look like we made the right choice for our products."

"Yeah, it seems that most of our customers are freshmen looking for paper and pencils. And most people come here looking for candy."

"We can't sell candy. It is against the lunch program regulations," Tiffany reminded him.

"Yeah, but we can sell mints. What kind of mints do you think we should sell?" Mike asked.

"We could create a survey about mints and have people in the school complete it during lunch," suggested Tiffany.

"We might also try adding a line of school spirit wear. We could target incoming freshmen. If we promote our Friday Spirit Days, they will want to be sure they have the right clothes to wear," Mike said.

"Where do you think we should get the spirit wear and the mints?" Tiffany asked.

"We'll be able to sell them at a better price if we can go directly to the manufacturer and purchase them," Mike said. "The mints would be easy, but the spirit wear would be harder to get because everything would have to be customized."

"Ms. Ward has a former student who has a custom apparel business," Tiffany said.

"Great idea! We'll have to ask her for that person's phone number. Once we get our new products, we'll have to decide how much markup to have. We want to make a profit, but let's make sure we keep the prices competitive."

"Hey, maybe we should start opening before school and even during lunch. Most students want a mint after lunch," Tiffany suggested.

"We're coming up with some great ideas! How do you think we can get the word out?"

"Well, Mike, we can purchase an advertisement in the school newspaper and we could get some publicity by writing a press release for the PTSA Newsletter. We could also get the media production department to do a feature about our store on the next edition of the school television program. And most of this stuff won't cost us a thing!"

"Tiffany, let's get started. We need to set some goals for our store and put all this in writing!"

What Do You Know?

1. Why can Tiffany and Mike offer a better price on their products if they purchase directly from the manufacturer?
2. Why is the school newspaper a better advertising medium than a community newspaper for the school store?
3. Why do you think it is important for Tiffany and Mike to set goals for the store?

The *Marketing* Mix— Product, *Distribution*, Price

Marketing your product or service is important to your business. Without marketing, your product won't succeed. Marketing makes people aware of your product or service. If they don't know about it, they won't buy it. To market your business well, you will need a marketing mix. A **marketing mix** is the blending of the four marketing elements of product, distribution, price, and promotion used to reach a target market.

PRODUCT

Once you have determined what kind of business you will run, you will need to make decisions about the products that you will sell. To select your products, think carefully about which products and services most appeal to your target customers. The different products and services a business sells is a **product mix.**

Luisa Ramirez, a 32-year-old entrepreneur, wants to open a gourmet food shop in her community. Luisa's Gourmet Luxuries will sell hundreds of different packaged goods, from Italian olive oil to Mexican rice to imported Italian pastas. She will also offer a wide selection of fresh foods, including cheeses, fruits, vegetables, and baked goods. To determine her product mix, Luisa lists the various departments she plans to establish in her store. She then lists the products that each department will carry.

SELECTING PRODUCT FEATURES In addition to identifying your product mix, you will have to select product features. Features include color, size, and quality. They also include hours, warranties, delivery, and installation. You will need to consider your target market when selecting product features.

Every product has features. For instance, Luisa has many choices to consider when she is deciding what types of olives to inventory in her store. There are green and black olives. There are olives stuffed with pimentos or garlic cloves. There are olives that come in jars, olives that come in cans, and gourmet olives that are available fresh. There are olives that are produced in the United States, in Italy, and in France. In fact, there are so many different types of olives there is no way Luisa can offer every single type to her customers. She needs to decide how many types of olives she can carry and then decide what kinds her target customer is most likely to buy.

Some automobiles are positioned as family cars.

Position Your Products or Services

Different products and services within the same category serve different customer needs. For example, both Hyundai and Jaguar sell automobiles. But these two products are positioned very differently in the marketplace. **Positioning** is placing a product in a certain market to get a desired customer response. Jaguar's pricey cars are positioned for the person wanting high quality and status. Hyundai positions its product to satisfy a need for an inexpensive family motor vehicle. Examining the competition's product mix will help you determine the best market for you to target.

Luisa knows that the other gourmet store in town is perceived as snobby. Because of this, Luisa decides to position her store as the friendly gourmet store. To do so, she plans to offer in-store cooking classes and free samples of food items. She knows that always being cheerful and helpful to customers will help her desired image. She also plans to hire experienced and courteous employees, which will support the image she wants.

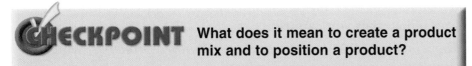

CHECKPOINT What does it mean to create a product mix and to position a product?

DISTRIBUTION

Luisa knows she must consider distribution in the marketing of her business. You will need to consider how you get the goods to sell, as well as how you actually get them into the customers' hands. To make sure you have goods to sell, you will need channels of distribution. **Channels of distribution** are the routes that products and services take from the time they are produced to the time they are consumed. You will need these channels for both the products and services you sell and the products and services you buy.

Channels of Distribution for Retail Goods

Retail businesses have many ways of selling products. As the owner of a retail business, you can distribute products in various ways.

- Stay open hours that are convenient for consumers, such as evenings and weekends.
- Use catalogs, fliers, and other advertisements to reach customers who live outside the area.
- Take orders by phone or fax and ship them directly to customers.

You can distribute your product or service on the Internet.

DISTRIBUTION ON THE INTERNET You could create a web site on the World Wide Web. People with access to the Internet can pull up your web site on their computers to learn about your products and services. They can also order from you directly over the Internet. More information on using the Internet can be found in Chapter 13.

Luisa's business is a neighborhood store, so she does not think she would get much benefit from catalogs, faxes, or customer ordering numbers. She does decide to stay open until eight o'clock on weeknights and have hours from ten until four on Saturdays and noon to four on Sundays. She also creates a web site that contains product descriptions and order forms.

Receiving Goods to Sell

All business types must receive goods from suppliers. Retailing businesses need to obtain goods to sell. All businesses, whether they sell goods to customers or not, need paper, computers, raw materials, and more to be able to function. A service business that grooms pets needs to buy cat and dog shampoos and flea combs. A business that manufactures blankets must purchase yarn or cotton to produce its product.

You can use various sources to locate distributors, wholesalers, and manufacturers. Your public library should have the following research materials you can use:

- *The American Wholesalers and Distributors Directory,* which lists suppliers in a wide range of industries
- *The Thomas Register,* which lists all manufacturing companies
- AT&T's *Business Buyer's Guide,* a national directory of toll-free numbers
- Magazines on your industry that may include articles about or advertisements by suppliers

Luisa will need to create relationships with wholesale distributors. She will need to find companies she can trust to deliver high-quality products quickly. Luisa will purchase some of her products directly from the companies that produce them, and others will be purchased through distributors. Her pastries come from a local baker. Distributors will supply her with imported and domestic canned goods, as well as meat, fruits, and vegetables.

NET WORTH

Point your browser to

http://www.ideas-in-action.swep.com

Complete the activity for Chapter 9.

Channels of Distribution for Service Businesses

Most entrepreneurs who own service businesses sell their services directly to customers. These service businesses have a single, direct channel of distribution because the production and consumption of a service happens at the same time. For example, electricians, restaurant owners, and tax preparation services deal directly with the people who purchase their services.

Some service businesses, such as film developers, use retail stores to distribute their services. In planning your distribution, keep customer convenience in mind.

Channels of Distribution for Manufacturing Businesses

Manufacturers usually don't sell directly to customers. Instead, they make their products and then sell the products to other businesses, such as retailers. The retail store then sells to the final consumer.

Some manufacturers distribute their products very broadly and use all possible channels of distribution. Other manufacturers distribute their products through selected outlets only. For example, high-priced cosmetics usually are sold in exclusive department stores. Inexpensive cosmetics are sold in discount and drugstores.

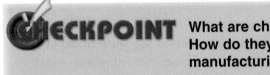

CHECKPOINT What are channels of distribution? How do they benefit retail and manufacturing businesses?

PRICE

Prices you charge must be low enough so that customers will buy from you and not from your competitors. To earn a profit, though, your prices need to be high enough so that revenues exceed expenses.

Set Price Objectives

Before you can select a pricing strategy, you will need to establish objectives for your pricing program. What is the most important thing you want the price to do? Examples of pricing objectives include:

- Maximize sales
- Discourage competition
- Increase profits
- Attract customers

Luisa thinks carefully about her pricing objectives. She determines that her first objective is to attract customers, so she sets low prices on her products as a way of building traffic in her store. Once she has lots of customers, she may slightly raise prices to increase her profits.

Determine Prices

There are three methods for determining price. One, two, or all three can be used. To determine which strategy is best for any one product or service you offer, you should remember your target customers. Why will they buy the item? How much will they pay?

COST-BASED PRICING **Cost-based pricing** is a price determined by using the wholesale cost of an item as the basis for the price charged. A **markup price** is a price determined by adding an amount to the wholesale cost of an item. A **markdown price** is a price determined by subtracting an amount from the retail price of an item. Usually, a set percentage is used to determine a markup or a markdown price.

Luisa buys artichoke hearts for $1.77 a can. To cover her expenses, she adds 40 percent to her wholesale cost, or $0.71. The new price $2.48 is her retail price.

wholesale cost × percentage markup = markup amount
$1.77 × 0.40 = $0.71

wholesale cost + markup = retail price
$1.77 + $0.71 = $2.48

Sometimes business owners purchase too much of a particular item and want to sell more of it quickly. To do so, they mark down the retail price of the product. You should be careful not to mark down an item too much. You should not lose money when you sell a product or service.

Luisa usually charges $10.50 for a large bottle of olive oil. To sell more of this item, she decides to mark down its retail price by 20 percent.

retail price × percentage markdown = markdown amount
$10.50 × 0.20 = $2.10

retail price − markdown amount = markdown price
$10.50 − $2.10 = $8.40

DEMAND-BASED PRICING Pricing that is determined by how much customers are willing to pay for a product or service is called **demand-based pricing.** If the bakery at Luisa's Gourmet Luxuries becomes widely recognized as the best in town, Luisa can probably charge high prices for her baked goods. People will be willing to pay the higher price for a loaf of bread because it is the best.

COMPETITION-BASED PRICING Pricing that is determined by considering what competitors charge for the same good is called **competition-based pricing.** Once you find out what your competition charges for an item, you must decide whether to charge the same price, slightly more, or slightly less.

Luisa's business will compete with The Gourmet Grocery, a gourmet shop that has been in her community for five years. She cannot expect to charge more than her competitor for items that customers could just as easily purchase there. So she decides initially to charge a few cents less than The Gourmet Grocery on all packaged goods. She keeps an eye on the competition to make sure she is always up to date on what they are doing.

 **CHECKPOINT** Name and explain the three methods of determining prices.

THINK CRITICALLY

1. In the market for blue jeans, which brands are positioned to satisfy customers' need for high quality and status? Which brands are positioned to satisfy a need for inexpensive clothing? Describe the consumers of each of the brands you name.

2. Which method of pricing do you think is most effective? Why?

MAKE CONNECTIONS

3. MATH A shoe store owner pays a manufacturer $54 a pair for a popular brand of athletic shoes. The store offers the shoe to customers for $129 a pair. What is the markup percentage?

4. COMMUNICATION Write a paragraph explaining all the possible channels of distribution for a tee-shirt manufacturer.

GOALS

USE advertising
to promote your
business.

STUDY publicity as
a promotional tool.

EVALUATE other
kinds of promotion.

The Marketing Mix— Promotion

No matter how much you work on product, distribution, and price, you will not succeed as an entrepreneur if customers do not know about your business. You will have to promote your business by making customers aware of the benefits of buying from you.

Promotion takes many forms, including advertising, publicity, sales promotion, and personal selling. Your strategy for promoting your business will use at least some, if not all, of these techniques.

ADVERTISING

Service industries, manufacturers, and retailers all advertise. **Advertising** is a paid form of communication sent out by a business about a product or service. Established businesses such as Kellogg and Coca-Cola spend millions of dollars each year on advertising.

Advertising can be very important for small businesses, particularly new ones. Advertising helps you communicate with potential customers. It lets them know what kinds of products and services your company offers and why they should buy from you.

Large companies generally use advertising agencies to create their advertisements. Highly creative and effective ads are usually the result. Using an advertising agency can cost a lot of money. As an owner of a small business, you probably will handle your own advertising.

Advertising should help a business convey a positive image. **Public relations** is the act of establishing a favorable relationship with customers and the general public. Advertising and promotion are public relations activities because they make potential customers feel good about your company. Keep in mind that public relations is more than just promotion. Anything that makes people feel good about your business is public relations. Getting involved in your community, making donations to charities, and being personable with your customers are also public relations activities.

CHOOSE YOUR MESSAGE Your advertising should clearly communicate the message and image you want. If, for example, your marketing strategy is to have low prices, advertisements highlighting those prices might be appropriate. If your aim is to target customers willing to pay higher prices for excellent service, advertising that describes your well-trained staff would fit your image.

Once you choose a message, you will need to decide which advertising medium to use. To choose a medium, you will have to consider both cost and effectiveness in reaching your target audience.

Television Advertising

Television advertising reaches millions of people every day. It is the best way to reach a large number of people quickly. Television advertising usually comes in the form of commercials or paid advertisements. *Commercials* are usually less than a minute in length and are run during breaks in television programming. They are very short promotions about a product or business. *Paid advertisements* can last a half hour or more and go into depth about the product being offered. Television advertising allows businesses to communicate through both sight and sound with potential customers. It can be creative and informative.

DISADVANTAGES OF TELEVISION ADVERTISING Advertising on television is very expensive. Producing even a low-budget commercial can cost thousands of dollars. And paying a network or cable station to broadcast the commercial can cost much more.

Television reaches too broad an audience to be effective for most businesses. If, for example, only 1 percent of the viewing audience is interested in a particular product, advertising on television is not likely to be cost effective.

Because of the excessive costs and the fact that she may not reach her target customer very effectively, Luisa decides that television advertising is not right for her business.

Radio Advertising

Radio advertising can be effective for small businesses. It is less expensive than television advertising. You also can be more certain you are reaching your target market. Radio stations tend to attract a particular kind of listener. Pop rock stations target teenagers and people in their twenties. Classical or talk radio stations usually attract older listeners. Selecting a station whose listeners share the same demographics as your target market can benefit your advertising. You can contact stations and ask for a demographic profile of their listeners to make sure it fits your target market profile.

DISADVANTAGES OF RADIO ADVERTISING Radio is a purely audio message and can't visually show your product. Radio listeners may not remember what they hear. They may not even listen to the ads.

Luisa Ramirez is targeting middle-aged, upscale customers. To reach this audience, she decides to advertise on the classical music station in her community. She receives a demographic profile of the radio station's listeners and determines that her business targets a similar type of person.

Newspapers are only one type of advertising medium.

Newspaper Advertising

Newspapers are the single largest form of advertising in the United States. Newspaper advertising is good for small businesses because:

- It is relatively inexpensive.
- It targets a limited geographic area.
- It reaches large numbers of people.

Luisa decides to advertise in several local newspapers. She places quarter-page ads in the morning paper serving the city-wide area. She also puts half-page ads in all of the free newspapers that serve her community. These papers reach a much smaller audience than the large city newspaper, but they target the audience Luisa is trying to reach. Advertising in newspapers represents a cost-effective way for Luisa to reach her target market.

DISADVANTAGES OF NEWSPAPER ADVERTISING Newspapers reach a large audience, but much of that audience may not be interested in your business. If, for example, you own a small gift shop that caters to people only in your surrounding area, advertising in your city newspaper may not make sense because you will be paying to reach thousands of people who will never become your customers.

Another disadvantage to newspaper advertising is the fact that your advertisement will compete with many others. Newspapers carry so many advertisements that yours may be overlooked by readers.

CHECKPOINT What are the advantages of television, radio, and newspaper advertising?

Telephone Directory Advertising

Telephone directories list the phone numbers of people and businesses in a certain area. Directory ads usually appear on a page close to the listing and phone number of the business placing the ad. Directory ads can look a lot like newspaper ads. Customers look in telephone directories again and again, making them a good advertising medium.

A disadvantage of directory advertising is that people only look in the directory when they are already in search of a particular type of business. It is simply a way to convince customers to try you instead of a competitor. But, knowing how important the phone book can be, Luisa decides to take out a quarter-page ad in the commercial directory distributed in her area.

Direct-Mail Advertising

Direct-mail advertising includes fliers, catalogs, letters, and other correspondence sent to target customers through the mail. The main advantage of direct-mail advertising is that mailing lists for target markets are available for purchase. If your business sells hospital beds, you can purchase targeted mailing lists of people who would purchase your product. You can also get lists for people based on the geographic areas you want to mail to. Companies that specialize in maintaining targeted mail lists can provide almost any kind of list for any kind of business.

Direct-mail advertising can be effective if people read it. But many throw out direct-mail advertising, which they say is "junk mail." To reach as many target customers as possible through direct-mail advertising, you will have to come up with an attention-grabbing design or other means of making people open and read your advertisement.

Luisa Ramirez decides to use direct mail to target residents living in four zip code areas near her store. She creates an attractive brochure with a catchy slogan on the outside cover, and she mails it to residents in the neighborhoods she is targeting.

Magazine Advertising

Magazines are an excellent way to aim products and services at specific markets. Running magazines are full of advertisements for shoes and other products purchased by runners. Magazines targeting teenage girls are full of advertisements for products that appeal to them.

Most magazines are nationally distributed. This can make them inappropriate for businesses that sell in a limited geographic area. Some large cities have local magazines, which would be an effective way to target a certain area.

The city in which Luisa will be opening her gourmet store has two local magazines. One focuses heavily on restaurants and entertaining. Luisa checks the demographics of the magazine's readership and finds that it targets the same market she is trying to reach. She decides to advertise in the magazine every other month.

Outdoor Advertising

Outdoor advertising includes billboards and signs. Such advertising can be effective in keeping the name of your business in a place where many people can see it. But because people view such advertising quickly as they drive by, it cannot include much information.

Luisa's advertising needs to provide too much information for outdoor advertising to be useful. Luisa is also concerned that outdoor advertising could not be used in a way consistent with the type of image she wants to create for her business. She therefore rules out this advertising medium.

Transit Advertising

Transit advertising is signs on public transportation. Transit advertising can be used to give more information about a business than can a billboard. Such advertising can be effective if the market you are trying to reach includes many people who use public transportation.

Luisa's target market lives in the suburbs and rarely uses public transportation. For this reason, she rules out transit advertising, which would not help her reach her target market.

 **CHECKPOINT** What is an advantage of telephone directory advertising? Of magazine advertising?

PUBLICITY

Publicity is free promotion generated by media coverage. Good publicity can be as helpful as advertising. Publicity is free, but staging an event or bringing in a celebrity to generate publicity usually isn't.

You should also know that publicity can be negative if the media coverage is unfavorable. For example, some community newspapers publish listings of restaurants that have violated health code laws. Customers may see this publicity and stop eating at those restaurants.

Luisa plans to have an open house to mark her first day in business. She hopes that the media will do a story on her grand opening. To increase this chance, Luisa hires a popular local jazz band to perform. She also invites her community's leaders and personalities. She writes and sends a press release to all of the local newspapers, magazines, and radio and television stations as well. A **press release** is a written statement meant to inform the media of an event or product.

To keep her name in the news, Luisa volunteers to write a weekly cooking column for one of the free newspapers in her community. She likes the opportunity to educate the public about gourmet cooking and to increase her store's visibility as a seller of gourmet foods.

 **CHECKPOINT** What are some ways you can generate publicity for your business? Why would you write a press release?

YOU CAN SAY THAT AGAIN!

" If you give the same effort to buying products or materials that you give to sales, the result will be increased gross profit. "

—*Beverly Miller, owner of Miller/Bevco, a wholesale distributor of packaging and labeling equipment*

GALA OPENING OF LUISA'S GOURMET LUXURIES

Come celebrate the opening of Luisa's Gourmet Luxuries on Friday, September 20, at 8:00 P.M. Hors d'oeuvres, imported champagne, and French pastries will be served at the event. Music will be provided by Glendale's leading jazz ensemble, Jazz Expressions.

The opening of Luisa's Gourmet Luxuries marks the realization of a dream by owner Luisa Ramirez. "As a specialty cook," she says, "I could not always find the products I needed. And I was never happy with the selection of produce and baked goods in town." Luisa decided to open a store that would offer the kinds of products she could not find elsewhere in town.

Luisa's Gourmet Luxuries offers an astounding selection of products, including 14 different kinds of olive oil, 12 different kinds of rice, and pasta products from several different countries. "Everyone's tastes are different," says Luisa, "so I offer a large selection."

For more information contact:

Luisa Ramirez, Proprietor

Luisa's Gourmet Luxuries

1610 Marbury Road, Glendale, CT

(275) 555-3983

OTHER TYPES OF PROMOTION

Advertising and publicity are not the only ways you can promote your business. You can also offer sales promotions, or use personal selling to promote your business.

Sales Promotions

Sales promotion is the act of offering an incentive to customers in order to increase sales. Examples of sales promotion include:

- contests
- free samples
- coupons
- rebates
- frequent purchaser programs
- gifts
- special events

Some companies offer rebates. A **rebate** is a refund offered to people who purchase a product. Customers who purchase a $12 bottle of olive oil may be entitled to a $2 rebate from the supplier. To make sure that customers are aware of products on which rebates are offered, Luisa posts a flier that includes a list of rebates.

As part of her sales promotions, Luisa also plans to give away a $25 gift certificate each month. She also offers free samples and distributes coupons good for discounts on selected merchandise.

Personal Selling

Personal selling is critical. When you have personal contact with your customers, it says that you care about the business they give you. Being courteous and helping customers helps people look at your business positively. Employees should also be friendly and knowledgeable. Many entrepreneurs already have good personal-selling skills. Some need to read books and take courses to improve their skills.

Luisa wants to be accessible to customers, and make them feel special about shopping in her store. Luisa also trains her associates to make sure that they are knowledgeable about the products they sell and that they know how to encourage customers to try new products.

What Went Wrong

Advertising/Promotion

Toothless in Seattle

Business: PerioDent, Seattle, Washington * In business, 6 months

Dr. George Nilsson, a periodontist, had built up his practice by using dentist referrals, word of mouth, and speaking at conferences. As a way to expand his business, he decided to develop a program for dentists that graphically tracked gum disease. It would take the guesswork out of whether a patient should go to a specialist or not. Dr. Nilsson designed a step-by-step program, including a video and printed guide. He started the PerioDent company, investing $150,000 in developing the program elements, another $40,000 for initial inventory, and $80,000 more for advertising and public relations.

PerioDent sent out mailings to dentists, periodontists, and schools. It took out full-page ads in professional journals. Unfortunately, after six months, sales were declining. There was a backlash of bad press from his peers. The majority of dentists saw the PerioDent program as questioning, even insulting, the way they had been diagnosing gum disease. Additionally, dentists accused it of reducing their income by pushing patients to periodontists. At the same time, periodontists accused George of blatant self-promotion and greed.

Think Critically

1. What were the major mistakes in the product's design?
2. What could have been done differently to advertise and promote the program?

Telemarketing

Telemarketing is using the phone to market your product or service. It can be a cheap, effective way to let people know about your business, or about special offers. Keep in mind that some consumers consider telemarketing to be annoying and would rather not be contacted while they are relaxing at home.

CHECKPOINT Give three examples of sales promotion. Why is personal selling important to business?

THINK CRITICALLY

1. Why is advertising important for a new business?

2. Describe some public relations activities businesses in your area have performed.

3. How would you decide which of the ways to advertise is the best and most cost-effective choice for your business?

4. Describe a time when you saw good publicity on the news. When have you also seen bad publicity?

MAKE CONNECTIONS

5. COMMUNICATION Interview an advertising sales representative from a local magazine, newspaper, direct-mail marketer, or radio or television station. Write a one-page report about the different advertising programs offered and their pricing structures.

6. PROBLEM SOLVING You are opening a new video store in town. Use the six-step problem-solving method to determine how to advertise your shop's grand opening.

GOALS

SET short-, medium-, and long-term goals for your business.

WRITE your marketing plan.

Set *Marketing* Goals

Once you have your marketing mix, you will need to set goals to help shape your marketing plan. These goals should reflect your short-term, medium-term, and long-term plans for your business. After you've worked out all the elements in your marketing plan, you should put it in writing.

ESTABLISH YOUR GOALS

What do you want your marketing efforts to achieve for your business? Do you want to offer additional products or services after one year? Perhaps you want to find a larger building, or add on to your current one, five years from now. Establishing short-, medium-, and long-term marketing goals ensures that the marketing you do today fits in with the vision you have for your business tomorrow.

Short-Term Goals

Short-term goals are what you want your business to achieve in the next year. They can be stated in terms of number of customers, level of sales, level of profits, or other measures of success.

Identifying your short-term goals will help you determine how to target your marketing. If your goal is to build a customer base, you

SHORT-TERM MARKETING STRATEGY FOR LUISA'S GOURMET LUXURIES

Element of Marketing Mix	Strategy
Product	• Offer wide selection of gourmet foods, including outstanding selection of fresh foods
Distribution	• Establish reliable network of distributors so that products are always in stock
Price	• Keep prices on packaged goods lower than main competitor
	• Keep prices on fresh products approximately 2 percent above competitor
Promotion	• Distribute 2,500 fliers describing the store and inviting customers to drop by for free bagel and pint of fresh-squeezed orange juice
	• Sponsor high-profile non-profit events, such as 5K races
	• Distribute discount coupons
	• Send press releases to local media, letting them know about the store's mission
	• Display merchandise attractively in the store

may decide to keep prices low and spend money on promotion. If your goal is to have a positive cash flow, you may decide to price your products or services higher.

In the short-term, Luisa Ramirez wants to generate traffic in her store. Because of that goal, her marketing strategy focuses on establishing a customer base. She creates a list of short-term goals using product, distribution, price, and promotion.

Medium-Term Goals

Medium-term goals describe what you want your business to achieve in the next two to five years. Although your marketing strategy will be determined largely by your short-term goals, you will need to make sure that the strategy you are planning will make it possible for your medium-term goals to be achieved.

Luisa's primary medium-term goal is to become the most successful gourmet shop in her community by having a market share of at least 55 percent. **Market share** is the percentage of a market owned by a business. The total market for a product must be known in order for a market share to be determined. For example, if people in Luisa's community normally spend $1,750,000 a year on gourmet food products and Luisa's store sells products amounting to sales of $192,500, her market share will be 11 percent.

$$\text{Amount of sales} \div \text{Total market size} = \text{Market share}$$
$$\$192,500 \div \$1,750,000 = 11\%$$

Your market share will depend on the level of competition in your market. If you create a market for an entirely new product, your market share will be 100 percent, since you will be the only supplier, at least for a period of time. If you enter a market with many competitors or one in which a few large companies dominate the market, your market share will be small at first.

If Luisa wants a market share of 50 percent, she will need to generate annual sales of at least $875,000. Companies increase market share in many ways. One way is to lower prices. Advertising and promotion can help, too. You can also network with potential customers. **Networking** is establishing informal ties with people who can help your business grow. Attending trade association meetings and other gatherings can give you good opportunities to network. As part of her networking efforts, Luisa plays softball in a local women's league in the summer.

In Class Activity

In small groups, brainstorm a list of short-, medium-, and long-term goals for one of the following new businesses: Mexican restaurant, office supply wholesaler, health-food store, advertising agency.

Entrepreneurial Timeline

| 1940 | 1960 | 1980 | 2000 |

A Business with Automatic Gains

When automatic transmissions first became popular in the late 1950s, there was a need for mechanics who knew how to work on them. In 1959, Anthony A. Martino met this need. He was 26 years old when he opened the first shop that specialized in the new transmissions in Philadelphia. He named his company AAMCO Transmissions, which was short for the Anthony A. Martino Company.

Anthony's store was a huge success, as all the newer cars were outfitted with automatic transmissions. With his initial profits, he spent a lot of money on advertising and quickly opened five more locations. He soon started franchising AAMCO, which means he sold the rights for people to use his company name to offer his service in certain areas of the country. By 1967, over 550 AAMCO stores were in business, generating over $100 million in sales.

A wealthy man at 33, Anthony retired from the transmission business only to fill another market need with a business called MAACO, which supplied good quality, reasonably priced car painting and body work.

She also attends Chamber of Commerce meetings monthly. She hopes that through both settings she will meet people who will become customers. She also hopes to meet lawyers, accountants, and other business owners who might help her run her business more efficiently.

Long-Term Goals

Long-term goals show where your business will be five, ten, even twenty years from now. Thinking about what you want to do in the long term can help you think about how to market the business today.

Luisa eventually would like to establish a mail-order division of her business. Luisa does not let her long-term plans for a mail-order division change her thinking about how to market her store today. Knowing what she wants in the long run, however, motivates her to work very hard to make her store a success so that she can use it as a starting place from which to develop a second business.

 **CHECKPOINT** What is the difference between a short-term and a medium-term goal? Why is it important to establish long-term goals for your business?

Once you have determined all your strategies and goals, you should write your final marketing plan. It will help you if you need financing for your business. A written plan will also help you determine whether your marketing plan is solid and all parts are consistent. Writing your plan is helpful because you can always review it

later to determine if it needs any revisions, or if you need to change the way you are marketing your business.

Your written marketing plan should identify your overall market strategy as well as your specific strategies for price, product, distribution, and promotion.

 **CHECKPOINT** **Why is it important to put your marketing plan in writing?**

THINK CRITICALLY

1. What is the relationship between short-term goals and medium-term goals?

2. Marjorie Lupica has opened a pet-grooming business. What kinds of networking could Marjorie become involved in to help her establish a presence in the community, and later, to help her business grow?

3. List some long-term goals that Marjorie might set for her pet-grooming business.

MAKE CONNECTIONS

4. MATH Marjorie estimates the annual size of the pet-grooming market to be about $325,000 in her community. There are two pet-grooming businesses in town already. If Marjorie achieves her five-year goal of capturing 45 percent of the market, how much will she earn in her fifth year?

5. COMMUNICATION Prepare an outline of a marketing plan for Marjorie's pet-grooming business.

CHAPTER SUMMARY

The *Marketing* Mix—
Product,
***Distribution*, Price**

1. When marketing your business, you will need to make decisions about product, distribution, price, and promotion.
2. You will need to decide what kinds of products you will sell. Your product mix is the different products and services you offer.
3. You will need to determine how you will distribute products and services to your customers. The routes that products take from production to consumption are channels of distribution.
4. There are several ways to price your products or services. To earn a profit, you need to be sure that your prices are high enough that revenues exceed expenses.

***The* Marketing Mix—**
Promotion

5. Advertising is a paid form of promotion. Your advertising message should convey the image and information you want.
6. Advertising media include television, radio, newspaper, telephone directories, outdoor advertising, and more.
7. Publicity is free promotion. It can have positive or negative effects for your business.
8. Sales promotion and personal selling can give your customers incentives to buy your product or service.

Set *Marketing*
Goals

9. You will need to set short-, medium- and long-term goals for your business. Short-term goals can be listed and determined for the next year or so. Medium-term goals should be determined for the next two to five years. Set long-term goals to decide where you want your business to be in five, ten, or twenty years.
10. You should put your marketing plan in writing. A written plan may help you get bank financing, and you will be able to easily review your plan.

What Do You Know Now?

Read *Build a Business* again. Then answer the questions a second time. How have your responses changed?

VOCABULARY BUILDER

Choose the term that best fits the definition.
Write your answers on a separate sheet of paper.

1. Price determined by adding an amount to the wholesale cost of an item
2. Refund offered to people who purchase a product
3. Free promotion generated by media coverage
4. Pricing that is determined by considering what competitors charge for the same good
5. Act of offering an incentive to customers in order to increase sales
6. Placing a product in a certain market to get a desired customer response.
7. Blending of the four marketing strategies about product, distribution, price, and promotion used to reach a target market
8. Percentage of a market owned by a business
9. Routes that products and services take from the time they are produced to the time they are consumed
10. Different products and services a business sells
11. Paid form of communication sent out by a business about a product or service
12. Written statement meant to inform the media of an event or product

a. advertising
b. channels of distribution
c. competition-based pricing
d. cost-based pricing
e. demand-based pricing
f. markdown price
g. market share
h. marketing mix
i. markup price
j. networking
k. positioning
l. press release
m. product mix
n. publicity
o. public relations
p. rebate
q. sales promotion
r. telemarketing

REVIEW YOUR KNOWLEDGE

13. What are the four areas you should consider when developing your marketing plan?
14. How do you identify your product mix?
15. What is the importance of the channels of distribution?
16. Name three methods of setting prices.

17. Why should established businesses advertise? Why do new businesses need to advertise?

18. How do you choose an advertising medium?

19. What are the advantages and disadvantages of publicity?

20. What are some ways you can generate publicity?

21. What is the purpose of sales promotions?

22. Why are personal-selling skills important?

23. What is the importance of identifying short-term goals?

24. What are some of the ways to increase market share?

25. Why do you need to set long-term goals for your business?

26. Why do you need to write a marketing plan?

APPLY WHAT YOU LEARNED

27. You are a home-improvement contractor. What role will channels of distribution play in your business? Detail the pricing method you will use. Which form of promotion will work best for you? Why?

28. You are planning to open a dry cleaning and laundry establishment. What are the products and services you will offer? What are the features of your product? What positioning statement will you use to differentiate your business from your competitors?

29. In what ways will you advertise your dry cleaning business? You have decided to run a sales promotion for your new business. What type of incentives will you use to attract customers? What other kinds of public relations might help promote your business?

30. Write out the short-, medium-, and long-term goals of your dry cleaning business.

THINK CRITICALLY

31. How does the product mix for a retail business differ from that of a service business? What product features can a service have?

32. What do you think are the best forms of promotion for retail businesses? Service businesses? Do you think manufacturing businesses need promotion? Why or why not?

33. Is increasing market share a goal that all businesses strive for? Why or why not?

MAKE CONNECTIONS

34. **MATH** You own a photography shop. The wholesale price for a digital camera is $225.00. You have decided to use cost-based pricing and will mark up the price by 35 percent. How much will you charge your customer for the digital camera? There is another photography store in your town that carries the same camera for less money. Should you lower your price? Why or why not?

35. COMMUNICATION You are opening a health club and spa. Because you have limited financial resources, you need to use your promotion budget carefully. Write a press release that you would send to the local newspapers and radio and television stations. You are also buying time on a local radio station. Write the commercial that will air on the radio. Write down some public relations activities that could promote your business.

36. COMMUNICATION Write a creative television commercial for one of the following businesses: car repair shop, travel agent, gift shop, restaurant, or furniture store. Use a video camera to tape your commercial. If necessary, ask classmates to play parts in your commercial. Use visual aids in your commercial, such as appropriate clothing and props. Show your commercial to the class.

37. RESEARCH You are opening a home entertainment store. Locate distributors, wholesalers, and manufacturers for one of your products. Choose three brands of one item and contact the distributor to obtain information about pricing and delivery. What is the wholesale price of each product? Find the same product in a local store. What is the retail price? What is the markup percentage?

38. MATH The annual sales of home entertainment equipment in your area is $23 million. You want to capture 15 percent of the market. How much will you have to sell to achieve your goal?

This Is Your Business Project

1. Determine the product mix for your business and the features of each product. How do you plan on positioning your products? Research possible suppliers, wholesalers, and retailers.

2. Locate three businesses that compete with your business and evaluate their pricing. Choose five products (or services) offered and compare the prices charged with what you want to charge. Are the prices very different? If so, why do you think there is such a difference? How much will you charge for each product or service? What pricing strategy are you using?

3. Get advertising rates for a local radio station, television station, and newspaper. Choose the medium that is best for your business and write an ad for that medium. To generate publicity, write a press release that you will send to the media.

4. Define your short-, medium-, and long-term goals. Write your marketing plan for each element of the marketing mix.

Chapter 10

HIRE AND MANAGE A STAFF

LESSONS

10.1 **Hire Employees**

10.2 **Create a Compensation Package**

10.3 **Manage Your Staff**

BUILD A BUSINESS

The Frazzled Photographer

"I've been so busy, Richard. I can't keep up with all the requests that are coming in for my photography services," Kim said.

"If you don't hire someone to help you, you're going to get so far behind you will never catch up," Richard cautioned.

"Yeah, but I don't have the slightest idea how to go about hiring someone. Can you give me some advice?" Kim asked.

"Well," Richard answered, "the first thing I do is decide exactly what I want the employee to do. I make a list of all their responsibilities and then write a job description."

"Okay, so once you've done that, what do you do next?"

"The next step is to recruit prospective employees," said Richard. "You can run an ad in the newspaper. You might contact the job placement center at the local college, too. They may have some photography majors who are looking for work."

"I like that idea! Okay, so when I'm ready to interview candidates, what do I do?"

"Kim, the first thing you want to do is be sure that the qualifications of the applicants match your job description. If the applicants don't have any experience in photography, don't waste your time interviewing them."

"I probably need to prepare a list of questions to ask them," thought Kim.

"Good idea!" Richard exclaimed. "Based on the interviews and reference checks, you can decide who you want to hire."

"Another big decision I need to make is about pay. I've got to decide how to pay them and if I am going to offer any benefits."

"You might consider paying your employee an hourly salary plus a commission on all the picture packages they sell. That often gives them an incentive to work a little harder."

"That's a good idea. I guess I should also decide how I'm going to train my new employee."

"Training is an essential part of getting good employees. It also makes them happier in their jobs, because they know what they need to do, and they know how to do it," said Richard. "And Kim, you already have the qualities to be a good manager. You're honest, you are enthusiastic, and you are a good listener."

"Hey, thanks for the compliment. Would you mind helping me come up with my very first job description?"

"Sure, I'd be glad to," Richard smiled.

What Do You Know?

1. What are some questions Kim should ask prospective employees in the interview?
2. What kind of benefits might Kim offer to the employee she hires?
3. Once Kim hires someone to work for her, what are some things she can do to be an effective manager?

Hire
Employees

To succeed, you probably will need to hire employees. Employees can help your business run efficiently. Good employees will help you attract customers and increase sales. But how do you know what kinds of employees you need? And how do you go about getting them?

IDENTIFY YOUR NEED FOR EMPLOYEES

Chances are, you will eventually need to hire employees. To find out your hiring needs, ask yourself these questions.

- What kind of employees do I need?
- What skills am I missing?
- What skills do I need daily?
- What skills do I need occasionally?

To answer these questions, make a list of all the duties in your business. Then try to identify how much time is needed to perform each of those duties. Your list should help you identify whether you need part-time, full-time, or temporary workers. You can also determine if you need managers or assistants and how many employees you need.

Write Job Descriptions

A **job description** is a written statement listing the duties and responsibilities of a job. It indicates the educational and professional experience required to perform a particular job. It often includes a salary amount, hourly wage, or a salary range.

Writing a detailed job description is important. You will need to understand exactly what every job in your company involves so that you can determine how much money to offer job applicants. A detailed job description

SAMPLE JOB DESCRIPTION
Title: Receptionist
Duties and responsibilities: Receives and directs phone calls, greets visitors, receives and sorts mail and packages, orders office and kitchen supplies, keys documents when required.
Qualifications: High school graduate. Needs good communication skills and ability to get along with people. Keying speed of 45 words per minute. Experience desirable but not necessary.
Salary: $15,000–$20,000, depending on experience.

will also make clear the responsibilities of all the workers. If a receptionist objects to ordering coffee supplies, his employer can remind him that this is included in his job description. Job descriptions also can be used to measure how well an employee performs a job.

Create an Organizational Structure

Once your company has several employees, you will need an organizational structure. An **organizational structure** is a plan that shows how the various jobs in a company relate to one another. Many businesses use a chart to represent the organizational structure.

In some small businesses, all employees may report directly to the company owner. In larger companies, lower-level employees usually report to a supervisor. This kind of organizational structure ensures that the owner of a company is not called upon to deal with relatively unimportant issues that could be handled more efficiently by a lower-level manager.

Sandra Wilson owns Northcliffe Publishing. Sandra has an organizational structure where the heads of the four departments report to the vice-president, Robert Gotting. Robert in turn reports directly to Sandra. This structure helps Sandra devote her time to long-term issues, such as expanding the company into new areas or increasing sales and market share.

 **CHECKPOINT** How do you determine the staffing needs of your business?

ORGANIZATIONAL CHART, NORTHCLIFFE PUBLISHING			
Sandra Wilson PRESIDENT		Robert Gottig VICE-PRESIDENT	
PRODUCTION	MARKETING	DESIGN	EDITORIAL
Rose Silver DEPARTMENT HEAD	Martine Landy DEPARTMENT HEAD	Stella Jackson DEPARTMENT HEAD	Orlando Smythe DEPARTMENT HEAD
EDITORS Ellen Bhattacharya Cynthia Williams Roger Wills Stephen Ortiz Mark Michaels Elizabeth Smith	ASSOCIATES Heidi Berger Ross Wingate Karen Yoshida Kevin Acton Phil Kelley	DESIGNERS Monroe Ross Maura O'Donnell	EDITORS Nancy Peters Rachel Roberts Suzanne Beck Paul Whitnery Samantha Evans
Rita Woo ASSISTANT	Anne Husayn ASSISTANT	Andrew Roberts RECEPTIONIST	Alan Berg ASSISTANT

Sample want ad

RECRUIT EMPLOYEES

To **recruit** is to look for people to hire. You can recruit employees in a variety of ways.

Classified Advertising

A *want ad* is a type of classified ad that announces a job opening at a company. It can be an effective way to recruit employees. Your want ad should briefly describe the position and tell the educational requirements and/or experience required. It should also identify any special job requirements, such as willingness to travel or to work evenings.

Employment Agencies

Employment agencies find employees for businesses and other institutions. These firms try to match people looking for jobs with businesses looking for employees. They charge businesses a fee when they are successful.

College Placement Centers

Most colleges and universities operate job placement centers. These offices collect information on career and employment opportunities, which they make available to their students and graduates. Generally, no fee is charged for using a college placement center. If college students or graduates might be suitable for your business, contact local colleges and universities and ask them what you need to do to have your business listed with their placement center.

Other Ways of Recruiting Employees

One of the best ways entrepreneurs find employees is by acting on referrals from friends, acquaintances, or employees. You can try to recruit employees by putting a help wanted sign in your store window or posting your job opening on the World Wide Web. If your company already has employees, the ideal candidate for a job you need to fill might already be working for you.

 **CHECKPOINT** List five ways you can recruit employees.

HIRE EMPLOYEES

Hiring employees is often difficult because it requires making very important decisions based on fairly limited information. How should you decide whom to hire?

Know What to Look for in an Employee

The job description identifies the specific requirements needed to perform a particular job. You should also look for personal characteristics that would make a person a desirable employee.

Screen Job Applicants

The first step in the hiring process is to screen candidates to remove people who do not have the right qualifications and are not right for the job. This allows you to concentrate on looking at the most qualified candidates.

DESIRABLE PERSONAL CHARACTERISTICS	
Dependability	Promptness
Sensitivity to others	Open-mindedness
Honesty	Flexibility
Enthusiasm	Maturity
Able to accept constructive criticism	Able to work in many environments
Willingness to listen	Willingness to learn

Michael Johnson, the owner of Johnson's Medical Supply, ran a want ad in his local newspaper. He was looking for a person with at least five years of experience selling medical equipment. He received more than 150 responses to his ad. However, 120 of the resumes he received were from people with no experience in the field. Michael immediately removed those from the stack of possibilities. Next, he carefully examined each resume and cover letter and selected ten candidates to interview, based on their experience.

Interview Job Applicants

The job interview provides you with the opportunity to determine if prospective employees would improve your ability to meet customer needs. Making the most of the job interview is as important for you as it is for the job candidate. To ensure that you use your time effectively, follow these basic rules.

1. ***Be prepared.*** Make a list of open-ended questions you want to ask. Review the job candidate's resume and application just before the interview begins.
2. ***Be courteous.*** Do not be late for the interview. Avoid taking phone calls during the interview. Try to put job candidates at ease by offering them something to drink. Make them feel welcome in your office.
3. ***Avoid dominating the interview.*** Remember that the interview is your opportunity to get to know the job candidate. To do so, be sure to allow the applicant plenty of time to speak.
4. ***Take notes.*** Throughout the interview, jot down your impressions of the candidate as well as any interesting information he or she reveals.
5. ***Look for warnings that the person may not be a good worker.*** These include frequent job changes, unexplained gaps in employment, and critical comments about previous employers.

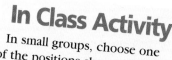

In Class Activity

In small groups, choose one of the positions shown on the organizational chart for Northcliffe Publishing. Write a job description for that position. Share your results with the class.

6. ***Don't make snap judgments about a candidate.*** Don't rule out someone until the interview is over.
7. ***Remain pleasant and positive throughout the interview.*** At the end of the interview, thank the candidate for coming and let him or her know when you plan to make a decision.
8. ***Write a summary of your impressions of the candidate.*** You should do this right after the interview while your thoughts are still fresh. Put this document in the candidate's file.

SAMPLE INTERVIEW QUESTIONS
1. What interests you about the job?
2. How can your skills and experience benefit the company?
3. What are your career plans? How does this job fit in with those plans?
4. What other positions have you held? What did you like and dislike about those positions?
5. What were your achievements at your previous jobs?
6. Why did you leave your last job?
7. How do you think your education has prepared you for this job?
8. What kind of work do you enjoy most? What makes a job enjoyable for you?
9. Describe a situation where you had to manage conflicting priorities.

Entrepreneurial Timeline

| 1830 | 1850 | 1870 | 1890 |

A Pattern for Good Business

In the mid 1800s, factory-produced fabrics and home sewing machines were changing the way clothing was made. Ellen Curtis Demorest had already established a number of her own successful hat shops. At her husband's suggestion, she became the first to offer mass-produced paper patterns for women's clothing in 1858. Ellen and husband William also began the publication *Mme. Demorest's Mirror of Fashions.* The magazine featured one clothing pattern per issue, and the nation's very first personal advice column. In addition, Ellen and a number of other women co-founded Sorosis, the first professional club for women in the United States. Ellen contributed to the American economy because her businesses created job opportunities for many women and African Americans.

Check References

Once you have two or three very qualified candidates, you need to check references. With the permission of the applicant, call his or her most recent employers to make sure he or she held the positions listed on the resume. Ask previous employers what they can tell you about the person. Describe the job the person has applied for and ask the previous employers if the candidate would perform well in such a position. Other questions can revolve around the personal qualities of the candidate, such as people skills and whether there were any problems with tardiness.

Make a Job Offer

When you have decided to make a job offer, contact the person by phone. Let the person know you were impressed with his or her credentials. Be sure to emphasize how much you would like the person to join your company. Clearly state the starting salary, benefits, and terms of employment. If the first applicant declines your offer, extend the offer to your second choice and then your third choice, if necessary.

Once a candidate accepts your offer, contact all of the other candidates. Thank them for interviewing with your business, and politely let them know that you have given the job to another applicant.

NET WORTH

Point your browser to

http://www.ideas-in-action.swep.com

Complete the activity for Chapter 10.

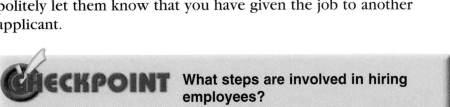

CHECKPOINT What steps are involved in hiring employees?

ALTERNATIVES TO ADDING STAFF

Adding employees to your payroll is costly. Paying wages or salaries to employees may strain your finances. In addition, it takes time and money to recruit staff. For these reasons, you may want to consider alternatives to permanent employees.

Hire Freelancers or Interns

Freelancers are people who provide services to businesses on an hourly basis or by the job. Business owners use freelancers when they need a job done but do not require a permanent full- or part-time employee. Examples of freelancers include bookkeepers, accountants, lawyers, graphic designers, window display artists, and advertising copywriters.

Interns are students who will work for little or no pay in order to gain experience in a particular field. To find out if interns are available in your community, contact local colleges and high schools.

Hire Temporary Workers

Businesses that need more workers often use temporary workers. Some temporary workers are seasonal employees. Other temporary workers are substitutes for employees who are sick or on a leave of absence. Temporary workers also can be used for long periods of time as an alternative to full-time hiring.

Temporary employment agencies provide trained temporary workers to various kinds of businesses. Businesses that use temporary agencies pay the worker's salary, plus a fee to the agency.

You might need a seasonal temporary employee if you own an orchard or farm.

 **CHECKPOINT** What are some alternatives to hiring employees?

THINK CRITICALLY

1. Why is it important for a company to have an organizational structure that allows the owner to focus on long-term issues?

2. List some advantages of using an employment agency.

3. Why do you need to check a job applicant's references?

4. What would be some disadvantages of hiring freelancers and temporary workers?

MAKE CONNECTIONS

5. COMMUNICATION Create an organizational structure for a 30 person local package delivery service. First, determine all the types of employees the business would have. Then create the chart based on your decisions.

6. COMMUNICATION Evan Goulet opened a motorcycle repair shop several years ago. He has decided to hire two mechanics and a receptionist. Write an ad to be placed in your local newspaper for each of the new positions.

Create a *Compensation* Package

A s an entrepreneur with paid employees, you will need to create a compensation package. The package should include wages or salary and may provide a variety of benefits.

WAGES AND SALARY

Wages are payments for labor or services that are made on an hourly, daily, or per-unit basis. **Salaries** are payments for labor or services done on an annual basis. Wages and salaries can be paid weekly, biweekly, or monthly.

Compensation Levels

In most markets, wages and salaries are competitively determined. This means that an employer who offers much less than the going wage or salary rate is not likely to find qualified workers.

PAY COMPETITIVELY To offer competitive wages or salaries, you will have to find out how much similar businesses in your area are paying their employees. You should also find out what people are earning in jobs with similar qualifications.

Once you know what the going wage or salary rate is, you will have to decide whether you want to offer more than, less than, or about the same as other businesses. Offering more than other businesses will attract the best employees.

Bob Aylward owns a limousine service. He knows that finding and keeping good drivers is difficult. To make sure his compensation package is attractive, he regularly finds out what other limousine companies are offering. He then sets a starting salary that is 3 percent higher. He also offers a few more days of paid vacation than his competitors. Bob hopes that these things will attract drivers that stay with his company for many years.

Types of Pay

There are many ways you can choose to pay your employees. A wage is a fixed amount of pay per hour or per unit. The paycheck for a person earning a wage will vary depending on how many hours are worked or how many units are manufactured. A salary is a fixed

In Class Activity

In small groups, brainstorm a list of conditions for receiving an employee bonus for salespeople working in the following types of companies: manufacturer of cardboard boxes, retail furniture store, neighborhood hardware store.

amount of pay for a certain time period. Employees who receive a salary might get paid once a week or once a month. Regardless of the number of hours the employees work in that time period, the amount of money they are paid does not vary. Employees can receive a **bonus,** which is a financial reward in addition to a regular wage or salary.

Some employees are on commission-based salary plans. A **commission** is a percentage of a sale paid to a salesperson. A **commission-based salary** is a salary that varies from month to month, depending on how much of a product or service is sold.

COMMISSION Some employees, especially those in sales, receive all of their salaries in commission. Commission-only plans are good for employers because commissions are paid only when sales are made. Some employees may not want to accept a commission-only position because they fear their income may rise and fall too much.

Lyn Kovacs works entirely on commission. Last year, Lyn sold $490,000 worth of electronic devices. She received 10 percent of her sales as commission. Her annual salary was $49,000.

Amount sold × Percent of commission = Amount of commission
$490,000 × 0.10 = $49,000

COMBINATION PLAN An employee may be on a combination plan. A combination plan includes a base salary plus commission. Employees may feel more comfortable accepting a position that offers this type of payment plan.

Veronica Marquez sells men's clothing at a local department store. She earns $6.75 an hour, plus 10 percent of whatever she sells. Last month, Veronica worked 158 hours and sold $11,500 worth of clothing. Her total monthly compensation was $2,216.50.

Hours × Hourly wage = Base wages
158 × $6.75 = $1,066.50

Amount sold × Percent of commission = Amount of commission
$11,500 × 0.10 = $1,150

Base wages + Amount of commission = Total pay
$1,066.50 + $1,150 = $2,216.50

CHECKPOINT **What are the different kinds of pay?**

Benefits are employment rewards for service, in addition to salary. They include paid days off from work and various kinds of insurance.

Paid Leave

Almost all employers offer paid vacation and paid sick leave. Both kinds of leave represent costs to employers because the employee is paid while he or she is not working. Be aware that some employees may abuse paid leave. Someone in your business should keep a record of the paid leave an employee takes.

VACATION Businesses handle vacation in various ways. Many offer one or two weeks of paid vacation a year to new employees. Employees usually gain more vacation time the longer they work at a business. Some businesses let employees carry vacation days from year to year, while others require employees to use their vacation time in one year.

SICK LEAVE Sometimes your employees will not be able to make it into work because of illness. The number of days of sick leave provided varies from business to business. Some businesses offer only five sick days a year. Others allow employees unlimited sick leave. You will have to develop a sick leave policy that is fair to your employees but not excessively costly to you.

Insurance

Most large businesses offer insurance as a benefit. This kind of benefit is less common among small businesses although many do provide such coverage. Usually, all full-time employees are eligible for this benefit. You can also decide to offer these benefits to part-time employees as well.

HEALTH BENEFITS Most Americans purchase medical insurance or join health maintenance organizations (HMOs). People with medical insurance or HMO coverage pay a monthly fee whether they are sick or not. In return, the insurance company or HMO agrees to cover most of their medical bills.

Entrepreneurs with many employees may be able to purchase group medical insurance or enroll employees in an HMO. You can offer either or both options to your employees as a benefit for working for your business.

YOU CAN SAY THAT AGAIN!

I promoted myself. I had to make my own opportunity! But I made it!

—*Madam C. J. Walker, a millionaire who made her fortune selling hair care products*

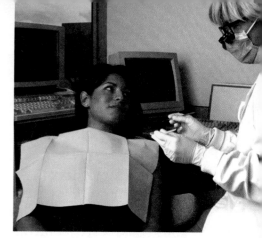

OTHER KINDS OF INSURANCE

Some businesses also offer other kinds of insurance. *Dental insurance* covers the cost of dental and orthodontic expenses. *Life insurance* is intended to provide financial support for families after the income earner dies. *Accident insurance* provides financial support to people who are in accidents.

Pension Plan

Large businesses generally offer their employees pension plans. Under a pension plan, the employer and the employee contribute money to a pension fund every month. The pension fund keeps this money in a special account, which it invests on behalf of the employees. When employees retire, they withdraw the pension funds. They use this money to support themselves during their retirements.

 **CHECKPOINT** List three types of nonsalary benefits your business might offer.

THINK CRITICALLY

1. Why might a combination plan be attractive to an employee?

2. Using examples, explain why employees' personal lives might influence their desire for different types of benefits.

MAKE CONNECTIONS

3. MATH You have received two job offers for similar sales positions. Company A pays a salary of $21,000 per year. Company B offers a combination plan of $12,000 per year plus a commission of 15 percent of sales. You are told that the average first-year salesperson at Company B has about $90,000 in total annual sales. Which job will you choose, and why?

4. COMMUNICATION Interview five adults you know who have full-time or part-time jobs. Ask them if they receive wages or a salary. Ask what types of benefits they receive. Ask which of these benefits is most important to them, and why. Put your findings in a chart.

Manage
Your Staff

O nce you have people working for you, you will become a manager. This means that you will no longer focus all of your efforts on doing your own job. Much of your time will be spent managing other people. As a manager, you will have to exhibit leadership and motivate your employees.

LEAD YOUR EMPLOYEES

To manage your staff effectively, you will need to develop good leadership qualities. Good leadership qualities will help you create a workforce that is dedicated to meeting customer needs and increasing sales.

Desirable Leadership Qualities

There are many personal characteristics that can help you be a good leader. Desirable leadership qualities include:

- Judgment—ability to make decisions carefully and objectively
- Honesty—ethical in your decisions and treatment of others
- Consistency—predictable and emotionally even
- Enthusiasm—ability to generate enthusiasm in others
- Cooperation—work well with others
- Communications—listen, speak, and write effectively
- Dependability—follow through on commitments
- Understanding—respect feelings and needs of people

Developing these qualities has helped Adam Stevenson create a team of dedicated employees at the busy tool rental shop he owns. Every month Adam posts the work schedule for the following month. He makes sure to assign the unpopular night and weekend shifts evenly among all his employees. Adam encourages employees who want to make schedule changes to discuss their needs with him. He tries to accommodate all reasonable requests. Adam urges all employees to come to him with suggestions for improving service. He also praises employees who have good ideas, and he lets others know of their contributions.

 **CHECKPOINT** List five desirable leadership characteristics.

Enforce Employee Policies

As the owner of your own business, you will establish policies concerning vacations, holidays, hours, acceptable dress, and other issues affecting your workers. You will need to make sure that all of your employees are familiar with these policies. This may mean gently reminding employees of policies if they fail to follow them.

Many companies communicate policies to staff by creating an employee handbook. These handbooks can be just a few pages long or they can fill a small binder, depending on the size of the company and the number of policies.

Train Your Employees

Well-trained employees perform their jobs well. They know what is expected of them, so they have higher morale and are less likely to quit. Poorly trained employees do not perform well. They become frustrated by lack of training and look for new jobs.

You will need to develop a training program for your new employees. This program should begin as soon as they are hired. Training should not end when the employee learns how things are done. Continuous improvement of employees will help your business.

What Went Wrong

Organization/Employees
Who Do You Trust?

Business: Motiva International, Chicago, IL * In business, 2 years

Bob Warren partnered with two business associates and formed Motiva International, a sales motivation and travel incentive company. The company designed and implemented programs to help clients motivate employees.

At weekly meetings, the partners shared and discussed confidential company details with their 18 employees. The employees appreciated the honesty. But the partners soon learned that there were some things it's best not to share.

Some employees did not want to know about the company's cash-flow problems, especially when it looked like the payroll could not be paid. At one meeting, Bob told his employees about a deal he was about to close with a new client. One excited employee told someone outside the company about the new client, which enabled a competitor to steal the new client. Losing that deal forced Motiva to lay off employees, go deeper into debt, and finally dissolve the company.

Think Critically

1. How do you determine what company information should be reserved to "management" and withheld from employees?
2. Would you have fired the employee who led to the loss of the new client?

There are techniques for providing training to employees. You may use different techniques for different job responsibilities. You will need to decide which is best for you, your business, and the employee.

1. **On-the-job training.** Employees learn new responsibilities by actually performing them at their place of business.
2. **Coaching.** Employees receive feedback and instruction from their manager on a constant basis.
3. **Mentoring.** One employee teams up with another more experienced employee to learn a job.
4. **Conferences and seminars.** Employees learn new techniques or duties from an expert in the field.

After training, you need to make sure employees are using that training, and that the training has been effective. Jennifer Reynolds needs to train her employees on the new computerized inventory program she wants to use. She brings in a representative from the software company to provide a training session. Jennifer will know the training was effective if employees understand the software and are able to use it.

SAFETY PRACTICES AND PROCEDURES Your employees should be thoroughly trained in safety issues. They should know how to operate equipment safely or wear any necessary protective gear. Employees should be briefed on emergency plans for fires, tornadoes, and other disasters. You should also map evacuation routes on your floor plan and post these throughout your building.

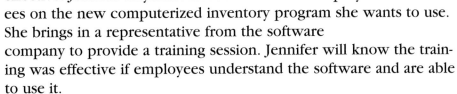 **CHECKPOINT** What are the different training techniques?

MOTIVATE YOUR EMPLOYEES

To get the most out of your employees, you will have to motivate them. You can do so in several ways.

1. **Pay them well.** When employees feel they are compensated well, they will be happier. They will perform to the best of their ability.
2. **Treat them fairly.** Everyone wants to be treated well. Be sure to treat everyone the same.
3. **Recognize them for the work they do.** Offer public recognition of good work. Praise employees frequently.
4. **Give them adequate responsibility.** Employees who are allowed to make decisions often work harder. They take pride in the fact that their work can make a difference.

Delegate Responsibility

Many entrepreneurs have difficulty delegating responsibility. To **delegate** is to let other people share workloads and responsibilities. Employees who are given more responsibility are better motivated and contribute more to the company. Delegating responsibility to them allows you to make the most of their talents.

Delegating allows you to focus on important items, such as expanding into new markets or offering new products. Paperwork and duties that someone else can perform will not bog you down.

Finally, delegating responsibility is essential if a company is to grow. When your business is small, you may be able to handle all areas of its management. If the company is to expand, though, you will have to let managers take on more and more responsibility.

Listen to Employees

Some entrepreneurs fail to listen to their employees. In doing so, they miss out on an opportunity to take advantage of valuable resources that can help them increase profits.

The people who work for you are very familiar with your business and may be able to offer fresh ideas. Listening to new points of view may help you come up with new, creative solutions. If you value the opinions of your employees, they will feel they are a valuable asset to your company. This means they will most likely be motivated to do a good job for you.

CHECKPOINT How can you motivate employees? Why should you delegate and listen to your employees?

Work as a Team

In many activities, working together as a team determines whether an effort is successful or not. A ball club cannot win if its players do not work together as a team. Astronauts working on the space station cannot complete their mission if crew members do not work together.

Teamwork is important in many businesses. Employees who work as a team are usually very committed. They are more likely to work harder and to come up with creative ideas for increasing profits.

What Makes a Good Team?

Creating an atmosphere in which employees feel part of a team is a big challenge. You should try to create an atmosphere in which all of your employees work toward a common goal. Respecting, communicating with, and getting along with other team members also is important.

As the owner of your own business, it will be up to you to provide the leadership that will allow your employees to work together as a team. To be an effective team leader you will need to

- Establish trust among team members and gain their trust.
- Make sure that all team members understand the goals you have set.
- Encourage team members to be creative and innovative.
- Make team members feel like partners in your business.
- Help team members learn from their mistakes.
- Build the team's commitment to achieving the goals you have set.

**CHECKPOINT** How can working as a team help your business succeed?

EVALUATE YOUR EMPLOYEES

At least once a year you need to evaluate how well employees are doing their jobs. Evaluating performance will help you determine whether an employee should be given a raise. It also will help you identify outstanding employees who should be promoted and problem employees who should be fired.

Create an Evaluation Procedure

Most businesses perform annual employee reviews in which they analyze each employee's performance and determine the increase in the employee's salary.

The original job description should be used when evaluating how well an employee has performed his or her job. If the employee has fulfilled all of his or her job responsibilities, that employee should receive a wage or salary increase.

You should record the review on an appraisal form. The employee's name and job title should be listed, as well as the manager's name, the date range the evaluation covers, job responsibilities and attributes, places for comments, goals for the next year, and a section for how the employee can improve. A ranking method can be used to easily mark how well the employee has performed.

Reviews in which you let employees know how they have performed during the year should be conducted face to face. A written summary of the review should be kept in your general employee file.

**CHECKPOINT** Why should you evaluate the people who work for you?

PERFORMANCE APPRAISAL

DATE: January 21, 20--
NAME: Daniel Tisdale
JOB TITLE: Marketing Director

Reports To: Laureen Stiles
Review Period: 1/1 to 12/31

ATTRIBUTE	WELL ABOVE STANDARD	ABOVE STANDARD	STANDARD	BELOW STANDARD	FAR BELOW STANDARD
Quantity of work		✓			
Knowledge of work		✓			
Ability to organize			✓		
Meets deadlines			✓		
Dependability			✓		
Judgment			✓		
Initiative	✓				
Communication				✓	
Manages others well			✓		
Teamwork			✓		

COMMENTS

You have done an outstanding job of increasing sales. Your hard work, dependability, and initiative are very much appreciated.

AREAS FOR IMPROVEMENT:

1. Increase technical knowledge so that quality of work matches quantity of work.

2. Improve written communication skills by enrolling in a business writing course.

3. Improve management skills, in particular by delegating more responsibility to your marketing assistants.

4. Increase ability to participate as part of team.

GOALS FOR COMING YEAR:

1. Increase store sales 12 percent.

2. Oversee completion of company web site.

3. Generate sales over World Wide Web of $75,000.

Employee: Daniel Tisdale

Manager: Laureen Stiles

Daniel Tisdale

Laureen Stiles

Promote Employees

Promoting good employees will help ensure that they remain interested in working for your business. However, employees compete with one another. Promoting one employee over another may cause problems. Be sure that you make all decisions fairly. Base your decision on solid reasons, such as volume of sales and quality of customer service.

Terminate Employees

Some employees may not work out. In fact, they may end up hurting your business. How will you handle such situations? As soon as you notice an employee not performing well, discuss the situation with him or her. If performance does not improve, issue a written warning. If there is still no improvement, you will need to fire that employee.

Once you decide to terminate an employee, do so immediately. Meet with the employee privately and explain why you are letting him or her go. Ask him to leave the workplace the same day. Record the date of the termination and the reason for termination in the employee's file.

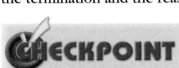 **Why is it necessary to promote or terminate employees?**

THINK CRITICALLY

1. Why do you think it is difficult for many entrepreneurs to delegate?

2. How is a work team similar to an amateur sports team? How is it different?

3. Why do you think it is important to keep a written summary of a performance evaluation?

MAKE CONNECTIONS

4. **COMMUNICATION** With a partner, role-play an evaluation for an employee who deserves a promotion. Make up the employer and job. Use the performance appraisal form in this lesson. Summarize the meeting in writing.

5. **PROBLEM SOLVING** Barry Sandler, owner of Sandler's Custom Computers, has decided to change the way sales associates are paid. Regular salary is currently used. Barry decides to gather the sales team together to get their suggestions on how to change. As a class, use the consensus-building problem-solving method to decide on a new compensation method for the company. Your teacher will role-play Barry Sandler.

CHAPTER SUMMARY

Hire Employees

1. In order to succeed as an entrepreneur, you will need to hire employees. Determine what skills and qualifications you need for your employees and write job descriptions that list the specific responsibilities of each job. You should also create an organizational structure that shows how the different jobs in your company relate to each other.
2. Use classified advertising, employment agencies, college placement centers, and word of mouth to recruit employees.
3. When hiring employees, you will first need to screen applicants and then interview those who seem good for the job. After you have interviewed several candidates, you should check their references and offer the position to the most qualified candidate.
4. In addition to hiring permanent employees, you can also hire freelancers, interns, or temporary workers.

Create a *Compensation* Package

5. Determine the wages, salaries, or commissions you will give your employees. Be sure to pay competitively.
6. You might also offer benefits, including paid leave, insurance plans, and pension plans.

Manage *Your* Staff

7. Having good leadership qualities will help you manage your staff effectively. Enforcing policies and offering training will help your employees perform better.
8. If you motivate your employees, you will get the most out of them. There are several ways you can motivate, including treating employees fairly and listening to them.
9. You should develop a training program for all your employees.
10. Teamwork is very important in businesses. You should try to create an atmosphere in which employees feel part of a team.
11. You should create a procedure for evaluating employees. Outstanding employees should be promoted, and problem employees should be terminated.

What Do You Know Now?

Read *Build a Business* again. Then answer the questions a second time. How have your responses changed?

VOCABULARY BUILDER

Choose the term that best fits the definition.
Write your answers on a separate sheet of paper.

1. Financial reward in addition to a regular wage or salary
2. Percentage of a sale paid to a salesperson
3. Plan that shows how the various jobs in a company relate to one another
4. Written statement listing the duties and responsibilities of a job
5. Students who will work for little or no pay in order to gain experience in a particular field
6. Payments for labor or services done on an annual basis
7. Payments for labor or services that are made on an hourly, daily, or per-unit basis
8. People who provide services to businesses on an hourly basis or by the job
9. To let other people share workloads and responsibilities
10. To look for people to hire

a. bonus
b. commission
c. commission-based salary
d. delegate
e. freelancers
f. interns
g. job description
h. organizational structure
i. recruit
j. salaries
k. wages

REVIEW YOUR KNOWLEDGE

11. Why is it important to write a detailed job description?
12. Why is it important to create an organizational structure?
13. What type of information should a classified advertisement contain?
14. What are some of the characteristics of a desirable employee?
15. List the things you should do while interviewing a candidate.
16. Why might you consider some alternatives to hiring permanent employees?
17. How are wages and salaries determined in most markets?
18. Name the five different types of pay.
19. What are some of the most common benefits?
20. Why are good leadership qualities necessary to manage a staff?
21. Why is it important to give employees adequate responsibility?

22. What are the methods for training employees?

23. Why is teamwork important in many businesses?

24. Why do you need to evaluate your employees?

APPLY WHAT YOU LEARNED

25. You have decided to hire three people to help in your custom drapery business: a receptionist, an interior designer (salesperson), and a tailor. What qualifications and skills must each of these employees possess? Write a job description for each position. For each job, establish a compensation package. Did you structure the compensation differently for each employee? How will you recruit these employees? Write a list of interview questions that you will ask each candidate.

26. Each of the employees in your drapery business has completed one year of service. Create a performance appraisal form for each position. For each employee, write a complete performance appraisal. What types of goals did you set for each employee? Are your employees entitled to a raise or promotion? Why or why not?

THINK CRITICALLY

27. Recruiting employees by acting on referrals from friends, acquaintances, or other employees is one of the best ways to find employees. Why do you think this is so? Are there any reasons why you might not want to act on a referral from someone you know?

28. To pay competitively, employers must know what similar businesses pay their employees. What are some of the ways to find out compensation levels at similar businesses? How do you decide whether you want to offer more than, less than, or the same compensation as other businesses?

29. Good leadership qualities are essential to manage effectively. Are good leadership qualities something that can be learned, or are you born with them? Why do you think so?

MAKE CONNECTIONS

30. MATH Jayne Smith sells vacuum cleaners under a combination plan. She earns $9.25 per hour plus 15 percent of whatever she sells. Last month, Jayne worked 160 hours and sold 9 vacuum cleaners. Five of the vacuum cleaners were top-of-the-line models with a price of $1,100 each. The remaining vacuum cleaners were $450 each. What was Jayne's compensation last month?

31. COMMUNICATION You are opening a new department store. Write a newspaper advertisement for the positions you will need to fill. Write the job description for two of the positions available. What skills are you seeking? Why? Write a list of interview questions. Interview two classmates for one of the positions.

Compare their answers and interview performance. Which candidate will you hire? Why?

32. **RESEARCH** Compare three advertisements for the same type of job. Are the qualifications requested the same for each? How are they different? Is any mention of compensation made? If so, how is it structured? Using the library and any other sources you can, find out what the going wage is for this position. What do you think is a fair wage for this job? Why?

33. **PROBLEM SOLVING** One of your employees is upset that another employee received a promotion. The first employee thinks she deserved the new job. How will you deal with the situation?

This Is Your Business Project

1. Your business has grown and you will need to add employees. Make a list of at least 5 jobs that need to be filled. Is each job a full-time job, part-time job, or occasional work? For each job, write a detailed job description. Create an organization chart for your business based on these new jobs.

2. Write a classified advertisement for each of the jobs that you need for your business. What characteristics are you looking for? What qualifications are you seeking? Write the interview questions that you will ask the candidates for each position. Write a list of questions you will ask their references.

3. For each position, write a complete compensation package that outlines wages, salary, and nonsalary benefits. Explain why you have structured the compensation package as such.

4. Prepare a company handbook that outlines policies concerning vacation, holidays, hours, acceptable dress, and any other issues that affect your workers. Write the policy and procedure for employee evaluation. Create a sample performance appraisal form. Will this form be the same for each position? Why or why not?

5. Determine the ways you plan to motivate your employees. Create at least one method of publicly acknowledging employees for their work. Write down your ideas.

6. In what ways will you train new and existing employees for your business? What aspects of your business require training, and what type of training is the best for each aspect? Write a short report about your decisions.

Chapter 11

RECORD KEEPING AND
ACCOUNTING

LESSONS

11.1 **Set Up a Record Keeping System**

11.2 **Understand Basic Accounting**

11.3 **Track Your Inventory**

BUILD A BUSINESS

CDs and Records

"You know, Raphael, I am getting pretty tired of paying 15 to 20 dollars for a CD and then listening to it for a few weeks and losing interest in it," Rita said as they were browsing at the local CD store one afternoon after school.

"I know what you mean," Raphael replied. "Sometimes I feel like I waste a lot of money. I bet I've got 100 CDs that I haven't listened to in six months."

"I bet our friends have this same problem. I've got a great idea!" exclaimed Rita. "Let's open a used CD shop. We can take our CDs and get some from our friends and sell them much cheaper than new CDs. We'll charge our friends a commission to sell theirs. If we don't have to purchase inventory, this will help keep our start-up costs low."

"Rita, that is a great idea! We might want to add computer games to our inventory, too," Raphael suggested. "I know lots of people who pay 50 to 75 dollars for a game and once they've mastered it, they lose interest."

"We will really have to keep good records to make this work," Rita advised. "We'll have to have a very good inventory system so that we know who we got items from, how long we have had them in stock, and to whom we owe commissions."

"In addition to inventory, we need to be very careful in keeping records of our money. It's important for us to know to whom we owe money when we sell an item and how much money we are making. After all, isn't that the main reason for doing this—money?"

"I hope we do make money," Rita replied. "Remember when we took accounting and we learned that you should keep business records separate from your personal records. I think the first thing we should do is open a business checking account."

"My sister works at the bank, maybe she'll help us get started. I know she'll give us a lecture about keeping our checkbook balanced. I always hear her telling my brother about that. It's really important!" Raphael replied.

"Another thing we need to think about is the journals we will use. We've got to decide if we want to use one journal for all transactions or separate them out into different journals based on the type of transactions we have," Rita responded.

"Right, Rita! Once we decide that and get our ledgers set up, then we'll be able to make financial statements. Then we'll know if we're making any money. After all, isn't that the main reason. . ."

"Wait! Let me finish this sentence for you," Rita interrupted, "for doing this—money? I hope we do make money. Then we can buy a computer to help with all this record keeping."

What Do You Know?

1. Why do you think it is important for Raphael and Rita to know what items they have and how long they have been in stock?
2. Why is it important to keep a checkbook balanced?
3. How do you think a computer can assist with record keeping?

237

Set Up a Record Keeping *System*

Good record keeping can help you make smart business decisions. Incomplete or inaccurate records can cause you to mismanage your business or can cause serious legal problems. You will need to keep accurate accounting journals and ledgers, as well as records of bank statements, payroll, and taxes you have paid. You can keep records on paper or electronically.

TYPES OF RECORDS

The records you will keep include journals and ledgers, bank records, payroll records, and tax records.

Journals

Journals are accounting records of the transactions you make. A **transaction** is a business activity that changes assets, liabilities, or net worth. Accurate journals help you keep track of how much money you have earned, how much you have spent, and how much profit you've made. Journals also show how much money you owe and how much people owe you. They also help you create financial statements.

TYPES OF JOURNALS Most businesses keep five journals for their accounting needs.
1. *Sales Journal.* This is used to record *only* sales of merchandise on account. Merchandise sold on account means that customers receive goods or services now that they pay for later.
2. *Cash Payments Journal.* This is used to record *only* cash payment transactions. Any cash or check payments a business pays out are recorded in this journal.
3. *Cash Receipts Journal.* This is used to record *only* cash receipt transactions. Goods paid for in cash at the time customers receive them are recorded in this journal.
4. *Purchases Journal.* This is used to record *only* purchases of merchandise on account. If you receive merchandise today but pay for it later, you should record this in the purchases journal.
5. *General Journal.* This is used to record any kind of transaction. Some businesses use only a general journal. Businesses that use the special journals described above record transactions that do not fit in the other four journals in the general journal.

Ledgers

Businesses also use a general ledger to which they post the items they record in their journals. **Posting** means copying information from a journal entry to a ledger account. Posting is generally done every one to two days to keep the ledger current.

Journals separate business transactions by *type.* Ledgers separate transactions by *account.* An **account** is an accounting record that summarizes all the information for a particular business item. Your business will have accounts for expenses, such as rent and utilities. You also will have accounts for cash and sales. A ledger allows you to view each separate account individually. It also aids in the preparation of financial statements you will need to run your business effectively.

SUBSIDIARY LEDGERS The only ledger a business needs is the general ledger. But, some businesses choose to keep subsidiary ledgers for certain types of accounts. A *subsidiary ledger* is a ledger that is summarized in a single general ledger account.

Subsidiary ledgers are commonly used for accounts receivable and accounts payable because they help you view at a glance money due to you and the money you must still pay. An *accounts receivable ledger* keeps track only of money owed to you by customers to whom you have sold merchandise on account. An *accounts payable ledger* keeps track only of money you owe to suppliers from whom you have purchased merchandise on account.

Maria Lopez wants to use subsidiary ledgers for accounts payable and accounts receivable to keep detailed records of transactions with her suppliers and customers. This information is then copied into the general ledger under accounts payable and receivable. These summaries make it easy for Maria to prepare her financial statements.

Journals and ledgers should always be kept up to date.

AGING TABLES An *aging table* is a record keeping tool for tracking accounts receivable. It shows a business how long it is taking customers to pay their bills. Maria can see by her aging table that one customer is over 61 days past due on a bill. She decides that she should not send this customer more merchandise until he has paid the outstanding bill.

Customer	Amount	0–30 days	31–60 days	over 61 days
E. Kwon	$175.23	$175.23		
P. Mossett	$106.20		$106.20	
M. Stern	$82.34			$82.34
Totals	$363.77	$175.23	$106.20	$82.34
Percent of total	100%	48%	29%	23%

 **What is the difference between a journal and a ledger?**

Bank Statements

You will need to open a checking account for your business. You will use your business account for all deposits and withdrawals related to your business. If you already have a personal checking account, you will still need a separate one for your business.

When you open your checking account, you will receive a set of checks and a check register. A **check register** is a book in which you record the dates, amounts, and names of people or businesses to whom you have written checks. Computer software is also available that can keep your account records electronically.

BALANCE YOUR ACCOUNT Every month when you receive your bank statement, you should balance your check register. Balancing your check register is very important because it will prevent you from accidentally writing checks when you do not have money in your account. Writing checks when you don't have enough money in the bank to cover them is illegal. If your checks do not clear, your suppliers may stop shipping merchandise to you. Most businesses and banks will charge you a fee for having written a bad check.

YOU CAN SAY THAT AGAIN!

Whether you think you can, or that you can't, you are usually right.

— Henry Ford

Payroll Records

If you have employees working for you, you will have to maintain payroll records. A **payroll** is a list of people who receive salary or wage payments from a business. Payroll records show how much your employees earn during a particular pay period. They also show any deductions that may have been made from those earnings.

Every pay period, you will need to create a *payroll register.* That register will include the following information:

- Employee's name
- Number of hours worked
- Regular and overtime earnings
- Federal, state, and local taxes deducted
- Social security and Medicare contributions deducted
- Other deductions (such as health insurance)

After you create the payroll register, you will prepare payroll checks. Most businesses use voucher checks for their payrolls. *Voucher checks* have a statement of earnings and deductions attached to them. The statement shows employees how their pay was calculated.

Tax Records

You will have to make several different kinds of tax payments. These include income tax, payroll deductions, and sales tax.

INCOME TAX Businesses that earn profits must pay income tax. These taxes are paid quarterly, or every three months. Income tax must be prepaid at the beginning of a quarter, so you will need to estimate your income taxes. If you fail to make these payments or you underestimate how much tax is due, you may have to pay a penalty. You could also be subject to criminal penalties for tax fraud.

PAYROLL DEDUCTIONS By law you are required to deduct taxes from your employees' paychecks and submit these taxes to the government. Your employees also may ask you to take voluntary deductions from their earnings to cover such programs as health or dental insurance.

SALES TAX Most businesses are required to charge sales tax on goods or services. If you own a business that collects sales tax, every month you will have to deposit the tax you collect in a special bank account that belongs to the government.

Sales tax is based on a percentage of sales. The actual percentage charged varies from state to state. It also can vary within states. You will need to find out the percent of sales tax you must charge in your area.

NET WORTH

Point your browser to

http://www.ideas-in-action.swep.com

Complete the activity for Chapter 11.

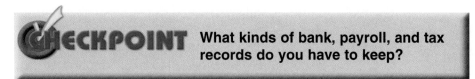

CHECKPOINT **What kinds of bank, payroll, and tax records do you have to keep?**

COMPUTERIZED RECORD KEEPING

Most small businesses use computer programs to handle their record keeping. These programs handle everything from sales records and payroll to accounts receivable and inventory.

Advantages of Computerized Record Keeping

Businesses large and small keep their records electronically. There are many advantages of computerized record keeping.

1. ***Store and Analyze Data.*** Computer programs allow you to store and analyze data more efficiently than you could with a pencil and paper. They also create reports that help you make sound business decisions.
2. ***Link Records.*** Computerized record keeping links all of the records you maintain. Every time you make a sale, your program

automatically records the change on your income statement. It also deducts the item sold from your inventory.

3. **Reduce Errors.** Although computers do not prevent all mistakes, they will prevent incorrect math calculations. Adding up many numbers by hand can lead to mistakes, or at least hard work. Computers can perform math calculations much faster than people can, and they are always correct.

4. **Correct Errors.** If you keep records by hand, you will have to erase any incorrect figures and replace them with correct figures. You will also have to check which other records were affected by your mistake and change all of those as well. Correcting errors is much simpler when your records are kept electronically. Making a change in one record automatically changes all other records that were affected by the change.

What Went Wrong

Computerized Record Keeping
All Your Eggs in One Basket

Business: JCP Distributors, Portland, Oregon * In business, 12 years

After working for six years at a Toyota dealership, Billy Wong borrowed money from his family and started Japanese Car Parts Distributors (JCP). The business grew, and in ten years it had twelve employees, thousands of parts in inventory, and hundreds of customers across the country.

Billy kept the books and records for the business by hand. Before long, his 18-year-old computer-whiz son Tommy wouldn't let him ignore the advantages of computerizing his record keeping. So Billy gave Tommy the task of setting up a computer system and transferring the accounts, inventory, and financial information from his paper records to the new electronic format. Tommy bought state-of-the-art computer hardware and software. He worked long hours transferring the handwritten data into computer files and creating applications to improve the way JCP did business. Within a year Billy stopped keeping handwritten records in favor of Tommy's computer, and in the next year the business ran more smoothly than ever.

Tragedy struck the business one December night when Tommy found robbers in the business office. Tommy was badly injured by the thieves and was rushed to the hospital. Sadly, he died on the way. If this wasn't enough for Billy to handle, the thieves that had killed his son had taken petty cash, the office phones, the stereo system, and the computer.

Billy had left all the electronic record keeping to his son, and he had no idea if Tommy had made backup copies of all the files that had been stored on the stolen computer. Billy found it would take months and a large amount of money to set up a new computerized record-keeping system. Whether it was the money and the aggravation, or that his heart was broken by Tommy's death, Billy sold JCP for ten cents on the dollar.

Think Critically
1. Was Billy wrong to trust his young son with so much responsibility?
2. Would JCP's problems have been solved if they found Tommy's disks?

Disadvantages of Computerized Record Keeping

Computers can help you run and track your business. But, you will need to be aware of some problems that can occur.

1. **Staff Resistance.** Some employees may have difficulty using computers or not know how to use them. For example, they might feel uncomfortable handling returns on a computerized cash register. They might be unable to make unusual transactions, such as the use of a gift certificate.
2. **Unauthorized Access.** Using a computer may make it easier for an unauthorized employee to introduce errors into your records. For this reason, you should limit access to files (see Chapter 13).
3. **Computer Problems.** Your computer hard drive can fail. Viruses can affect the files on your computer. To protect yourself against these kinds of problems, always keep copies of your files on floppy disks or on a secured server. Also, install an anti-virus program to check your hard disk for viruses that could hurt your files.

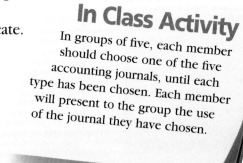

In Class Activity

In groups of five, each member should choose one of the five accounting journals, until each type has been chosen. Each member will present to the group the use of the journal they have chosen.

 **CHECKPOINT** What are some of the advantages and disadvantages of using a computer to handle your record keeping?

THINK CRITICALLY

1. Elisha Conner owns a small clothing boutique. Elisha uses her personal checking account for both business and personal needs. How would you convince Elisha that she should open a separate bank account for her business?

2. How would you overcome resistance from employees who object to using computers?

MAKE CONNECTIONS

3. MATH You create an aging table for your business. The total accounts receivable is $1,098.61. One customer owes you $281.90. What percent of the total is this?

4. COMMUNICATION Conduct research into computer viruses currently posing a problem for computer systems. Write a one-page report on your findings.

GOALS

DEMONSTRATE understanding of balance sheets, income statements, and cash flow statements.

DETERMINE whether you need a professional to help you with your record keeping and accounting.

Understand Basic *Accounting*

To run your own business, you will need to know how to read and understand financial statements to determine how well your business is doing. These financial statements are also important when you are trying to raise capital for your business. Some entrepreneurs prepare financial statements themselves. Others hire accountants to prepare these statements for them. Whether or not you prepare these statements yourself, you will need to understand how to read and interpret them.

TYPES OF FINANCIAL STATEMENTS

The balance sheet, the income statement, and the cash flow statement all serve different purposes. You need to know what each statement tells you about the condition of your business.

The Balance Sheet

In Chapter 7, you learned a balance sheet is a financial statement that lists what a business owns, what it owes, and how much it is worth *at a particular point in time.* It does so by identifying a business's assets, liabilities, and owner's equity. **Owner's equity** is the difference between assets and liabilities.

The balance sheet is based on an equation called the accounting equation. This financial statement is called a balance sheet because the two sides of the accounting equation must always be in balance. This means that

Assets = Liabilities + Owner's Equity

The Income Statement

An income statement shows how a business performed *over a period of time,* usually a year. It shows a business's revenues, expenses, and profits. An income statement can be used to:

1. Examine how sales, expenses, and income are changing over time.
2. Forecast how well your business can expect to perform in the future.
3. Analyze your costs to determine where you may need to cut back.
4. Identify categories of expenditures you may want to increase or decrease, such as advertising.

The income statement consists of four main parts: revenue, cost of goods sold, operating expenses, and net profit before taxes.

REVENUE The dollar value of the goods or services a business gives to customers over a certain period is **sales.** Sales is what drives your revenue. Revenue includes sales for which you received payment and sales that you have made but have not yet been paid for.

Janet Wiskowski owns The Framing Place. Last year Janet sold $41,000 worth of custom frames, $34,000 worth of packaged frames, and $8,000 worth of prints and posters. Her total sales were $83,000.

COST OF GOODS SOLD The cost of the inventory a business sells during a particular period is called **cost of goods sold.** Only businesses that have inventory have a cost of goods sold. This means most service businesses do not have this expense.

Janet's cost of goods sold on the custom frames was $24,000. The cost of goods sold on the packaged frames was $21,000. The cost of goods sold on the prints and posters was $5,000. Totalling these three categories, Janet's total cost of goods sold was $50,000.

$24,000 + $21,000 + $5,000 = $50,000

In Class Activity

In small groups, create an imaginary income statement for a service business. Have one group member present your income statement to the rest of the class.

OPERATING EXPENSES The expenses necessary to operate a business are **operating expenses.** They include salaries, rent, advertising, and utilities. All businesses pay operating expenses.

Janet spent $14,000 on salaries, $6,000 on rent, $1,400 on advertising, and $1,200 on utilities last year. She also paid $400 in other expenses. Janet had $23,000 in total operating expenses last year.

$14,000 + $6,000 + $1,400 + $1,200 + $400 = $23,000

NET PROFIT BEFORE TAXES Net profit before taxes is the amount remaining after the cost of goods sold and operating expenses are subtracted from your sales. It shows how much you earned before taxes have to be paid.

Janet's cost of goods sold was $50,000 and her operating expenses were $23,000. Subtracting these sums from her total sales of $83,000 leaves net profits before taxes of $10,000.

$83,000 − $50,000 − $23,000 = $10,000

 **CHECKPOINT** What are the four parts of the income statement?

Entrepreneurial Timeline

| 1800 | 1865 | 1930 | 1995 |

An Empire Built on Soap and Candles

In 1837, two men settled in Cincinnati, Ohio. The two met when they married a pair of sisters, and their new father-in-law suggested they become partners. And that's how the business of William Proctor and James Gamble was begun. Proctor & Gamble started out making candles and soap. By 1859, sales had reached one million dollars. P&G was a pioneer in market research. Marketing campaigns for the company's products, including radio "soap operas," helped consumer demand grow so much, the company began setting up manufacturing plants in other cities. Over the years, the company has expanded its product line and now has international offices in more than 70 countries.

The Cash Flow Statement

A **cash flow statement** is an accounting report that describes the cash that flows in and out of a business. For many businesses, it is the most important of the three basic financial statements. This is because the cash flow statement shows how much money you have.

As discussed in Chapter 7, an income statement is different from a cash flow statement. A cash flow statement deals with actual cash coming in and going out. An income statement deals with revenues and expenses you have incurred but may not have yet received or paid out.

Net cash flow is the difference between cash receipts and disbursements.

Cash receipts − Disbursements = Net cash flow

Cash receipts include cash sales, accounts receivable that have been collected, tax refunds, and loans. *Disbursements* include payments made to cover your payroll, equipment, supplies, materials, rent, utilities, loan repayments, tax payments, and other expenses.

POSITIVE OR NEGATIVE CASH FLOW If cash receipts are greater than disbursements, your business has a positive cash flow. You can put this money in the bank or use it to expand your business. If cash disbursements are greater than cash receipts, your business has a negative cash flow. You won't be able to pay bills. You will either have to borrow money or ask your creditors to give you more time to pay.

 **CHECKPOINT** Explain why the three financial statements are important.

Many small businesses use professionals to help them keep their records and prepare their financial statements. Accounting assistants or certified public accountants can help you with accounting records.

An accounting assistant is a staff employee who records business transactions. Accounting assistants work with journals, ledgers, tax records, and payroll records, and keep them all up to date.

CERTIFIED PUBLIC ACCOUNTANT Many entrepreneurs use certified public accountants (CPAs). CPAs are accountants who have passed a series of demanding accounting examinations. They are licensed by the state in which they work. Because they have more training than accounting assistants, they are more expensive to use.

Having a CPA prepare your financial statements may make sense if you are not familiar with accounting procedures. Your CPA will prepare your statements in compliance with generally accepted accounting principles. Your CPA can also help you prepare your tax return and offer you advice on the financial management of your business.

 **CHECKPOINT** Why do some businesses hire accounting professionals?

THINK CRITICALLY

1. Would it be a good idea to look at your balance sheet and your income statement every few days? Why or why not?

2. Green Golf Course has a positive cash flow six months of the year. What should the owner do with the extra cash during these months?

3. If you decide to hire the services of a CPA, what criteria would you use to decide among candidates for the position?

MAKE CONNECTIONS

4. **MATH** In May, Green Golf Course had receipts of $22,200 for greens fees, $18,250 for cart fees, $2,500 for merchandise, and $2,740 for snacks. What were total sales for May?

5. **MATH** June sales at Green Golf Course were 25 percent more than May sales. If cost of goods sold was $2,500 and other operating expenses were $8,600, what was the net profit before taxes?

Track *Your* Inventory

Most businesses have to keep the products they sell in stock as a convenience to their customers. To avoid running out of items your customers want to buy, you will need to use a tracking method to keep a careful eye on your stock. You will also need to manage your inventory by determining how much you can afford to keep in stock at any given time.

TRACK YOUR INVENTORY

Inventory is the stock of goods a business has for sale. Every business must track inventory levels. Tracking your inventory can be done in two different ways. You can use the perpetual inventory method or the periodic inventory method. Regardless of the inventory method you use, you will need to take a physical inventory at least once or twice a year.

Perpetual Inventory Method

The **perpetual inventory method** keeps track of inventory levels on a daily basis. This method can make your business more efficient. It can also ensure that you never run out of stock. This method uses stock cards or a computer to keep track of the inventory you have. A **stock card** is a paper record for a single item. Many entrepreneurs do not use stock cards any longer. It is much easier and faster to keep inventory records in an electronic format. Regardless of whether you use stock cards or a computer to track your inventory, you should record the following items:

- a description of the item
- a stock number for identification purposes
- any receipts of inventory, the number of units received, and the date of the transaction
- any sales of inventory, the number of units sold, and the date of the transaction
- the amount of inventory you currently have
- the minimum amount you want to keep in inventory, often referred to as the *reorder point*. When inventory reaches this number, you should place an order to receive more units.
- the maximum amount you want in inventory at any time

Lei Woo owns a toy store. Lei uses her computer to track inventory levels on a daily basis. She makes a list of items that are at the reorder point, then creates a low stock report. That report shows which items she needs to reorder. It also shows how many units of each item Lei needs to order so that she can restock to the maximum level.

LOW STOCK REPORT				
ITEM	STOCK NUMBER	MAXIMUM	REORDER POINT	NEED TO ORDER
Building blocks	Q323	15	7	8
Doll houses	K393	4	2	2
Playing cards	S222	25	12	13
Stickers	S494	50	20	30

USE A COMPUTER Businesses that sell hundreds of items usually use a computer to track inventory. You will need to purchase special software that connects your electronic cash registers to your computers. Every time a sale is made, the register deducts the item sold from your inventory. It automatically calculates a new balance.

Take a Physical Inventory

Your actual inventory may differ from that listed in your perpetual inventory system. The difference can be caused by many things, such as failure to record sales, theft, or damage to merchandise. Taking a physical inventory means counting the number of items you have in stock. You will take a physical inventory at least once or twice a year. To take a physical inventory, you will need to record the date on which you are taking the inventory, the stock number of the item, a description of each item, and the actual number of units in stock.

At least two people should be involved in taking a physical inventory. One person should count the items on your shelves while the other records the information found. This information can later be entered in a spreadsheet for easy use.

Putting your inventory records into a computer spreadsheet is a good idea.

Periodic Inventory Method

Some businesses use the **periodic inventory method.** This method involves taking a physical inventory of your merchandise. That inventory will tell you how many units of each item remain in stock. You can then compare your inventory figure to the maximum figures listed on your low stock report to determine how many units of each item you need to order.

Businesses that use the periodic inventory method take their inventory frequently. Some check it weekly. Others check it monthly.

ECKPOINT **Describe the two different inventory tracking methods.**

The level of inventory you keep in stock depends on three factors:
- the cost of carrying inventory
- the cost of losing a sale because you are out of stock
- the frequency with which you sell your inventory

Costs of Carrying Inventory

Holding inventory can be very costly. These costs are known as *carrying costs.* A business with inventory will always have carrying costs. But carrying costs can become too high if you have too much inventory. Costs can increase due to:

According to the U.S. Department of Commerce, holding inventory can cost you as much as 25 percent of the cost of the inventory itself.

- **Obsolescence.** Inventory can be held too long and become old and outdated. People do not want to buy a computer made two years ago. You may be stuck with merchandise you can't sell.
- **Deterioration.** Inventory can deteriorate, forcing you to throw it away or sell it at a discount. If you own a garden store, some plants will need to be sold within a few weeks because they will begin to die.
- **Interest fees.** Suppliers charge interest on money due to them. If you cannot pay your suppliers until you sell your inventory, you will incur an extra expense.
- **Insurance.** You may have to carry insurance against theft, fire, or other problems.
- **Storage.** Inventory takes up space. If you run out of room, you will need to lease additional space.

Costs of Being Out of Stock

Being out of stock can cost you money because if you have nothing to sell, you lose sales. You may also lose customer loyalty due to out-of-stock situations. You will need to weigh the costs of being out of stock with the costs of carrying more inventory.

Stuart Alton owns a rug store. Last week, a young couple came into his store to buy a $700 area rug. Unfortunately, Stuart was out of stock on the rug. The couple left the store without making a purchase.

Turnover Rates

A supermarket might sell hundreds of cans of soft drinks every day but only twelve jars of marmalade. The **stock turnover rate** is the rate at which inventory of a product is sold and replaced with new inventory. It shows how many times a year you sell all of your merchandise. A store that purchases inventory four times a year and sells all of its inventory in that same year has a stock turnover rate of 4.

Stock turnover rates vary from industry to industry. You should contact the trade association for your industry or talk to other entrepreneurs in your field to find out the turnover rate for the items you inventory.

DETERMINING INVENTORY Turnover rates can help you determine how much inventory to keep in stock. To find out how many months of inventory you should keep in stock, divide 12 (the number of months in a year) by the stock turnover rate.

Brad Wilson owns a retail store. The stock turnover rate in his industry is 6. This means that he needs to keep two months worth of inventory in stock at all times.

Months in year ÷ Stock turnover rate = Months of inventory to stock
$$12 \div 6 = 2$$

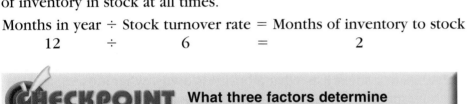

CHECKPOINT **What three factors determine the amount of inventory you keep in stock?**

THINK CRITICALLY

1. What do you think are the benefits of using the periodic inventory method? The perpetual method?

2. Do you think you could still manage your inventory well if you did not know the turnover rate for a product? Why or why not?

MAKE CONNECTIONS

3. COMMUNICATION Using the perpetual inventory method, create an inventory tracking report on the computer for at least five inventory items a grocery store would carry.

4. RESEARCH Find out the stock turnover rate for five products of your choice. Write a short report, including where you found your information, what industry the product belongs to, and an example of a store that might inventory that product.

Review

CHAPTER SUMMARY

Set Up a
Record Keeping
System

1. Journals are accounting records of the transactions you make. Accurate journals help you keep track of how much money you have earned, how much you have spent, and how much profit you've made. Journals separate accounting records by type.
2. Ledgers separate accounting records by account. Ledgers make it easy to view any one account for your business.
3. Other types of records you will keep are bank statements, payroll records, and tax records.
4. You can use computers to handle your record keeping. An advantage of computerizing your record keeping is that it is very efficient. A disadvantage is that employees may not feel comfortable using a computer.

Understand Basic
Accounting

5. A balance sheet lists what a business owns, what it owes, and how much it is worth at a particular point in time.
6. An income statement shows how a business performed over a period of time. Included in an income statement are sales, cost of goods sold, operating expenses, and net profit before taxes.
7. A cash flow statement shows the cash that flows in and out of a business. This statement will help you determine whether you have a positive or negative cash flow.
8. Some businesses hire professionals to help keep records. You can hire an accounting assistant or a certified public accountant.

Track *Your*
Inventory

9. You can track inventory using the perpetual inventory method or the periodic inventory method.
10. There are costs associated with keeping inventory. To help manage your inventory, you should find out the stock turnover rate for your inventoried items and determine how many months of inventory you should keep on hand.

What Do You Know Now?

Read *Build a Business* again. Then answer the questions a second time. How have your responses changed?

VOCABULARY BUILDER

Choose the term that best fits the definition. Write your answers on a separate sheet of paper.

1. A business activity that changes assets, liabilities, or net worth
2. A list of people who receive salary or wage payments from a business
3. Copying information from a journal entry to a ledger account
4. Book in which you record the dates, amounts, and names of people or businesses to whom you have written checks
5. The difference between assets and liabilities
6. Cost of the inventory a business sells during a particular period
7. Accounting report that describes the cash that flows in and out of a business
8. The difference between cash receipts and disbursements
9. The stock of goods a business has for sale
10. Rate at which inventory of a product is sold and replaced with new inventory
11. Expenses necessary to operate a business
12. Keeps track of inventory levels on a daily basis

a. account
b. cash flow statement
c. check register
d. cost of goods sold
e. inventory
f. net cash flow
g. operating expenses
h. owner's equity
i. payroll
j. periodic inventory method
k. perpetual inventory method
l. posting
m. sales
n. stock card
o. stock turnover rate
p. transaction

REVIEW YOUR KNOWLEDGE

13. What is the purpose of maintaining accounting journals?

14. What are the five types of journals that businesses keep?

15. Why do some businesses use computers for record keeping?

16. What are the three types of financial statements?

17. Why do some small businesses use professionals to help them keep records and prepare financial statements?

18. Describe the two methods of managing inventory.

19. Why should business owners take physical inventory from time to time?

20. Why is holding inventory costly?

APPLY WHAT YOU LEARNED

21. You plan to open a retail sportswear store. What types of journals do you need to keep for such a business? Why? What kinds of bank, payroll, and tax records will you have to maintain? Which type of inventory method will you use? Why? How will you use a computer to help you keep and manage your records?

22. You are planning to start a hospital supply business. What would be the advantages of using a computer program to handle your record keeping? Do you think it is necessary to hire a CPA for this business? What are the carrying costs for this type of business? What would be the advantage of using an electronic perpetual inventory system?

THINK CRITICALLY

23. What are some of the ways that incomplete or inaccurate record keeping can affect a business? What types of decisions do business owners have to make based on their records? Why do you think entrepreneurs need separate bank accounts for their businesses?

24. Do you think you still need a basic understanding of accounting, if accounting professionals help you with your business? What is the difference between the balance sheet and the income statement? Can a business owner prepare one without preparing the other? Why or why not?

25. What inventory method do you think supermarkets use? Why do you think they use this method? Can you think of businesses that sell goods but do not need to keep inventory? What are some of the ways to reduce your inventory carrying costs?

MAKE CONNECTIONS

26. **MATH** You own a bookstore. The stock turnover rate in the bookstore business is four. How many months worth of inventory must you keep on hand?

27. **COMMUNICATION** You own a kitchen equipment store with a partner. You would like to use a computer to track inventory, but your partner is resisting. Write a letter to your partner with a proposal to implement a new inventory system. What reasons will you give for using a computerized system? How will you convince your partner to implement the plan?

28. **MATH** You own a pet-supply business. Last year you sold $42,000 in dog food and $53,000 in cat food. The cost of goods sold on the dog food was $13,000, and the cost of goods sold on the cat food

was $14,000. Operating expenses for the business were $4,500 for rent, $13,000 for salaries, and $900 for advertising. What is your net profit before taxes?

29. **RESEARCH** For each business listed below, contact the appropriate trade association and at least two business owners to find out what the stock turnover rate is. A. Supermarket, B. Jewelry store, C. Car dealership, D. Office supply store, E. Computer store. Was the information you collected from each source the same? If not, why do you think there was a variation?

This Is Your Business Project

1. Determine what types of journals you will keep for your business. For each type give an example of a transaction that will be recorded in that journal. What accounts will your business have? If your business collects sales tax, find out what the rate is in your state or county.

2. Contact two local banks and obtain information about commercial checking accounts. What are the rates? What types of special services or products are offered to small business owners?

3. Create a payroll register for your business. Contact your state and/or county government to find out what taxes (and the rates of each) must be deducted from employees' pay. Are there any other deductions that will be made?

4. If your business has inventory, list all of the items you will have in inventory and your cost for each. Using the perpetual inventory method, create an inventory tracking report for your business. How did you determine your reorder point? What inventory carrying costs are relevant to your business? How can you reduce your carrying costs?

5. What are the operating expenses for your business? List all of your operating expenses on an annual basis. Estimate your first year sales. What do you estimate your net profit before taxes to be for your first year of business?

6. Contact three CPAs and ask about the services they offer to small business owners. Do they prepare taxes and offer financial advice? What are the charges for these services? Do you think your business will need the help of a professional accountant? Why or why not?

Chapter 12
FINANCIAL
MANAGEMENT

LESSONS

12.1 Manage Your Cash Flow

12.2 Analyze Your Financial Performance

12.3 Hire Experts

BUILD A BUSINESS

Financing and Web Pages

Alex and Leo had their own web design business. They were always very busy, but for some reason, they didn't seem to be making any money. Some weeks they could barely pay themselves for their work.

"Leo," Alex said, "We need someone to take a look at our business and give us some advice."

"Let's go visit Dr. Mori," suggested Leo. "One of my friends has taken some of her accounting courses. She might be willing to take a look at our financial records and give us some advice."

Alex and Leo contacted Dr. Mori and made an appointment for the next day. When they arrived at Dr. Mori's office, Alex and Leo explained a little about their business and showed her their business records. Dr. Mori asked, "When do you require payment for your work?"

Alex answered, "We don't really have a set time for people to pay us. Most of our customers are students like us, and they don't always have a lot of cash on hand."

"That can be a problem," Dr. Mori advised. "If you are going to perform services for people you need to be sure you get paid promptly. You might consider charging a 50 percent deposit before you begin a web page and then full payment before you upload it. You could even give a discount for full payment before you start. You might also look for some professional clients."

"Those are good suggestions," Leo said.

"What kind of expenses do you have?" Dr. Mori asked.

"Our biggest expenses are our computers. We need to keep them up-to-date," Alex responded.

"And our online service charges run pretty high," Leo added.

"You need to construct a cash budget," Dr. Mori told them. "A cash budget will help you know when to expect a cash shortage and when you might have a surplus that you could use for expanding or upgrading your business."

"We could do that with a spreadsheet program," Alex thought.

"You also need to consider your break-even point," Dr. Mori continued. "This will tell you how many web pages you have to complete before you make a profit."

"We need to know that," Leo agreed. "Obviously we haven't reached that point yet!"

"Alex and Leo, you made a wise decision by looking for outside help with your financial management. I wish you good luck and hope that you will call on me again in the future."

What Do You Know?

1. What would be the advantage for Alex and Leo if they give a discount for full payment of web pages before they begin working?
2. How do you think Alex and Leo could reach their break-even point more quickly without increasing the number of web pages created?
3. In addition to an accountant, who are some other professionals that small business owners might look to for assistance?

GOALS

CREATE a cash budget.

IMPROVE your business's cash flow.

Manage Your Cash *Flow*

As the owner of your own business, you will need to make sure that you have enough cash to cover your expenses. To do so, you will have to create a cash budget. You will also have to learn how to manage your cash flow.

CREATE A CASH BUDGET

As you learned earlier in this text, the cash flow statement is the single most important financial statement you will deal with. It shows you how much money you have available to pay your bills.

Construct a Cash Budget

A cash budget should show the projections of your cash coming in and out, but it should be based on actual past revenue and operating expenses to ensure accuracy. A cash budget looks very similar to a cash flow statement, but it has slight differences. Three columns are used to show the estimated cash flow, the actual cash flow, and the difference between the two. This information can help you budget your resources. If your cash budget shows you will be short of cash in six months, you can begin arranging financing or generating capital now. If your cash budget shows you will have a surplus of cash two years from now, you might use that information in planning how to expand your business.

Total cash receipts, disbursements, and net cash can be shown on the cash budget itself. You can also show these totals on a separate summary form.

USE AN ELECTRONIC SPREADSHEET Just a few decades ago, constructing cash flow spreadsheets was time consuming. Today, however, many businesses use electronic spreadsheets (see Chapter 13). These computer programs automatically perform calculations on the figures you provide. This allows you to examine changes in your cash flow.

Mark Matson owns a snow removal business, which he runs from his home. He uses an electronic spreadsheet to create a budget for the first three months of the coming year. In his first month, Mark's receipts were higher than he anticipated. But so were his expenses. Even so, Mark came out ahead in his overall net cash amount.

CASH BUDGET MATSON PLOWERS Month One, 20—

	A	B	C	D
		Estimated	Actual	Difference
1	**Cash receipts**	**$14,000**	**$18,000**	**$4,000**
2	Cash sales	$2,000	$4,000	$2,000
3	Accounts receivable payments	$11,150	$13,150	$2,000
4	Tax refund	$850	$850	$0
5	Total cash receipts	$14,000	$18,000	$4,000
6	**Cash disbursements**	**$8,300**	**10,125**	**−$1,825**
7	Salaries	$4,500	$5,500	−$1,000
8	Gasoline	$2,500	$3,125	−$625
9	Vehicle maintenance	$350	$400	−$50
10	Utilities	$50	$50	$0
11	Advertising	$150	$300	−$150
12	Insurance	$500	$500	$0
13	Other	$250	$250	$0
14	Total cash disbursements	$8,300	$10,125	$1,825
15	**Net cash increase/decrease**	**$5,700**	**$7,875**	**$2,175**

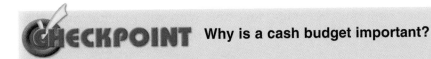

CHECKPOINT Why is a cash budget important?

IMPROVE YOUR CASH FLOW

If your cash receipts will not cover your expenses, you will need to take action to improve your cash flow. You can increase cash receipts, decrease disbursements, or perform both actions.

Increase Your Cash Receipts

One way to improve your cash receipts is to decrease your accounts receivable by getting customers who owe you money to pay more quickly. To encourage faster payment:

- Offer discounts on bills paid right away.

- Establish tighter credit policies (decrease the amount of time your customers have to pay their bills from 60 days to 30 days).

- Establish a follow-up system for collecting unpaid accounts receivable. Consider contacting a collection agency, which will track down customers who owe you money.

- Hold shipments to customers with large unpaid bills, or insist that such orders be paid in advance.

In Class Activity

In small groups, brainstorm expenses, such as advertising, that can be cut in the short term to improve a business's cash flow.

Two businesses with the same level of sales and expenses may have very different cash flows. One business may have a positive cash flow, while the other may have a negative cash flow and be unable to cover its expenses. The difference may reflect a different pattern of cash receipts.

INCREASE YOUR CAPITAL Businesses can have cash flow problems if they start off with too little capital. If your cash flow is inadequate, you may want to try to obtain more capital for your business. This means taking out a loan, financing your business with your own money, or finding investors who will provide you with capital in return for a share of your future profits.

Reduce Your Disbursements

Another way of improving your business's cash flow is to reduce your disbursements. This can be done by gaining better control over your inventory and payroll, slowing the rate at which you pay your bills, or reducing your expenses.

CONTROL INVENTORY AND PAYROLL Two large categories of expenses over which you have some control are inventory and payroll. Reducing these expenses will improve your cash flow.

You know that carrying inventory is costly. If your business has cash flow problems, check to make sure that you are not holding too much inventory. Reducing your inventory will reduce your accounts payable because you will not be purchasing as much. This will improve your cash flow.

Reducing your payroll can also improve your cash flow. One way of reducing your payroll is to reduce the size of your work force, either by laying off workers or by reducing the number of hours employees work each week.

Payroll is one disbursement you can control.

SLOW BILL PAYMENT Your suppliers probably offer credit terms. This means that they may agree to accept payment at a later date if you pay interest charges. If your cash flow needs to be improved, you may want to consider taking advantage of the longest possible credit terms your suppliers will give you or charging your purchases on a credit card.

Mark Matson usually pays cash for the gasoline and oil he needs to power his snowplows. But in December, his expenses are particularly high and cash receipts are low. In this month, he charges his expenses to his credit card. By delaying payment until the following month, Mark improves his cash flow in December. When the credit card bill comes in January, he will have received payment from his customers for the work he did in December and won't have any problems paying the bill.

CUT OTHER EXPENSES Some expenses, such as rent, are fixed, at least in the short term. You can't reduce them. You do have control over other categories of costs, however, such as advertising. Reducing special expenses will improve your cash flow.

 **CHECKPOINT** What are some ways you can improve your cash flow?

THINK CRITICALLY

1. How will constructing a cash budget using an electronic spreadsheet make this financial report more helpful to an entrepreneur?

2. What are the disadvantages of using the longest possible credit terms offered by suppliers?

MAKE CONNECTIONS

3. **MATH** Margot Belville, owner of Flowers on Main, projects the following cash receipts and disbursements. Based on these amounts, what would her projected net cash flow be for each quarter?

	Quarter 1	Quarter 2	Quarter 3	Quarter 4
Cash receipts	$52,000	$48,000	$42,000	$60,000
Cash disbursements	$24,000	$22,000	$21,000	$31,000

4. **PROBLEM SOLVING** If your business were experiencing a negative cash flow, how might you use the six-step problem-solving model to help you?

Analyze Your *Financial* Performance

Your financial statements can tell you a lot about how your business is performing. You have to be able to understand and analyze these statements to determine how well you're doing. You will also need to know how to use the information in your statements to determine the level of sales you need to achieve to earn a profit.

ANALYZE FINANCIAL STATEMENTS

Businesses keep many kinds of records and create different kinds of financial statements. Your records and statements can help you analyze your sales and profits, as well as set and meet profit goals.

Analyze Your Sales

Your sales records show sales trends and patterns. You can use these records to forecast future sales and make good business decisions.

ANALYZE SALES BY PRODUCT Analyzing your sales by product can help you make decisions about the kind of inventory to stock. It can help you increase sales and profits.

Emily Lee owns a garden and patio store. Her store has four departments: outdoor furniture, outdoor grills, plants, and garden tools. Emily's sales figures show that almost 57 percent of her annual sales come from the outdoor furniture department.

$$\text{Sales of outdoor furniture} \div \text{Total sales} = \text{Percent of sales}$$
$$\$110,000 \div \$194,000 = 56.7\%$$

DEPARTMENTAL SALES • LEE GARDEN AND PATIO

Department	Sales	Percent of total
Outdoor furniture	$110,000	56.7
Outdoor grills	37,000	19.0
Plants	24,000	12.4
Garden tools	23,000	11.9
Total	$194,000	100

The plant department accounts for only a little over 12 percent of sales. Based on these data, Emily decides to reduce the size of the plant department and increase her inventory of outdoor furniture.

Analyze Net Profit on Sales

Your income statement shows whether or not your business is earning a profit. It also tells you how profitable your business is. This information can be very useful in helping you set and meet profit goals.

The rate of profit a business earns is often shown as the ratio of its net profit to its sales. This ratio is calculated by dividing net income after taxes by net sales.

Net income after taxes ÷ Net sales = Net profit on sales

In order to calculate net profit on sales, a business must first perform math calculations to determine net income after taxes and net sales. All of these calculations are found on the income statement.

CALCULATE NET SALES Jack Hendrick owns a retail store that sells automotive supplies. He wants to find out his net profit on sales. First he must determine his gross sales and net sales. **Gross sales** is the dollar amount of all sales, including returns. **Net sales** is the dollar amount of all sales after returns have been subtracted. Jack sold $235,000 worth of merchandise and had $3,200 worth of merchandise returned. Therefore his net sales amount is $231,800.

Gross sales − Returns = Net sales
$235,000 − $3,200 = $231,800

**CHECKPOINT** How do you analyze sales by product? What is the difference between gross sales and net sales?

HENDRICK'S AUTOMOTIVE SUPPLY
INCOME STATEMENT   YEAR 20—

Revenue from sales	
Gross sales	$235,000
Less returns	3,200
Net sales	231,800
Cost of goods sold	150,000
Gross profit	81,800
Operating expenses	
Salaries	26,200
Advertising	1,200
Rent	8,400
Utilities	1,800
Insurance	1,300
Other	1,000
Total expenses	39,900
Net income from operations	41,900
Less interest expense	2,400
Net income before taxes	39,500
Less income tax paid	12,245
Net income after taxes	27,255

CALCULATE NET INCOME AFTER TAXES

Three calculations must be performed to enable you to determine your net income after taxes. You must calculate:

- Gross profit
- Net income from operations
- Net income before taxes

Gross profit is profit before operating expenses are deducted. Last year, Jack spent $150,000 for merchandise that he sold. This amount represents his *cost of goods sold*. Jack subtracts his cost of goods sold from his net sales to find his gross profit.

Net sales − Cost of goods sold = Gross profit
$231,800 − $150,000   = $81,800

Jack's operating expenses include rent, salaries, and similar business expenses. Last year his operating costs were $39,900. Gross profit minus operating expenses equals **net income from operations.**

Gross profit − Operating expenses = Net income from operations
$81,800   − $39,900   = $41,900

To calculate net income before taxes, Jack has to subtract one more expense that has not yet been taken into account: interest on loans he has taken out. Last year, Jack paid $2,400 in interest. He subtracts this from his net income from operations to get his net income before taxes. If a company has no additional expenses, the net income from operations equals the net income before taxes.

Net income from operations − Interest expense = Net income before taxes
$41,900   − $2,400   = $39,500

To compute his after-tax income, Jack subtracts the amount he paid in income tax last year, $12,245, from his net income before taxes. This gives him his net income after taxes for his automotive supply business.

Net income before taxes − Income tax paid = Net income after taxes
$39,500   − $12,245   = $27,255

WHY NET PROFIT ON SALES IS IMPORTANT Using the net profit on sales ratio, Jack determines that his profits represented 11.8 percent of his net sales.

Net income after taxes ÷ Net sales = Net profit on sales
$27,255   ÷ $231,800 =   0.118

Jack can use this figure to assess his profits in two ways. First, he can compare his profit ratio this year with his profit ratio in previous years. If his profit ratio has declined, his business has become less profitable. If the ratio has increased, his business has become more profitable. Jack can also compare his profit ratio with average profit ratios in his industry. If his ratio is lower than the industry average, he may want to figure out what he can do to improve his profitability.

Set and Meet Profit Goals

To run your business effectively, you will need to set profit goals. These goals will reflect the amount of profit you hope to earn from your business during a particular year.

Jack Hendrick would like to increase his profit ratio to 15 percent. He decides to try to increase his sales and reduce his expenses. He begins a frequent-buyer program and offers discounts on bulk purchases. Jack will talk to suppliers in the hopes of reducing his cost of goods sold.

Jack would like to increase his profits even more by opening several more stores. He hopes that purchasing his inventory in large quantities will lower his costs significantly.

 **CHECKPOINT** **Name and describe the three calculations that must be completed to determine net income after taxes.**

Entrepreneurial Timeline

1800   1850   1900   1950

More Than Gold in California

During the California Gold Rush, thousands of would-be millionaires traveled across North America to see if they could find their fortune. However, you might be surprised to know that many entrepreneurs made their money without even panning the rivers for gold. There were many business opportunities for creative entrepreneurs. Women offered cooking and cleaning services, or ran hotels and boarding houses. Diaries document women earning a hundred dollars a week washing clothes, $25 a plate for dinner, and $200 a week running boarding houses.

Men were also able to cash in without becoming miners. One thoughtfully bought up all the carpet tacks in California, successfully cornering the market. He was able to ask high prices from buyers. And did you know that one man stitched up the first pair of canvas pants and sold them to miners? His name was Levi Strauss. There were definitely lots of people who used their shovels to get rich during the Gold Rush. But there was also an equal number of people who used their wits and thought of creative ways to make money in 1848 and 1849.

You can determine how increased sales affect your profits by conducting break-even analysis and identifying your break-even point. The **break-even point** is the volume of sales that must be made to cover all of the expenses of a business. Below the break-even point, your expenses will exceed your revenues and you will be losing money. Once you reach the break-even point, your sales will equal all of your expenses. This means that at this level of sales, you will neither make nor lose money. Once you exceed the break-even point, you will begin to earn profits.

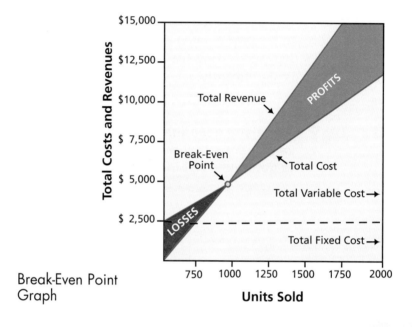

Break-Even Point Graph

Measure Costs, Sales, and Profits

In order to calculate your break-even point, you will have to know your total fixed costs, your selling price per unit, and your variable cost per unit. You also will have to know the level of your sales.

Businesses have fixed and variable costs. Fixed costs remain the same regardless of how many units you sell. Variable costs go up or down, depending on your level of sales.

Charlene Mason owns a small manufacturing business that produces refrigerator door magnets. The total variable cost of producing magnets varies depending on her level of sales at any given time. She must figure out her current variable costs in order to determine the break-even point. She totals her cost of goods, salaries she pays to employees, and advertising costs. She then divides this number by 30,000, the number of magnets she makes each year. Her variable cost per unit is $0.95.

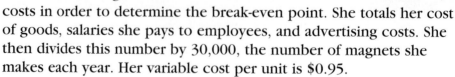

Total variable costs ÷ Number of units = Variable cost per unit
$28,500 ÷ 30,000 = $0.95

Calculate Your Break-Even Point

The break-even point shows the volume of sales you need to reach to earn a profit. If your sales are below the break-even point, you will not earn a profit and will have to increase your prices, increase the quantity you sell, or reduce your costs. The formula for calculating the break-even point is

$$\frac{\text{Total fixed costs}}{\text{Selling price per unit} - \text{Variable cost per unit}} = \text{Break-even point}$$

Charlene's fixed costs are $40,000 a year. Her selling price is $3.50 per unit. Her variable cost is $0.95 per unit. Using these numbers in the formula, she gets

$$\frac{\$40,000}{\$3.50 - \$0.95} = 15,686 \text{ units}$$

If she sells 15,686 magnets, she will break even. If she sells more, she will earn a profit. If she sells fewer, she will not cover her expenses and will lose money.

CHECKPOINT What does the break-even point indicate?

THINK CRITICALLY

1. Which goals do you think are more important to meet: sales goals or profit goals? Explain your answer.

2. What is the importance of knowing the break-even point for your business?

MAKE CONNECTIONS

3. MATH Marlo Castille owns Castille Imports. The business had $52,200 in sales of 2,088 porcelain vases one quarter. How much did she charge for each vase?

4. MATH If the variable cost per vase is $2.90, total fixed costs are $25,056, and sales were the same as in exercise 3, what is Castille Imports' break-even point for porcelain vases?

Hire *Experts*

You will handle many aspects of running your business yourself. Only you can find the perfect location for your business. Only you can decide which products to offer. Other aspects of your business may be better handled by a professional. Using a person who is specially trained to create your financial statements or who can give you financial advice may be good for your business.

HIRING A PROFESSIONAL

Many entrepreneurs prefer to let professionals prepare their financial statements and advise them on the financial management of their businesses. Some hire experts because they do not feel comfortable dealing with this aspect of their business themselves. Others simply prefer to devote their time to other aspects of their business. People who spend all of their time dealing with financial statements may be able to offer businesses valuable advice.

Types of Professionals

Various kinds of professionals provide financial management services. They include bankers, attorneys, certified public accountants (CPAs), financial planners, and investment brokers.

BANKERS Bankers can help you read and understand your financial statements. They can help you analyze your balance sheet, income statement, and cash flow statement to come up with ways to increase your profits.

ATTORNEYS Attorneys can provide assistance because they know financial laws. They should also keep you informed of changes in specific laws that could affect your business. For instance, if the government passes a new law for regulating manufacturing businesses, an attorney would be able to discuss the effects of the new regulation on your business.

ACCOUNTANTS As you learned in Chapter 11, many entrepreneurs use certified public accountants (CPAs) to prepare their financial statements. CPAs can also provide financial advice. If you are already using a CPA to prepare your financial statements and you require financial management assistance, it may make sense to turn to your CPA.

FINANCIAL PLANNERS Financial planners are professionals who help individuals and businesses manage their assets. Some financial planners charge an hourly fee for advising their clients. Others charge no fee for their services but earn a commission on any financial services they sell.

INVESTMENT BROKERS Investment brokers will offer you free advice on investing your excess cash. Their income comes from the commission they charge on buying and selling stock for you.

How to Choose a Financial Advisor

Many people will be willing to offer you advice on managing your business's finances. To make sure that you make the right choice in selecting an advisor:

1. *Research financial management so that you are familiar with the issues you need to deal with.* Books and articles can provide important information. Consider taking a course on financial management.
2. *Consult other people in your industry.* Find out if anyone you know can recommend a financial advisor.
3. *Consider choosing a financial advisor who charges a fee, not a commission, for services.* Commissioned salespeople may want to sell you a particular financial service, even if it is not the best service for you.

Reading newspaper articles and contacting people in your industry can help you find the right advisor.

Financial advisors who charge fees are more likely to give you unbiased advice.

 **CHECKPOINT** What professionals provide financial management assistance?

Financial experts can help you with various kinds of planning. These include financial, strategic, and tax planning.

Financial Planning

Financial planning involves analyzing financial statements in order to make decisions about the future. A financial expert can examine your balance sheet, income statement, and cash flow statement. An expert can make recommendations on ways you can increase sales and reduce costs and can also analyze the financial health of your business.

Strategic Planning

Strategic planning involves making decisions that affect your business in the long term. Deciding to enter a new market or offer a wider range of products are examples of strategic decisions.

Professionals who help businesses make these kinds of decisions are called *strategic planners*. Entrepreneurs sometimes hire strategic planners when they want to expand in a new direction.

What Went Wrong

Financial Records

That Takes the Cake

Business: My Just Desserts, New York City * In business, 6 months

When Angela became a widow, she was left with a small insurance benefit, a huge credit card debt, and her 71-year-old mother to support. Angela and her mother moved into the same place to save money. To supplement their income, they began baking Italian cheesecakes at home and selling them to neighborhood restaurants for $20. After just two months, they were selling 48 to 50 cheesecakes each week, making $11 profit on each cake. They were netting about $500 a week. After buying two more ovens, they were baking 130 cakes a week and making a $1,400 weekly gross profit.

Unfortunately, the building manager noticed a spike in the electric bill. He put it together with the constant aroma of cheesecakes and told Angela she couldn't run the business out of the apartment any longer. Angela scrambled to find a storefront to rent, line up commercial ovens, obtain licenses, and get a business loan. However, with no financial records for the business and no real business plan, she couldn't get anywhere. When she finally found a consultant to help her get her business going, most of her customers had turned to established bakeries to meet their needs.

Think Critically
1. Do you think the $20 price for a cheesecake was realistic?
2. How would a potential lender evaluate her $1,400 weekly gross profit?

Tax Planning

Filing your income tax return correctly is very important. If you are not careful, you could end up paying too much or too little tax. Paying too much tax can leave you short on cash. Paying too little tax can cause financial and legal problems.

Most entrepreneurs hire accountants to prepare their tax returns. Accountants who specialize in taxes stay informed of changes in tax laws that affect their clients. They can help you minimize the amount of tax you will have to pay by taking advantage of certain tax laws and incentives. Accountants will also make sure that all tax forms are correctly filled out.

TAX AUDIT The Internal Revenue Service (IRS) randomly selects individuals and businesses to investigate. An IRS investigation of a tax return is an **audit.** If your business is audited, you will have to meet with an IRS agent and explain how you came up with the numbers you included in your tax return. If you have your taxes prepared by a professional tax preparation specialist, such as an accountant, you should ask that person to accompany you when you meet with the IRS agent. Although you will ultimately be responsible for any error that may have been made on your return, the person who prepared your tax return may be better able to explain how the return was prepared.

CHECKPOINT What are some services financial experts provide?

THINK CRITICALLY

1. Do you think it is necessary for entrepreneurs to understand how financial statements are created? Why or why not?

2. For the three types of planning discussed in this lesson (financial, strategic, and tax), tell whether each is an example of long-term, medium-term, or short-term planning.

MAKE CONNECTIONS

3. COMMUNICATION Research one of the three kinds of planning using library or Internet sources. Write a one-page report about what types of services are offered and the typical fees.

4. COMMUNICATION Write an essay about the entrepreneur's role in preparing the company's tax return.

Review

CHAPTER SUMMARY

Manage Your Cash *Flow*

1. A cash budget should show the projections of your cash coming in and out, but it should be based on actual past revenue and operating expenses to ensure accuracy.
2. Cash flow can be improved by increasing your accounts receivable. Discounts on bills paid promptly and tight credit policies can help increase cash receipts.
3. Cash flow can also be increased by reducing disbursements. Inventory, payroll, and bill payment are disbursements that can be controlled to improve cash flow.

Analyze Your *Financial* Performance

4. In order to assess how well a business is doing, financial statements must be analyzed. Sales should be analyzed by product, and net profit on sales must be calculated.
5. In order to calculate net income after taxes, three calculations must be performed first: gross profit, net income before operations, and net income before taxes.
6. To figure out the level of sales needed to achieve to make a profit, the break-even point must be calculated. If sales are below the break-even point, the business is losing money. If sales are above the break-even point, the business is making money.
7. To calculate the break-even point, a business must know its total fixed costs, the selling price of an item, and the variable cost per unit.

Hire *Experts*

8. Some entrepreneurs hire professionals to handle some aspects of the financial management of their businesses. Bankers, accountants, and financial planners can all help a business with its financial management.
9. When selecting a financial advisor, you should be familiar with financial management so you know the issues you will deal with.
10. Professionals can help you with financial planning, strategic planning, and tax planning.

What Do You Know Now?

Read *Build a Business* again. Then answer the questions a second time. How have your responses changed?

VOCABULARY BUILDER

Choose the term that best fits the definition. Write your answers on a separate sheet of paper.

1. An IRS investigation of a tax return
2. Gross profit minus operating expenses
3. Dollar amount of all sales after returns have been subtracted
4. Profit before operating expenses are deducted
5. Volume of sales that must be made to cover all of the expenses of a business
6. Dollar amount of all sales, including returns

a. audit
b. break-even point
c. gross profit
d. gross sales
e. net income from operations
f. net sales

REVIEW YOUR KNOWLEDGE

7. What is the benefit of having a cash budget?

8. What are some of the ways to increase your accounts receivable?

9. What are the three disbursements you can easily control?

10. How can your records and statements help you analyze your sales and profits?

11. Why should you set profit goals for your business?

12. What information do you need to identify in order to calculate your break-even point?

13. What are some of the reasons entrepreneurs hire professionals to prepare financial statements?

14. Why do most entrepreneurs hire accountants to prepare their tax returns?

APPLY WHAT YOU LEARNED

15. You own a hardware store and have a negative cash flow. What are some of the ways you will increase your cash receipts? Which way do you think is best? Why? What are your fixed and variable costs in this business? Do you think you will be able to manipulate these costs to help your cash flow? Why or why not?

16. You want to analyze your sales by product for your hardware store. Your total sales are $140,750. The sales of each department in your store are as shown in the table. What percent of sales does each department generate for your store?

Seasonal merchandise	$25,525
Lumber	$40,211
Tools	$38,524
Lighting	$15,235
Kitchen cabinets	$21,255

THINK CRITICALLY

17. Two businesses with the same level of sales and expenses may have very different cash flows. How is this possible? Why is cash flow so important to a business? Is it possible to have a negative cash flow and still make a profit? Why or why not?

18. What is the relationship between profit and the break-even point? Why is it important for an entrepreneur to conduct a break-even analysis? What are some of the ways that entrepreneurs can change their break-even point?

19. Many entrepreneurs hire financial advisors. What are some of the advantages of hiring a financial professional? What do you think are some of the dangers of making the "wrong" choice in selecting a financial expert? What do you think qualifies a person to be a financial advisor? What qualifications do you think strategic planners need? Why?

20. You want to expand your architecture firm. What kinds of professionals will you hire to help you? What role will each of these professionals play in your expansion? What information do you need to know before hiring each of these professionals? What results will you expect from them?

MAKE CONNECTIONS

21. MATH You own an ice cream shop. Last year you sold 13,500 ice cream cones at $1.25 each. Your variable cost for each ice cream cone is $0.52. Your fixed costs are $7,000. What is your break-even point? What was your profit on ice cream cones last year?

22. **MATH** You own a store that sells CDs, cassettes, computer games, and video tapes. Last year your gross sales were $325,000. Your customers returned $2,300 worth of merchandise. What were your net sales last year? Your cost of goods sold was $215,000. What was your gross profit? Your operating expenses totaled $75,000. What was your net income from operations?

23. **COMMUNICATION** Your business has had a negative cash flow because of a relaxed accounts receivable policy. Write a letter to your customers that outlines your new accounts receivable policy. How will you enforce this policy?

24. **RESEARCH** Using the library, magazines, and the Internet, locate information about financial management of small businesses. What do these articles advise entrepreneurs to be aware of? Contact a local college and obtain information on financial management courses. What are the costs of these courses? Obtain a copy of the syllabus from the professor or department secretary. What material is covered in the class? Do you think this would be a good class for an entrepreneur? Why or why not?

This Is Your Business Project

1. Based on actual revenues and expenses, create a cash budget for your business for the next three months. If possible, use a computer spreadsheet. Using a piece of paper or a word processor, write down the profit goals for your business. Do you need to improve your cash flow to meet those goals? What do you think is your best strategy for improving your cash flow?

2. Analyze your sales by creating a table that lists each of your products and the total sales for each (or estimated sales). What is the percentage of total sales for each product? What changes, if any, will you make to your inventory management based on this information?

3. Perform a break-even analysis for your business. How many units do you need to sell to break even? Is this a feasible number? Why or why not? Can you think of ways to lower the break-even point?

4. Locate and contact two professionals in your area who specialize in strategic planning. What are their credentials? What are their fees? Do you think that either of them would be helpful to your business? Why or why not?

Chapter 13

USE
TECHNOLOGY

LESSONS

13.1 Technology and Your Business

13.2 Learn about the Internet

13.3 Purchase Technology

276

BUILD A BUSINESS

Getting Up to Date

"**B**urt, do you think you could give me a hand?" Katrina asked her son. "I need to update the technology I use in my clothing boutique. I know things have changed since I opened ten years ago. I want to buy computers and other technology that will help me run my business better."

"Sure, Mom. What do you want to talk about first?"

"Truth is, I don't even know where to start."

"Well, Mom, I know you have a computerized cash register. I'm sure that keeps up with your cash and credit card sales each day."

"Yes, it does. I also use it to transmit my credit sales to the bank every day."

"It sounds like you've got that pretty well covered, I wouldn't change that part of your business. So what else do you think technology might help you do?"

"I need a way to communicate with my suppliers quickly. Often I need to get a copy of an invoice to them when there's a discrepancy in what I ordered and what I received."

"All you need for that is a fax machine, Mom," Burt said. "Do you write letters a lot?"

"Two or three a day at least!" Katrina exclaimed.

"Then you should buy a computer and a printer. Along with getting word processing software to write your letters, you could use a spreadsheet to calculate payroll and a database to keep up with your customer information and inventory. You could also use e-mail software to write messages to your suppliers. And, you could use the computer to make advertising fliers for your boutique."

"I knew I kept you around for something!" Katrina kidded her son. "These are great ideas! Okay, now that I know what I want, how do I know what to buy?"

"We should research hardware options by using magazines and newspapers. We might want to talk to some salespeople at computer stores. We should also decide what software programs would benefit your business. It's important to know exactly what you need before you go buying technology."

"Goodness, there is so much to learn!" said Katrina.

"If this is confusing you, Mom, just wait until I start talking about the Internet and all the things it can do for your business! The Internet and the World Wide Web are definitely tools you should take advantage of."

"I guess it's a good thing I have you to help me, huh?"

"Well," Burt said, "computer consultants can help you decide what technology to buy. They charge a fee for their services, so I guess you owe me. . . ."

"Guess again!" Katrina laughed.

What Do You Know?

1. List all of the business uses for word processing, spreadsheet, and database software that you can think of.
2. How could a clothing boutique use the Internet?
3. Why is it important to research computer systems before making a purchase?

Technology and Your Business

Computers have changed the face of business. Tasks that were once performed by hand are now done on computers. These include simple tasks, such as ringing up a sale and calculating income taxes. They also include complicated tasks, such as taking inventory and analyzing profits.

Whether you own a bakery or an automobile dealership, you probably will use a computer and related equipment, such as a printer and a modem.

COMPUTER HARDWARE

Computers used to be huge machines that filled entire rooms. Only corporations and other large institutions, such as banks and insurance companies, used them. But today, millions of people use small but powerful desktop or laptop computers every day. Computers help people create documents, store data, and perform calculations.

Computers and the equipment used with them are known as **computer hardware.** Hardware includes desktop computers, portable computers, printers, and modems.

Desktop Computers

Desktop computers are computers that people use at home or in their offices. Desktop computers are able to fill the needs of almost all small businesses. The type of computer you purchase will depend on the kind of business you own. It will also depend on the ways in which you plan to use computers to run your business. The first decision you will have to make will be to choose between the two basic kinds of computers: personal computers and Macintosh computers.

PERSONAL COMPUTERS Most computers used by businesses and individuals are personal computers (PCs), also known as IBM or IBM-compatible computers. PCs are ideal for most basic needs, such as word processing, electronic spreadsheets, database programs, and Internet access. They can also do more advanced functions, such as graphics and design.

MACINTOSH COMPUTERS Macintosh computers, also known as Macs, are very easy to use and provide excellent graphics options, and are better tools than PCs for this special need. Because of this, Macs are used in companies where graphics and design are a part of business, such as advertising and publishing companies.

Portable Computers

Portable computers, also known as laptop computers, are computers that can be transported easily from place to place. They are generally lightweight and easy to carry. They can be plugged into an electrical outlet and used at a desk or kitchen table. They can also be operated by a battery pack and used on an airplane or at a coffee shop.

Laptop computers are smaller than desktop computers, but they can be very powerful. Both personal computers and Macintosh computers are available in portable models.

ADVANTAGES OF PORTABLE COMPUTERS Portable computers can be used anywhere. This feature makes them useful for people who travel and need their computers while they are away from their places of business.

Thomas Wilson owns a company that creates web sites. He uses his laptop computer on the train every morning as he commutes to his office. The laptop allows him to work wherever and whenever he wants.

DISADVANTAGES OF PORTABLE COMPUTERS Portable computers may be more expensive than desktop computers. They also have smaller keyboards, which makes typing difficult. Portable computer screens are smaller and may not have as clear an appearance as a desktop model. Also, if there isn't a place to plug in your computer and your battery pack is not charged, you cannot access your computer.

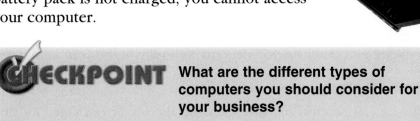

CHECKPOINT What are the different types of computers you should consider for your business?

Printers

To print out the documents you create, you will need to purchase a printer. There are three different kinds of printers available: laser, ink jet, and dot matrix. The printer you choose will depend on how you plan to use the printer and on how much money you want to spend.

NET WORTH

Point your browser to

http://www.ideas-in-action.swep.com

Complete the activity for Chapter 13.

LASER PRINTERS Laser printers are the most popular printer for most types of business. They produce high-quality documents in the fastest time. They come in both black-and-white and color models. Because color printers are more expensive to purchase and to operate, most small businesses use black-and-white printers.

INK JET PRINTERS A popular type of printer for general use is the ink-jet printer. These printers are slower than laser printers but may be less expensive. You can purchase a black-and-white ink-jet printer or a color printer.

DOT MATRIX PRINTERS Dot matrix printers are the least costly printers, but also the slowest. These printers do not produce high-quality documents. However, they are the only printers that can print multi-part forms, such as invoices, which often have several copies.

In Class Activity

In small groups, brainstorm the types of computer hardware the following businesses might need: gift basket business, retail wallpaper store, copy shop, dance studio.

Modems

A **modem** is an electronic device that allows information to be transmitted over telephone lines from one computer to another. You need a modem to access the Internet.

Some computers have modems built into them. Others need to have an external modem installed. High-speed modems allow you to access another computer's information more rapidly. Low-speed modems are slower but cost less.

CHECKPOINT Name the three types of printers and an advantage of each.

COMPUTER SOFTWARE

In order to run, your computer requires software. **Software** refers to the programs that control computer hardware and direct its operation. The software you purchase will depend on how you use your computer.

Types of Software

Software can be custom-made for a specific use or packaged for the mass market. Custom computer programming is very expensive. Larger companies with very special needs generally use custom-built software.

Mass-packaged programs include word processing, spreadsheet, database, and other kinds of programs. Most computers purchased today come with software already loaded on them. You can learn about software by reading the instruction manual, by the online help contained in the software, or by purchasing "how-to" books. Special training centers and colleges also teach people how to use software programs.

WORD PROCESSING PROGRAMS Word processing programs help you process word-based documents, such as business letters and reports. With a word processing program, you can easily make changes to text, create attractive documents, and automatically check and correct spelling. Most word processors also have grammar-checking tools, thesaurus capabilities, graphics options, and more.

SPREADSHEET PROGRAMS Spreadsheet programs enable you to report, analyze, and compile numerical data easily. They also allow you to create graphs of your data. They can be used to prepare budgets, measure performance, and create the kinds of financial statements you learned about in Chapter 11. Spreadsheet programs use formulas to perform basic arithmetic as well as to calculate percentages and complex mathematical formulas.

Spreadsheets are made up of columns and rows. Columns are labeled with letters. Rows are labeled with numbers. Each column letter and row number identifies a grid box, known as a cell. For example, the cell located in column A and row 5 is cell A5.

Jason Waters uses a spreadsheet program to calculate his monthly

	A	B
1	**Expense category**	**Monthly expense**
2	Salaries	$2,150
3	Advertising	$200
4	Rent	$525
5	Utilities	$195
6	Insurance	$50
7	Other	$125
8	Total	$3,245

What Went Wrong

Technology/Internet

Ice-Cold

Business: Sydney's Skiwear, Glens Falls, New York * In business, 4 months

Dick and Lucy Ross ran a few successful ski shops in upstate New York. Ski equipment rental, clothing, and accessories were their main business. When the Internet first began to get big, they eagerly adopted the new technology. They assumed it would be a simple extension to a global marketplace. They hired a web designer, bought computers and servers, and hired an Internet manager. But they were met with an avalanche of challenges.

Dick and Lucy offered more than 150 items online. But it took too long for the images of each item to download, and customers wouldn't wait. Dick and Lucy upgraded their technology and reduced the number of items offered. They also found they needed more staff because every sale involved a 6 to 8 minute phone call to their toll-free number. Dick and Lucy also found that intelligent buying and creative advertising for retail and for the Internet were very different. By the end of winter, their Internet venture was sapping cash flow, focus, and energy from the primary business. Dick and Lucy cut their losses and shut down.

Think Critically

1. Where could Dick and Lucy have invested more money to make the business work: people, technology, or advertising?
2. What alternatives did they have to shutting down the web site?

operating expenses. In the first column, he lists expense categories. In the second column, he enters the amount of each expense. To calculate his total monthly expenses, he adds the six expense categories by entering a formula into cell B8. This formula instructs the program to add cells B2 through B7.

DATABASE PROGRAMS Database programs store, sort, and analyze large volumes of data. These programs are very useful for entrepreneurs with large customer bases. You identify the *fields,* or the information you want to store in your database. Each field contains a certain piece of information. You may want a field for customer name, a field for phone numbers, and a field for entering what a customer has purchased from you. A collection of fields on a particular customer is known as a *record.* All of your records make up your entire database.

Jane Peterson runs a direct-mail business for children's clothing. She keeps a database full of customer information. When she was ready to mail out a catalog, Jane had her database sort out customers who had purchased at least $100 worth of clothing.

CHECKPOINT   List three kinds of software and explain what they do.

MORE TECHNOLOGY FOR YOUR BUSINESS

Technology is always growing. It seems like every day, additional developments are being made to make it even easier to do business.

Additional Software Programs

You have already learned about word processing, spreadsheet, and database software. Other mass-marketed software programs include:

1. *Graphics programs.* These programs make it very easy to design flyers, books, advertisements, and more on a computer screen. The images can be loaded into the graphics program, or they can be created with the help of the program.
2. *Scheduling programs.* Some people prefer to keep their daily schedules electronically. Software of this type can be set up to remind a person when a meeting has been scheduled.
3. *Zip compression utilities.* If you send very large files to other people, this software will condense the files so they can fit easily on floppy disks or be sent via e-mail. The person receiving the file unzips the file to be able to use it.
4. *Presentation software.* This software creates visually appealing presentations for business meetings.

Other Technologies to Consider

There is much more than just computer software and hardware to help you do business more quickly and easily. Some other items you should consider using in your business include:

1. **LCD Projector/Panel.** This device allows you to project your computer screen onto a wall for presentations.
2. **Fax capabilities.** You can use a fax machine or fax software to send hard copies of documents to people who also own a fax.
3. **Photocopier.** Using a photocopier is a fast, efficient way to keep documents for your files or send copies to other people.
4. **Scanner.** Similar to a photocopier, a scanner allows you to copy a document and make it a computer file.
5. **File Transfer Protocol (FTP).** Files can be corrupted when sent over e-mail. FTP allows you to post a file to a computer server, which can then be downloaded by the person who needs it. FTP can only be accessed if you know the server name and password.

 **CHECKPOINT** What other technological items might you use in business?

THINK CRITICALLY

1. What breakthrough in technology led to smaller computers? (If possible, use an online encyclopedia or the Internet to research the answer to this question.)

2. Do you think that having custom computer software created for a new small retail business would be reasonable? Why or why not?

3. Name two or three types of data that might be useful to a company if stored in a database. Tell how the data could be collected for each of these applications.

MAKE CONNECTIONS

4. **MATH** Make up a list of sales categories for a computer hardware store. Assign an amount representing monthly sales for each category. Using spreadsheet software, if possible, add up total monthly sales for the business.

5. **COMMUNICATION** Write a one-page report about the ways a small business could use computer software to its advantage. Write your report on a computer using word processing software, if possible.

Lesson 13.2

Learn about *the* Internet

The **Internet** is a worldwide computer network that allows people to communicate with each other electronically. It allows you to send or receive electronic mail and to access the World Wide Web. In recent years, it has also become a major means of buying and selling.

LOG ON TO THE INTERNET

To access the Internet, you will need to sign up with a service that will allow you to connect to a central computer through your telephone line. Companies that provide this service are known as **Internet service providers,** or ISPs.

Choose an Internet Service Provider

All ISPs provide connections to the Internet. Some also provide other benefits, including information services and the ability to post web pages. You can choose from many different ISPs. Some are small local providers, while others are giant national providers. In choosing your ISP, you will want to consider three main factors:

1. *Will you be able to connect easily to the ISP?* Some are easier to connect with than others.
2. *Can you connect to the ISP from anywhere in the country without paying a long-distance charge?* If the ISP you choose is based in your home city, you may have to pay surcharges to log on when you are out of town.
3. *What monthly charges will you have to pay?* ISPs may charge based on how much time you actually spend online, or they may have a flat rate charge.

Beth Cheng owns a manufacturing company that produces cellular phones. She employs 20 full-time salespeople, each of whom covers a different region of the country. Beth wants her salespeople to be able to connect to the Internet from anywhere in the country. She therefore signs up with an ISP that does not charge long-distance rates when her employees use the Internet while out of town.

YOU CAN SAY THAT AGAIN!

I devised the name myself. The letter 'K' had been a favorite with me . . . It became a question of trying out a great number of combinations of letters that made words starting and ending with 'K.'

—George Eastman, founder of Kodak Film Company, on how he came up with the company name.

Use Electronic Mail

Electronic mail, commonly known as *e-mail*, is used to send and receive electronic messages from anyone in the world. E-mail addresses are necessary to send or receive these messages. E-mail is a very popular form of business communication for several reasons:

1. *E-mail is convenient.* E-mail messages are received almost instantaneously. Many problems can be solved the same day they occur.
2. *E-mail is inexpensive.* There is no charge for sending or receiving e-mail. The only charges are the fees you must pay to your ISP and the cost of local telephone service.
3. *E-mail is not intrusive.* Telephone calls often catch people at inconvenient moments. In contrast, e-mail messages can be read at the recipient's convenience.
4. *E-mail messages can be saved.* Your e-mail program can save all of the messages you send and receive. This means that you can refer to messages received weeks, months, or even years ago.
5. *E-mail messages are less formal than letters and memos.* E-mail messages need not be carefully formatted, although they should use good business language. They are therefore less time-consuming to create.

Rob Miller runs a small business that provides nursing homes with supplies and equipment. Last week, one of Rob's suppliers used e-mail to let Rob know an order couldn't be filled. Rob, in turn, sent an e-mail message to other suppliers to try to find an immediate replacement.

Rob uses e-mail to communicate with his customers as well. Many of the 17 nursing homes he serves place orders with him over the Internet. He immediately e-mails a response confirming their orders and letting them know when the orders will be filled.

Surf the World Wide Web

The World Wide Web can be a very valuable resource for entrepreneurs because it contains thousands of web pages, many of them business related. A **web page** is a file accessible through the World Wide Web which greets visitors and provides information. A software program called a *browser* allows you to view the World Wide Web on your computer screen. Each web page has a special address that no other web page can use. This address tells a browser what file to show on the screen.

Entrepreneurial Timeline

1940　　　　　　1960　　　　　　1980　　　　　　2000

From Computers to Clothing

Bill Mow, the founder of Bugle Boy Industries, started his entrepreneurial career in the technology industry. In 1969, he established Macrodata, a company that built testing equipment for integrated circuits, the precursor of today's computer chips. Mow figured if he could make high speed technology, he could also handle retail clothing. Mow founded a clothing import company that in time became Bugle Boy Industries. But running a clothing company wasn't as easy as Mow thought it would be. The company met with some problems, including stocking too much inventory of Bugle Boy's first big hit—the parachute pant. The company made it through pitfalls like this one because Mow kept finding different ways to market and sell his products. Not only did he open a national chain of Bugle Boy outlets, but he also established the company on a world wide basis. Over the years, Bugle Boy Industries has become a multi-million dollar company. Not every clothing company—or technology firm—can say that.

How can the World Wide Web benefit you?

There are special web sites called search engines that allow you to search, or "surf," the Web using words and phrases. Searching the Web by using a search engine helps you find sources for products and services you need to run your business.

Leslie Wells owns a retail store that sells 1920s jewelry and clothing. She searches the Web for products her customers might want to buy. Last month, Leslie located a web page that described several vintage evening gowns she thought her customers would like. She used her credit card to buy the dresses over the Web.

CHECKPOINT What are some of the advantages of using e-mail and the World Wide Web?

PROMOTE YOUR BUSINESS ON THE INTERNET

Many businesses have web sites, which are collections of interlinked web pages, to promote their business. These sites often include information about a company's history, products and services, policies, and staff. They tell customers how to order products or services and can even advertise job opportunities with the company.

Do You Need a Web Site?

If your business targets only customers who live near you, you probably will not need a web site. If you sell services or products that can be used by people all over the country, you may want to consider electronic marketing. To use the World Wide Web to market your business, you will need to find an ISP that will post your web site. Your web site will also need to be designed. You can learn how to design it yourself, or you can hire a web site designer.

WHAT SHOULD YOUR WEB SITE INCLUDE? Marketing your business online is similar to marketing your business in more traditional ways. Your web site should:

- describe the products and services your business offers
- provide information and graphics that will convince potential customers that they should buy your products or services
- let customers know how they can place an order
- allow customers to contact you through e-mail if they have questions about your products or services

 **CHECKPOINT** What are some of the things a web site should include?

TRANSACT BUSINESS OVER THE INTERNET

Some businesses allow customers to place orders online. Selling products or services over the Internet is known as electronic commerce, or **e-commerce.** This kind of selling is expected to play a growing role in the U.S. economy in the coming years.

Businesses of various types and sizes engage in e-commerce. Some of these businesses sell millions of dollars worth of merchandise over the Internet every year. Others are small businesses that sell everything from fresh flowers to used books online.

Establish an Electronic Customer Base

Accepting orders over the Internet is much more complicated than promoting your business electronically. Creating an e-commerce site also is costly. Because of the expense involved, you should first establish a web site to promote your business over the Internet. Once you establish a solid base of electronic customers, you can then think about modifying your site to facilitate e-commerce.

Did You Know?

Nearly half the retailers participating in e-commerce claim they are profitable selling online.

Select Software

To set up an e-commerce site, you will have to purchase special software. It will perform three essential functions:

1. **Customers can charge purchases over the Internet.** The software will check a customer's credit card number to verify that it is valid. It will then bill the customer's account for the purchase.

2. **Credit card numbers will be confidential.** Customers must feel confident that their credit card numbers will not be used to make unauthorized purchases.

3. **The site will link up with an inventory database.** By tying your inventory database to your e-commerce site, the software will enable your customers to determine whether an item is in stock.

CHECKPOINT How can you use the Internet to sell your products and services?

THINK CRITICALLY

1. In your opinion, what are the advantages and disadvantages of using e-mail to communicate with co-workers, vendors, and customers?

2. You are thinking about creating a web site for your travel agency, Destinations. What could you include in this web site that would set it apart from other similar sites on the Web?

3. Why might customers be unwilling to make purchases over the Internet? What can a business do to overcome this?

MAKE CONNECTIONS

4. **COMMUNICATION** Conduct a phone interview with one or more Internet service providers in your area. Find out (1) what type of computer system you need in order to connect, (2) if you can connect to the ISP without paying a long-distance charge, and (3) the billing options offered by the ISP. Present your results orally in class.

5. **PROBLEM SOLVING** Using the information you collected in exercise 4, apply the six-step problem-solving model to solve the problem, "Which ISP should I choose for my home-based business's Internet connection?"

Lesson 13.3

Purchase
Technology

GOALS

ASSESS your business's need for technology.

DETERMINE where to purchase your technology.

Before you purchase technology for your business you will have to assess your needs carefully. Only by determining how you will use technology will you be able to make the right purchasing decisions.

ASSESS YOUR TECHNOLOGY NEEDS

Plenty of sophisticated technology exists to help you run your business. Some of this technology is very expensive. And much of it may not be appropriate for your business. Your job as an entrepreneur will be to determine which technology will help you best meet your customers' needs and increase your profits.

What Kind of Computer Technology Do You Need?

Once you decide to start your own business, you will probably want to buy at least one computer. Before you make your purchases, prepare a list of all of the ways you would like to use your computer. Then try to identify hardware and software that will help you do so.

PURCHASE HARDWARE Many people who are not computer experts end up purchasing much more than they really need. Some of the sources that can help you determine how much and what kind of hardware to purchase include:

- magazines aimed at entrepreneurs and small businesses
- computer magazines (especially "buying guide" issues)
- *Consumer Reports*
- the Small Business Administration
- the Service Corps of Retired Executives (SCORE)
- computer salespeople

PURCHASE SOFTWARE Your computer requires software to perform the functions you want. To identify the software you need, list all of the tasks you would like to carry out on your computer. Then try to find software that will help you perform these tasks.

Purchase Technology • Lesson 13.3   289

Write a Technology Plan

You will need a technology plan to help you avoid wasting money on technology that you don't need. A plan will also keep you from waiting too long to buy technology that could increase sales or reduce costs. To create a technology plan, write down specific goals you have for your business and describe how technology could be used to meet those goals cost-effectively.

Enrique Sanchez has identified several ways to use new technology to increase profits at his health and racquet club next year. As part of his technology plan, he lists his goals and the technology he plans to use to meet those goals.

Technology Plan for

RUXTON HEALTH AND RACQUET CLUB

Goal: Increase number of customers who pay bills within 30 days.

Solution: Purchase database program to track accounts and generate billing letters. Use program to identify late payers and generate mailing list. Contact late payers, reminding them of importance of paying on time.

Goal: Identify most profitable product lines in order to fine-tune marketing efforts

Solution: Purchase spreadsheet program to analyze profitability of various product lines (health club membership, tennis memberships, racquet shop, snack bar).

CHECKPOINT How can you assess your business's need for technology?

MAKE YOUR PURCHASE

Now you are ready to talk with vendors about purchasing equipment. You can contact a computer consultant or buy what you need from a retail source.

Computer Consultants

Computer consultants design computer systems for businesses. Consultants make sure all the parts of your system are compatible and that the equipment you buy meets your needs.

Don Hannahs owns a tax preparation service. Last year, Don upgraded the computers in his office. He wanted the new computers to be compatible with the printers he bought several years ago. He also wanted to be able to send files directly to the new computerized photocopier he planned to purchase. So Don contacted a company specializing in advising businesses on purchasing computer hardware.

Retail Sources

If your business is small and your needs are limited, you can purchase what you need at a retail store that sells office technology. Some of these stores have salespeople who understand the products and can help you determine which products will best meet your needs.

However, be aware that some store personnel are not knowledgeable. For this reason, it is important that you know what you want to buy before you shop. Retail stores also offer service warranties on the products they offer. Many also service the equipment they sell.

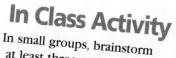

In Class Activity

In small groups, brainstorm at least three more goals Enrique Sanchez might add to his technology plan. Write a solution for each, stating how technology can be used to help reach the goal.

MAIL-ORDER AND INTERNET COMPANIES

If you know exactly what you need, you can buy computers, computer programs, and other technical products from a mail-order or Internet company. If you don't mind the loss of personal service, you may decide to purchase your technology through these vendors and suppliers.

 **CHECKPOINT** Where should you purchase the technology you need?

THINK CRITICALLY

1. Do you think it is important to consult current sources of information about hardware and software when you are ready to buy? Why or why not?

2. Arlon King sells plumbing equipment for manufacturers and is setting up an office in his home. Should he use a computer consultant or a retail source to purchase his computer system? Explain your answer.

MAKE CONNECTIONS

3. PROBLEM SOLVING Write two or three goals and solutions that Arlon King might put in his technology plan (see exercise 2). Use goals and solutions that are different from those shown in the example.

4. RESEARCH Interview a computer consultant. Find out what types of services the consultant provides, the profile of the typical customer, and what the consultant charges for services. Report your findings to the class.

5. COMMUNICATION Find various newspaper or magazine advertisements for computer hardware. Write a letter to a computer vendor describing the system you want for a new business. Ask for price quotes on each part of the system. Turn the letter in to your teacher.

CHAPTER SUMMARY

Technology and Your Business

1. Computer hardware consists of desktop computers, portable computers, printers, and modems. You need to determine what types of hardware you will need for your business.
2. Computer software refers to the programs that direct the computer. Software includes word processing, spreadsheet, and database programs.
3. Other technological elements you may add to your business include graphics programs, presentation software, LCD projectors, and scanners.

Learn about the Internet

4. The Internet is a computer network that allows people to communicate electronically and access the World Wide Web.
5. To connect to the Internet, you will need to sign up with an Internet service provider.
6. You can use electronic mail to send and receive messages.
7. You can surf the World Wide Web to find information on businesses and other resources.
8. You can promote your business over the Internet, and you can participate in e-commerce, or selling products or services over the Internet.

Purchase Technology

9. You should figure out what kind of technology you need to run your business. Then you should contact vendors and purchase the needed hardware and software.
10. It is important to write a technology plan for your business. It will help you determine how much equipment you need and will enable you to know exactly when you need to buy what technology.

What Do You Know Now?

Read *Build a Business* again. Then answer the questions a second time. How have your responses changed?

VOCABULARY BUILDER

Choose the term that best fits the definition.
Write your answers on a separate sheet
of paper.

1. A file accessible through the World
   Wide Web that greets visitors and
   provides information
2. System used to send and receive
   electronic messages from anyone in
   the world
3. An electronic device that allows
   information to be transmitted over
   telephone lines from one computer
   to another
4. Computers and the equipment used with them
5. A company that provides connections to the Internet through
   your telephone
6. Programs that control computer hardware and direct its
   operation
7. Selling products or services over the Internet

a. **computer hardware**
b. **e-commerce**
c. **electronic mail**
d. **Internet**
e. **Internet service
   provider**
f. **modem**
g. **software**
h. **web page**

REVIEW YOUR KNOWLEDGE

8. What is the difference between computer hardware and computer
   software?

9. What are some of the tasks that business owners use computers
   for?

10. What would you use a word processor program for? A spreadsheet
    program?

11. What are some of the ways to learn how to use software?

12. Why might you purchase presentation software? Graphics software?

13. What are the three factors you need to consider when choosing an
    Internet service provider?

14. List at least three advantages of e-mail.

15. What type of information usually is included on a company's web
    page?

16. What three functions must e-commerce software perform?

17. What are some of the sources you can use to help you decide what technology equipment you need to purchase?

18. What should you put in a technology plan?

19. What do computer consultants do? Under what circumstances would you need to hire one?

APPLY WHAT YOU LEARNED

20. You own a health food store. How will technology help you in your business? What type of computer equipment do you need to run your business? Using newspaper ads, magazine ads, catalogs, and the Internet, investigate the types of equipment you would like to purchase for your business. Write a report that outlines the hardware and software you need, and the total cost of all the equipment you must buy. Do you think your business would benefit from having Internet access or a web site? Why or why not?

21. The plumbing supply store that you own has been very successful in the local market. You would like to expand your business and do business on the Internet. What factors do you need to consider before engaging in e-commerce? What information will your web page contain? For each type of information, include the reason why you will include it on the web page.

THINK CRITICALLY

22. Why do business owners need to understand the different types of computer hardware and software? What are the advantages and disadvantages of pre-packaged software? Under what circumstances would an entrepreneur need custom software? Do you think that there are businesses that do not require computers at all? If so, what are they?

23. What types of businesses would benefit from using electronic mail? Why? What advantage do you think businesses gain by using the Internet? What factors should influence an entrepreneur's decision to promote his or her business on the Internet?

24. What is the best way to assess your business's need for technology? Why should you write a technology plan for your business? Do you think most business owners do this? Why or why not?

MAKE CONNECTIONS

25. **MATH** You are choosing an Internet service provider. One service charges $279.00 for an entire year of unlimited service. An alternate provider charges $4.95 per month. This provider gives five free hours per month, and each additional hour is $2.00. There are no long-distance charges to connect to either provider. You estimate your Internet use to be about 30 hours a month. Which provider should you use?

26. **COMMUNICATION** Contact two local computer programmers who write custom software programs for businesses. Interview them and find out what businesses they have written custom software for and the approximate cost for this service. Why did these businesses need custom software? Write a report that summarizes all the information you find out.

27. **RESEARCH** Using magazines, newspapers, catalogs, and the Internet, obtain prices for three laptop model computers and three desktop model computers. Make a chart that shows the features and price of each computer. Create another chart that compares features of two inkjet printers and two laser printers (black and white). Which products would you buy and why?

28. **RESEARCH** Using the library, telephone directory, and the Internet, locate four sources that would provide training on various types of software. Contact each company/trainer/school and find out what types of software they provide training for. Which is the most popular course? Why? What are the costs for this type of training?

This Is Your Business Project

1. Assess the technology needs for your business by preparing a list of all of the ways you would like to use your computer. Research and identify the type of hardware you will need. Compare three products by drawing a chart that outlines each product's features and price. Which product will you purchase and why?

2. What type of software will you need to run your business? Does this software exist pre-packaged or must it be custom made? If it already exists, compare three products that may work for your business. Draw a chart that outlines the features and price of each product. How will you learn how to use this software? Is formal training necessary? Why or why not? Contact two computer programmers who write software for your type of business. How does the software they write compare with the pre-packaged software? What is the cost?

3. Contact five Internet service providers that provide Internet service to your area. What services does each offer? What are the prices for each service? Which provider would you choose for your business based on this information? Why?

Chapter 14

MEET YOUR
LEGAL,
ETHICAL,
AND SOCIAL
OBLIGATIONS

LESSONS

14.1 **Understand Your Legal Requirements**

14.2 **Ethical Issues in Business**

14.3 **Meet Your Social Responsibilities**

BUILD A BUSINESS

Reasons for Regulations

"Mom, what's this little symbol on my shoe?" Andy pointed to the ™ next to the brand name of his gym shoe.

"It's a trademark," Joni responded. "It means that only the company that made your shoes can use that name."

"I remember during the Olympics that people got in trouble for using the Olympic logo without permission."

"That's a good example, Andy. You know, there are a lot of regulations that are put in place by the government to protect both businesses and the public."

"Zoning must be one that protects the public. Someone wants to put a shopping center right across the street from our school and I heard Dad saying that the community doesn't want the property to be zoned for a shopping center."

"Yes. That property is zoned as residential right now. People who live here do not want a shopping center there," said Joni. "The government also enforces laws that make the products and services we buy safe."

"Is that why we have USDA stamps on the meat we buy?"

"Exactly," said Joni.

"Does the government also regulate cosmetics and shampoos?" asked Andy. "The shampoo I use says 'this product was not tested on animals' on the bottle."

"Actually, that's something the company does on its own," explained Joni. "Businesses know people care about the environment, animals, and the Earth. The company is making a decision between right and wrong when it decides to test its products in a certain way."

"I know you always tell me to do the right thing, Mom! Doesn't everyone know that?"

"Some people get so involved with making money, they forget about doing the right thing! They do not treat customers with respect, or they are not honest. They need to realize if they are not ethical, pretty soon they won't have many customers left."

"Do business owners have special rules about how they treat the people who work for them?"

"Oh, yes," Joni continued. "Some include providing a safe workplace and prohibiting discrimination based on age, race, or gender. And remember when you wanted to get a job when you were 10 and I told you that you were too young?"

"I thought that was your rule."

Joni laughed. "Oh, no! It's part of the Fair Labor Standards Act."

"And all this time I thought you made all the rules, Mom."

"My rules are just the beginning, Andy. Get ready! There's a whole world full of rules."

What Do You Know?

1. Name some ways the government protects consumers, employees, and businesses.
2. Why do you think businesses should participate in ethical practices?
3. As an entrepreneur, why is it important for you to be responsible toward your customers and community?

Understand Your *Legal* Requirements

L aws affect almost every aspect of your business, including your dealings with employees, customers, suppliers, and governmental bodies. Laws affect where you can set up your business and how much of its profits you can keep. Advertising claims you make about your products or services are also governed by laws.

As an entrepreneur, you will have to become familiar with the government regulations that affect your business. You will also need to know when to contact a lawyer.

REGULATIONS THAT PROMOTE COMPETITION

As you learned in Chapter 3, most businesses face competition. To make sure that competition is fair, federal, state, and local governments have enacted various laws.

Antitrust Legislation

Beginning in 1890, laws were created that made monopolies in certain industries illegal. A monopoly is also called a trust, and these laws were called antitrust laws. Antitrust laws also ban other types of business activities that do not promote competition. It is important to become familiar with these laws so you do not do anything illegal.

1. ***Sherman Act***—makes it illegal for competitors to get together and set prices on the products or services they sell. This means that you and your competitors cannot together decide to keep prices at a certain level. Discussing prices with competitors is illegal.

   Pete Williams and José Pulido used to work together at Johnson Fencing, a small business that installed residential fences. Each now owns his own fencing company. Last month Pete called José to see if he would raise his prices by the same amount Pete was planning to raise his prices. José told Pete he could not, because José knew that fixing prices with a competitor was against the law.

2. ***Clayton Act***—states that it is illegal for a business to require a customer to purchase one good in order to be able to purchase another good.

   A distributor of computers, for example, cannot make customers purchase software when they purchase a computer. Customers must be free to buy only the products or services they want.

3. *Robinson-Patman Act*—makes it illegal to charge different prices to different groups of non-retail consumers.

If you own a retail store, you can charge different prices to different customers, such as giving discounts to senior citizens. If your business sells to other businesses, you must offer the same terms to all those businesses.

4. *Wheeler-Lea Act*—bans unfair or deceptive actions or practices by businesses. False advertising is an example. Under the Wheeler-Lea Act, businesses also are required to tell consumers about possible negative features of their products.

Drug companies, for example, must let people know of any side effects they may experience from using a medication.

Government Agencies that Protect Competition

The Antitrust Division of the Justice Department and the Federal Trade Commission are two government agencies that make sure competition remains fair. Other agencies, such as the Federal Aviation Administration or the Food and Drug Administration, oversee business practices in particular industries.

JUSTICE DEPARTMENT The Antitrust Division of the United States Justice Department takes legal action against any business it believes has tried to monopolize an industry. It also prosecutes businesses that have engaged in other activities that violate the antitrust laws.

FEDERAL TRADE COMMISSION The Federal Trade Commission (FTC) administers most of the laws dealing with fair competition. Some of the kinds of activities the FTC monitors include:

- price setting by competitors
- false or misleading advertising
- price discrimination
- misrepresentation about the quality, composition, or place of origin of a product

 **What kinds of business practices do antitrust laws prohibit?**

Government regulations were put in place to protect both businesses and the public. Laws that protect businesses include patent, copyright, and trademark laws. Laws that protect the public include licensing laws, building codes and zoning laws, and consumer protection laws.

Laws that Protect Businesses

Roller skates were first patented in 1819.

Three special government regulations give legal rights to creators of inventions, literary or artistic works, and brand names. The regulations give businesses or individuals the exclusive right to profit from what they have created. No one else can use their creations to make money. If you violate another person's patent, copyright, or trademark, you could be sued.

PATENTS A **patent** is a legal document that gives an inventor the sole right to produce, use, and sell an invention. A patent lasts for 20 years. During this period, no business or individual can copy or use the patented invention without permission from the patent holder.

COPYRIGHTS A **copyright** is the legal right to exclusive publication, production, sale, or distribution of a literary or artistic work. All books must have a copyright. A copyright lists the publisher of the work and the year in which the work was published. Copyrights remain in effect for 70 years after the death of the author.

Jessie Castille is a graphic artist who owns her own business. Jessie's copyrighted designs appear on tee shirts and posters. Last year, she found that a tee-shirt manufacturer in another city was illegally using her designs. She sued the manufacturer for violating her copyright.

TRADEMARKS A **trademark** is a name, symbol, or special mark that can be used only by certain businesses. Products that are trademarked are identified by the ™ or ® symbol. Examples of trademarks include Band-Aid™ and Kleenex™.

Laws that Protect Consumers

In addition to laws that protect businesses, the government also has regulations that protect customers. They include licenses, zoning regulations, and consumer protection laws.

LICENSES State and local governments require some businesses to have licenses. Beauty salons, restaurants, and health and fitness centers are just some of the companies that must carry licenses.

If you own a business that requires a license, you may have to have regular inspections by state and local authorities. Failure to meet certain standards could mean the loss of your license and the closing of your business.

ZONING LAWS Local governments often establish zoning regulations that control what types of buildings can be built in what areas. In many communities, certain areas are zoned for residential use only. This means that business buildings cannot be built in those areas. Other areas are zoned only for commercial businesses or for multiple purposes.

All businesses must obey zoning regulations. Before you choose a location for your business, you will have to check that the area you have selected allows your type of business to operate there.

In Class Activity

In small groups, make up several business scenarios that involve violation of antitrust laws. Role-play one of the scenarios for the class.

CONSUMER PROTECTION LAWS A variety of laws and government agencies protect the public against harmful products. You will have to make sure that the products you manufacture or sell meet all consumer protection standards.

The Federal Food, Drug, and Cosmetic Act bans the sale of impure, improperly labeled, falsely guaranteed, and unhealthful foods, drugs, and cosmetics. The Food and Drug Administration (FDA) enforces this law. The FDA has the power to force producers to stop manufacturing products that are unsafe.

The Consumer Product Safety Act of 1972 sets safety standards for products other than food and drugs. When the Consumer Product Safety Commission determines that a product is unsafe, it can make businesses recall and stop selling the product.

Automobiles are commonly recalled for safety reasons.

CHECKPOINT What laws protect businesses and the public?

REGULATIONS THAT PROTECT EMPLOYEES

In addition to protecting businesses and the public, the government has enacted laws that protect employees. These laws involve hiring, firing, time away from work, working conditions, and minimum wages.

Workplace Discrimination

Laws exist to guard against discrimination in the workplace. Their purpose is to give every person an equal opportunity in any company.

EQUAL EMPLOYMENT ACT This act bans discrimination against employees based on age, race, color, national origin, religion, or gender. This law means that you cannot turn a person down for a job based on any of these factors. It is illegal for you to discriminate against or fire an employee based on these criteria. An employee who has been discriminated against illegally can file a complaint with the Equal Employment Opportunity Commission (EEOC). The EEOC enforces the laws against discrimination in the workplace.

PROTECTION FOR DISABLED PEOPLE The Americans with Disabilities Act (ADA) bans discrimination against employees based on disabilities. It also requires businesses with 15 or more employees to accommodate the needs of employees with disabilities, even if the businesses currently do not have any disabled employees. Further, all businesses that are open to the public must be accessible to people with disabilities.

Having doors that open with a button is a way to accommodate the needs of disabled individuals.

Mark Rogers owns a two-story record store. To comply with ADA regulations, Mark installed ramps outside his store so that people in wheelchairs can enter the store easily. He also installed an elevator so that people who cannot use stairs can move from floor to floor.

Safe Working Conditions

The Occupational Safety and Health Act requires that employers maintain safe working conditions for their employees. The law is enforced by the Occupational Safety and Health Administration (OSHA).

To comply with OSHA regulations, you will have to keep records that show the steps you have taken to make your workplace safe. If your employees work with dangerous equipment or substances, you will also have to provide the workers with special training. If OSHA suspects that your business has unsafe practices, its inspectors will examine your facility. You may be required to make changes.

Family Medical Leave Act

This act requires businesses with more than 50 employees to provide employees up to three months of unpaid leave if a serious health condition affects the employee, the employee's child, or the employee's parent or spouse. The Family Medical Leave Act also makes it possible for male and female employees to take leave in the event of a birth or

The Justice Department uses a formula to determine whether corporations that merge are following antitrust laws. The formula calculates what the market share for the product in question will be after the merger.

adoption of a child. To be eligible for such leave, an employee must have been employed by a business for at least one year.

Wages

The Fair Labor Standards Act establishes the maximum number of hours employees can work. It includes rules for children under the age of 16 who work and rates for overtime work. The national minimum wage is also outlined by the Fair Labor Standards Act. Congress reviews the minimum wage every few years and makes adjustments if necessary.

 **CHECKPOINT** **What are the laws that protect the rights of employees?**

GET LEGAL ADVICE

You may be able to learn about some of the laws that affect your business. However, you may also need to hire a lawyer.

Learn about Laws Affecting Your Business

You should learn about some of the basics of the law so that you can handle a few issues yourself. If you are thinking of starting a home-based business, you could check the zoning laws and land-use restrictions rather than ask a lawyer to do so for you. You can learn about the law by reading books or by taking a course in business law. The Internet can also be a good source of information.

Hire a Lawyer

At some point, you probably will need a lawyer's advice. Your Chamber of Commerce may have a list of lawyers who specialize in small businesses. Other business owners in your community may also be able to suggest a lawyer. Lawyers can help you with a variety of legal issues affecting your business.

HOW LAWYERS CAN HELP YOU		
Help you choose a legal structure for your business	Create documents such as lease and purchase agreements	Develop partnership agreements
Inform you of regulations and licenses	Give advice on insurance coverage	Advise you on taxes
Help you apply for patents and trademarks	Help you plan for your future (drafting a will, retirement plans)	Defend you in a lawsuit, or file one for you

YOU CAN SAY THAT AGAIN!

I have maintained the ...
belief that if I have perseverence,
I will learn what I need to
learn and meet the people I
need to meet to make
my goals become a reality.

—Carmen Ramos, founder of
Quality Management Resources, Inc.

PREPAID LEGAL PLANS You can pay for a lawyer on an hourly basis, or arrange a prepaid legal plan. Participants in prepaid legal plans pay a monthly fee, whether or not they use the service. In return, they have the right to legal services and consultation time whenever they need it.

 **CHECKPOINT** What kinds of services can lawyers provide?

THINK CRITICALLY

1. Think of three examples of how a business might misrepresent a product it sells. Explain each example.

2. Besides Band-Aid and Kleenex, think of at least three other products that are trademarked.

3. Do you think it would be better to pay your lawyer an hourly fee or to sign up for a prepaid legal plan? Explain your answer.

MAKE CONNECTIONS

4. RESEARCH Use the newspaper, Internet, or visit your local library to find information on what the process is for applying for a patent. Also find out how much a patent costs, how many patents have been granted to date, and what the criteria are for obtaining a patent. Write a short report on your findings.

5. COMMUNICATION Create an advertisement for a product that would demonstrate a violation of the Wheeler-Lea Act.

Ethical Issues in **Business**

A s the owner of your own business, you will be forced to deal with what is right or wrong. You will have to make ethical decisions about the way you want to run your business. Thinking about ethical issues in advance will help you handle conflicts when they arise.

WHAT IS ETHICS?

Ethics is the study of moral choices and values. Ethics involves choosing between right and wrong. Behaving ethically means behaving in an honest manner.

Culture and Ethics

Different cultures define ethical behavior differently. In some countries, it is considered unethical to take bribes. In other countries, paying bribes may be an accepted business practice. In some countries, employers may treat employees badly. In other countries, employers are expected to respect their employees' rights.

Codes of Ethics

Even within the same culture, individuals develop different standards, or codes, of ethics. A **code of ethics** is the level of ethical behavior demanded by an individual, a business, or a culture. Some individuals have very high standards of ethics and do what is right in every situation. Other individuals don't develop a standard of ethics at all. They act without thinking whether their actions are right or wrong.

Jan Sommers has a high personal code of ethics. Last week, she received a duplicate refund check from one of her suppliers. Jan knew that the check had been sent to her by mistake. She immediately called the supplier to report the error.

CHECKPOINT What does it mean to have a high code of ethics?

ETHICS AND BUSINESS

Ethical questions arise in every type of business. Large corporations, small companies, and home-based businesses all deal with ethical dilemmas at one time or another. **Business ethics** is the application of the principles of right and wrong to issues that come up in the workplace.

Set High Standards

Business and ethics used to be considered unrelated to each other. Over the past hundred years, this view has changed dramatically. Businesses today recognize that they must behave in an ethical manner.

MYTHS ABOUT BUSINESS AND ETHICS Some people believe that entrepreneurs need not concern themselves with ethical issues. They believe that their only goal should be increasing profits. They might think that acting ethically can hurt their profits. In fact, using ethics in business can help you avoid disasters. It also can make customers and suppliers more willing to do business with you.

CONSUMER AWARENESS Consumers and business owners are both sensitive to business ethics. Because consumers are so aware of ethical issues, businesses find ways to show customers that they practice ethics in their daily operations. Manufacturers of some shampoos and cosmetics print on their packaging that they do not test their products on animals. Consumers who have strong opinions about animal rights may be more willing to purchase such products.

Establish an Ethical Workplace

As the owner of your business, it will be up to you to inspire your employees to behave ethically. You will want to establish an ethical workplace for several reasons.

1. You want to do the right thing.
2. You want to serve as a role model to others.
3. You want to be proud of the way you conduct yourself, and you want others to be proud of you.
4. Ethical behavior is good for business because it gains the trust of customers.

What Went Wrong

Modern Day Pirates?

Business: MarCom Dynamics, Englewood, New Jersey * In business, 28 months

Within two years of starting business, MarCom Dynamics (MD) had grown explosively. Their major client was a large pharmaceutical company with breakthrough products. MD produced brochures, videos, and sales seminars to support this client's sales force. The VP of sales approached MD with a last-minute idea for a video to introduce her strategy for regaining market share. MD wrote a script about the company's "'Captains Courageous'. . . Sale-ing the high-seas in search of pirates, to regain their plunder."

The project was on a short time frame and a tight budget. MD decided to use scenes from old pirate movies they rented and edit them to the soundtrack. They knew that using the footage violated the copyright laws. But there wasn't time or money to get a license to use it. They reasoned that no one except the company's sales reps would ever see it. The video was a hit at the sales meeting, and the VP was thrilled.

When the Los Angeles sales representative returned from the meeting, he told his father about the great battle scenes in the video. His father had worked as a major movie studio's stunt-coordinator for several pirate movies made in the 1950s. At his Thursday night poker game, the father mentioned it to his friend Herb, who was head of licensing for that movie studio. On Monday a subpoena for the video landed on the VP of sales' desk. The fines and legal fees were about $40,000. The VP was embarrassed, felt betrayed, and canceled all projects with MD. With the sudden loss of their largest client, MD was sunk.

Think Critically

1. Who appears to have been left out of MD's decision to produce the video using the pirate scenes?
2. Do you think the decision not to obtain permission to use the movie clips was ethical? Why or why not?

---

5. Employees are more likely to act ethically if they see the business owner acting in an ethical manner.
6. Acting ethically reduces the possibility of being sued.

CREATE A WRITTEN CODE OF ETHICS One way that you can communicate your ethical beliefs to the people who work for you is by creating a written code of ethics. Such guidelines will help you and your employees make ethical decisions.

You should create a code of ethics as soon as you begin your business. Even if you are your business's only employee, you should create a written code of ethics.

In Class Activity

In small groups, brainstorm several ethical dilemmas that entrepreneurs might need to deal with. Then determine what decisions you would make if you were faced with these problems.

You should also establish company policies and procedures to let you and your employees know how to behave in certain situations.

To create an ethical code for your business, think about ethical dilemmas that may arise and come up with solutions for dealing with them. Talk to other business owners to see what kinds of ethical problems they have encountered.

Jacki Rand owns a large discount store. Every month, salespeople from various manufacturing companies come to his company to sell their services or products. They meet with the head of the purchasing department, Ellen Chao. Last month, a manufacturing representative offered Ellen a free vacation for two. Not sure whether she should accept the gift, Ellen checked the company handbook. It clearly stated that gifts worth more than $100 should never be accepted from manufacturing representatives. The guidelines helped her solve an ethical dilemma.

 **HECKPOINT** Why is it important for entrepreneurs to establish and write a code of ethics?

THINK CRITICALLY

1. All businesses should practice ethical behavior. Can you think of some ways a convenience store cashier can practice ethical behavior?

2. Is it important for entrepreneurs always to act in an ethical manner? Why or why not?

MAKE CONNECTIONS

3. **COMMUNICATION** Interview someone you know who grew up in a different culture or at a different time in our culture. Ask the person if there are any ethical differences between the cultures or times. Present your findings to the class.

4. **PROBLEM SOLVING** One of your competitors approached you and other companies about setting common prices for your products. You refused but know that the others did not. Use the six-step problem-solving model to help decide whether or not you should turn them in to the Justice Department.

Meet Your Social Responsibilities

Entrepreneurs have responsibilities to the people they work and deal with. They also have responsibilities to the communities in which they are located. They even have a responsibility to the environment. What are these responsibilities, and how can you meet them?

SOCIAL RESPONSIBILITIES

As an individual, you have responsibilities to yourself, to your family, and to your friends. As an entrepreneur, you have responsibilities to your customers, your suppliers, your investors, your creditors, and your community.

Responsibilities to Customers

Your customers are your most important asset. You will need to treat them correctly, or they will no longer use your services or buy your products. When dealing with customers, you should:

1. *Treat all customers with respect.* No one likes to be treated badly.
2. *Be honest.* Never take unfair advantage of customers who do not know everything about the product or service they want to buy. Help your customers make good purchasing decisions.
3. *Avoid exaggerating the merits of your products or services.* Remember that customers who are not happy with what they purchase will not do business with you again.
4. *Inform customers of possible dangers of the products you sell.* Remember that this is also a legal requirement.
5. *Handle all disputes fairly.* Try to see both sides of an issue when there is a disagreement with a customer.

Responsibilities to Suppliers

You depend on your suppliers to provide you with the goods you need to manufacture or sell your products. To make sure that you maintain good relationships with them, you will need to:

1. *Treat all suppliers with respect.* If you respect them, they will respect you.
2. *Refuse to participate in dishonest schemes your suppliers may suggest.* If a supplier asks you to pay cash in order to conceal the payment from the Internal Revenue Service, don't do it.
3. *Give suppliers time to fill your order.* Try not to wait until the last minute to ask for merchandise.
4. *Handle all disputes fairly.* Try to see both sides of the issue and work out a solution that is fair to both you and the supplier.
5. *If you change suppliers, let your current supplier know the reason for your decision.* This is a courtesy to the supplier as well as a good business practice.

Responsibilities to Creditors and Investors

Creditors and investors have shown faith in your ability to succeed. To repay their confidence in you, you should run your business as carefully as possible. You should also let creditors and investors know when things are not going well. Never conceal losses from them.

Entrepreneurial Timeline

| 1850 | 1900 | 1950 | 2000 |

A Beautiful Empire

Did you know that Elizabeth Arden, one of the top cosmetic and fragrance companies in the world, was started by an entrepreneur? Canadian-born Florence Nightingale Graham moved to New York City in 1908. She worked as a bookkeeper at a pharmaceutical company, where her fascination with the product development told her she needed a career change. Graham's first business was a partnership with Elizabeth Hubbard. When the two went their separate ways, Graham saved money on replacing the store sign by only painting over the last name of her former partner. From then on, her company was called Elizabeth Arden. Graham used experimentation to invent her own cosmetic products for women. Her products met with success, and Elizabeth Arden salons began opening all over the world. Elizabeth Arden's innovation, packaging, and promotion all helped to establish the retail cosmetics industry and made Graham one of the world's richest women. Graham died in 1966, but her company continues on as part of International Unilever Prestige Personal Products.

Responsibilities to Your Community

Business owners have a special responsibility to contribute to their communities. They can do so in various ways, including donating money, products, or services. They can also get involved in community issues or activities.

CONTRIBUTE MONEY Business owners donate money to charities, cultural institutions, or causes they believe in. They enjoy giving something back to the community. Not all business owners can make large contributions, but any donation is welcomed.

DONATE PRODUCTS OR SERVICES Some businesses donate the products or services their business sells. Used clothing stores donate unsold clothes to charities. Computer companies sometimes send technicians to community agencies to help the staffs learn about computers.

Carrie Shapiro owns a restaurant. She used to discard all the left-over food every evening. But now, Carrie donates this food to the local soup kitchen. Food that Carrie would have thrown away is enjoyed by dozens of people who otherwise might not have eaten a good meal.

GET INVOLVED You can contribute to your community in other ways as well. Some entrepreneurs get involved in issues affecting their local governments, such as changes in zoning laws or establishment of local parks. Others get involved with charitable organizations, volunteering both their time and money.

In Class Activity

In small groups, brainstorm a list of ten ways an entrepreneur can get involved in the community.

CHECKPOINT What are some responsibilities entrepreneurs have to suppliers, customers, and the community?

RESPOND TO CHANGES IN THE WORKPLACE

Whenever society changes, businesses have to respond. In order to attract and retain good employees, you will have to become sensitive to the needs of the people who work for you.

Accommodate Your Employees' Family Needs

Many people today need to take time off from work to deal with personal issues. An employee may need to leave work early to attend a teacher conference or take a parent to the doctor. As an employer, you will need to establish policies that deal with these kinds of issues.

Ginny Sanders owns a data processing business that employs many people with children. To accommodate their needs, Ginny tries to let these employees work at home on days when school is closed because of bad weather.

Consider Flexible Work Hours

Some of your employees may prefer to work hours other than the standard hours you have set. Some may like to get to work very early in the morning and leave in the afternoon. Others may prefer to work four long days rather than the traditional five. Not all businesses can permit employees to work flexible hours. If your business can be operated with a flexible schedule, you should consider whether offering this option will benefit your employees.

Patrick Perkins has worked in the billing department of Regent & Sons, a small manufacturing company, for 14 years. Recently, he moved to a distant suburb. Patrick would like to carpool to work with his son, who leaves the house at 5:45 A.M. Patrick explained his situation to Tania Regent, the owner of the company. Rather than lose one of her best employees, Tania decided to let Patrick work from 6:30 A.M. to 3:30 P.M.

 **CHECKPOINT** Why is it important to consider the needs of your employees?

RESPECT THE ENVIRONMENT

Damage to the environment comes from many different sources. The burning of coal and oil for energy pollutes the air. Release of toxic chemicals pollutes the ground, air, and water. Disposal of billions of tons of garbage every year also creates environmental problems.

Businesses have a major impact on the environment. As an entrepreneur, you will have an obligation to do as little harm as possible to your surroundings. To meet your environmental responsibilities, you should:

 **NET WORTH**

Point your browser to

http://www.ideas-in-action.swep.com

Complete the activity for Chapter 14.

1. *Protect the environment from pollutants.* Don't knowingly dump hazardous material on the ground or in lakes and rivers.
2. *Conserve nonrenewable resources, such as coal and oil, by using them efficiently.* Nonrenewable resources are not easily replaced once they are gone. It takes hundreds of years to regenerate a nonrenewable resource.
3. *Reduce waste and dispose of waste responsibly.* Recycle materials such as paper, plastic, aluminum, glass, and steel.

4. *Use environmentally safe and sustainable energy sources to meet your business needs.* Electricity is a good example, as it can be replaced quickly and does not pollute the environment.

5. *Sell products that cause as little damage to the environment as possible.* For example, don't sell a car-wash solution that kills plants.

LAWS GOVERNING THE ENVIRONMENT In 1970, the federal government created an agency to enforce the laws governing the environment. The Environmental Protection Agency (EPA) enforces federal laws concerning clean air and water. If your business handles hazardous materials, you will need to become familiar with these laws.

**CHECKPOINT** As a business owner, what are some things you can do to protect the environment?

THINK CRITICALLY

1. At what point do you think the owner should tell creditors and investors if the business is not doing very well? Why?

2. Al Parker is one of your best employees. His mother has just returned from the hospital after having a heart attack. Al wants to take vacation to care for her. This is your company's busy season. What should you do?

MAKE CONNECTIONS

3. COMMUNICATION Maytown Mattress believes that customers are its most important asset. Make a poster that Maytown will display expressing this belief.

4. MATH Jade Yorida will donate 12 percent of her company's net income to the community if she makes her profit projections. How much will Jade donate if she makes her projected income amount of $235,000?

Review

CHAPTER SUMMARY

Understand Your *Legal* Requirements

1. Antitrust laws have been developed to promote fair competition in business. These laws include the Sherman Act, the Clayton Act, the Robinson-Patman Act, and the Wheeler-Lea Act. The Antitrust Division of the U.S. Justice Department and the Federal Trade Commission are government agencies that ensure fair competition.

2. Laws that protect businesses include patents, copyrights, and trademarks. Laws that protect consumers include license requirements, zoning laws, and consumer protection laws. There also are laws that prohibit discrimination in the workplace.

3. Work conditions must be safe for employees. Businesses also must make sure that they comply with the Family Medical Leave Act and the Fair Labor Standards Act.

4. You may need to seek the advice of a lawyer to make sure that your business complies with all regulations.

Ethical Issues in Business

5. Ethics is the study of choices and values. A code of ethics is the level of ethical behavior demanded by an individual, a business, or a culture.

6. You should write a code of ethics for your business. These guidelines can help determine what to do if an ethical dilemma arises.

Meet Your Social Responsibilities

7. You have the responsibility to treat your customers and suppliers honestly and with respect.

8. You can contribute to your community by donating money, donating products or services, and/or getting involved in community organizations.

9. You will need to establish policies to accommodate your employees' family needs. You might consider flexible work hours.

10. You need to make sure you are not damaging the environment. Some things you can do include reducing waste, recycling, and protecting the environment from pollutants.

What Do You Know Now?

Read *Build a Business* again. Then answer the questions a second time. How have your responses changed?

VOCABULARY BUILDER

Choose the term that best fits the definition.
Write your answers on a separate sheet
of paper.

1. Legal document that gives an
   inventor the sole right to produce,
   use, and sell an invention
2. Legal right to exclusive publication,
   production, sale, or distribution of a
   literary or artistic work
3. A name, symbol, or special mark
   that can be used only by certain businesses
4. Study of moral choices and values
5. Level of ethical behavior demanded by an individual, a business,
   or a culture
6. Application of the principles of right or wrong to issues that
   come up in the workplace

a. **business ethics**
b. **code of ethics**
c. **copyright**
d. **ethics**
e. **patent**
f. **trademark**

REVIEW YOUR KNOWLEDGE

7. What practice does the Sherman Act make illegal? The Clayton Act?

8. How do government agencies such as the Federal Trade
   Commission protect competition?

9. What exclusive right do patents, copyrights, and trademarks give
   to companies?

10. How do zoning laws protect consumers? How does the Federal
    Food, Drug, and Cosmetic Act protect customers?

11. Describe two workplace discrimination laws that protect employees.

12. How does the Occupational Safety and Health Act help protect
    employees?

13. Describe the Family Medical Leave Act.

14. What are some of the legal issues that require a lawyer?

15. How does culture affect ethics?

16. What are some of the reasons to establish an ethical workplace?

17. What are some of the responsibilities you have to your customers
    and suppliers?

18. Why do you have the responsibility to inform creditors and investors when your business is not going well?

19. List the ways entrepreneurs fulfill responsibilities to their communities.

20. How can business owners accommodate employees' family needs?

21. How can businesses meet their environmental responsibilities?

APPLY WHAT YOU LEARNED

22. Would you be in violation of the Clayton Act if you gave customers the option to buy a printer cartridge at 50 percent off when they purchase a color printer? The customer would be able to buy the cartridge without buying the printer, but would not get the discount.

23. You are an independent consultant to the state hired to inspect paving work on a highway site. The paving company must complete the job on time or will pay a fine to the state. Although the paving company did not follow the specifications in the contract, the president of the company has asked you to approve the job in exchange for a large sum of money. What are the ethical issues that you face? What do you think would be the best way to resolve this issue? Why?

24. You have opened a delicatessen in your town. What are some of the responsibilities you have to your customers? In what ways can your business benefit the community? How do you think fulfilling these responsibilities will help your business?

THINK CRITICALLY

25. Antitrust laws were enacted to make competition fair. Why do you think the government places so much value on fair competition? Can you think of examples of companies that have violated antitrust laws? What was the punishment? How do you think licensing laws protect the consumer? Why are licensing and zoning laws necessary?

26. Give examples of ethical dilemmas that may arise in corporations, small companies, and home-based businesses. How can using ethics in business help make customers and suppliers more willing to do business with you? Do you think consumers are concerned about a company's business ethics? Why or why not?

27. Why is it important for business owners to donate money and get involved in community activities? Do you think this behavior helps their businesses? Why or why not?

MAKE CONNECTIONS

28. COMMUNICATION Use newspapers, magazines, the Internet, and other tools to find examples of two companies that are environmentally responsible and one company that has violated environmental laws. Give a presentation to the class that details the company's actions and their impact on society.

29. RESEARCH You want to start your own beauty salon. Contact your local government and obtain information about zoning laws. Do the zoning laws in your area prohibit you from opening a salon in your home? What areas of your city or town are zoned for businesses? What are the state licensing laws for a salon? Will your business have to pass a state inspection?

This Is Your Business Project

1. Contact your state and local governments and obtain information about licensing and zoning regulations. How will these regulations affect your business?

2. If you will have employees, you must maintain safe working conditions. Obtain a copy of the Occupational Safety and Health Administration regulations for your type of business. What steps do you need to take to make your workplace safe?

3. Write a code of ethics for your business that includes company policies and procedures for dealing with particular situations. What are some situations that are specific to your type of business that may pose an ethical dilemma?

4. Write an environmental policy for your business. What are some of the actions your business will take to protect the environment? Are these actions required by law? If not, why will you incorporate them into your policy?

LESSONS

15.1 Develop a Strategy for Growth

15.2 Global Trends and Opportunities

15.3 Culture and Business

BUILD A BUSINESS

Gavin's Business Grows

"I feel very fortunate when it comes to my print shop business," Gavin said to his wife, Leanne. "Things are going so well. But you know what I've been thinking about?"

"No, but I think I am about to find out," Leanne teased.

"I think I need to expand. One thing that I thought about initially was putting a sandwich shop inside my store. But the more I thought about it, I decided that probably wasn't a very good idea. I don't really know anything about restaurant management and most people who come in my print shop are in a hurry."

"Well," thought Leanne. "Since you know printing and that's what you're good at, you could add services related to printing. You could buy computer systems with word processing and desktop publishing software. Customers who don't have access to computers or who get to your shop and decide they need to make a last minute change can use the computers and printers for an hourly fee."

"That's a good idea, Leanne," said Gavin. "I'll do some market research with my customers and the Chamber of Commerce just to make sure this is a good way to grow. You know, it's always important for a business to have a growth strategy, because it helps ensure success."

"You've always planned every step for your business, Gavin," replied Leanne. "You analyzed all decisions before making them; and you have been good to your employees and your customers."

"If all this works out, maybe I'll think about opening a shop in another part of town."

"Why not another part of the world?" Leanne said.

"Hey, that's an idea," thought Gavin. "I speak Spanish fluently. That would go a long way in opening up a store in Mexico or Spain!"

"And you already know two suppliers in Mexico City. Don't you import a lot of copier toner from them?" asked Leanne.

"I sure do. I guess I'll also have to research global possibilities when I go to the Chamber of Commerce. Having a shop in another country could be a good way to increase my sales."

"Maybe you should talk to my friend Roberta. She has family that lives in Mexico. I think it would be a good idea to know as much as you could about the culture there before you open a print shop," suggested Leanne.

"Do you have her number? This is exciting, I want to call her right away!"

What Do You Know?

1. What do you think Gavin should consider when deciding whether to expand his business?
2. Increased sales is a benefit of competing globally. Can you think of another? Can you name some disadvantages of competing globally?
3. Why is it a good idea to research the culture of a country when you are considering opening a business in that country?

GOALS

DETERMINE when your business is ready to expand.

MANAGE the growth of your business.

SELECT a growth strategy.

Develop a *Strategy* for Growth

Sooner or later, you will consider expanding your business. Some businesses have difficulty growing. Others expand too quickly. To expand successfully, you will need to determine both when and how to expand. You also will need to control your growth.

DETERMINE WHEN TO EXPAND

Determining when to expand depends on two main factors: the condition of your business and the economic conditions in the market in which your business competes.

Consider the Condition of Your Business

How do you determine when it is time to expand your business? Some of the signs you should look for include:

- Your business is recognized by your community and industry.
- Your sales are rising.
- You have a customer base that regularly buys from you.
- You are hiring more employees and now have managers.
- You need more space.

Assess Economic Conditions

If the condition of your business shows that you should expand, you should next analyze the economic climate that controls the business. You should ask the following questions:

1. How is the national economy doing? Are people worried about spending money, or are they spending freely?
2. What are the economic conditions in your industry or region?
3. Have the demographics of your market changed?
4. Is demand for your product or service expected to remain strong?
5. Does your business face new competition?

CONTROL YOUR GROWTH

Growing rapidly may sound like a great thing for a business. But, uncontrolled growth may be just as bad as no growth at all. Businesses that grow too quickly often find that they don't have the resources to support their growth. They can lack money, employees, supplies, and more. As a result, they often overextend themselves. Sometimes they are even forced to go out of business.

Joshua King owned a successful bookshop, Pegasus Books. Excited over his success, Joshua opened a second shop. But, he underestimated the costs involved in running a second store. The stress of managing two stores was overwhelming, and Joshua found he could no longer provide the personal service his customers wanted. After nine months, Joshua had to close both of his bookstores.

Create a Plan for Growth

To make sure that your business expands successfully, you will have to control its growth. This means you will need to come up with a plan for expansion that should include strategies for:

- attaining measurable objectives and goals (examples are sales goals, increasing your customer base, opening another store)
- hiring managers and supervisors
- financing expansion
- obtaining resources for expansion (capital equipment, inventory, materials, supplies)

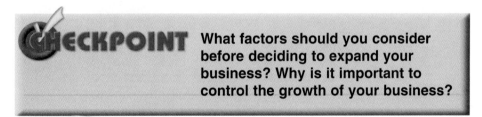

CHECKPOINT What factors should you consider before deciding to expand your business? Why is it important to control the growth of your business?

CHOOSE A GROWTH STRATEGY

You can expand your business in various ways. You can get more people to buy your products or services. You can expand into other geographic areas. You can also find new products and services to sell.

Penetrate the Market and Expand Geographically

Market penetration and geographic expansion are two strategies for increasing your sales. **Market penetration** is increasing market share for a product or service within a given market in a given area. *Geographic expansion* is when you decide to market your service or product in another town, city, county, or state.

Superior customer service can increase market share.

MARKET PENETRATION You can increase sales by increasing the number of people in your target market who buy from you. If total sales for your target market are $500,000, and your business attracts 5 percent of that market, your sales will be $25,000. If you raise your market share to 15 percent, your sales will be $75,000.

You can try to increase your market share by:

- increasing your advertising
- offering customers special deals, such as frequent buyer cards, incentives to purchase, and discounts
- offering superior customer service

Increasing your market share costs money. You may spend more on advertising, or you might have to give customers two items for the price of one. Spending money now will pay off with larger profits in the future if you obtain a larger market share.

GEOGRAPHIC EXPANSION You can also expand your business by targeting customers in other geographic areas. Sheila Fagan owns a business that builds sunrooms in the northern part of her state. To increase sales, Sheila started advertising throughout the entire state. She has already received calls from interested consumers 100 miles away.

Diversify with New Products or Services

Market development is a strategy for expanding the target market of a business. A business expands its target market by diversifying, which means selling new products or services in addition to what you already offer.

Entrepreneurial Timeline

| 1960 | 1970 | 1980 | 1990 |

Music to His Ears

How many entrepreneurs can say they own the largest company in their industry? Ralph Mercado can, although he'd probably be modest about it. He became involved in the music business in the 1960s and quickly saw that Latino musicians had a need for competent management. He opened Ralph Mercado Management Inc. in 1972. The company started with only three clients, but did such a great job managing their music appearances, other artists signed up. Mercado's company has grown considerably since 1972. The RMM Corporation, which deals in music bookings, concerts, audio and video production, films, and more, has become the largest entertainment company in the Latin music industry.

Sue Ann Rader owns a musical instrument store. Three years ago, she added a sheet music department to her store. She reduced her inventory of instruments to make room for the new department. Sheet music now contributes 25 percent of her annual profits.

Businesses can fail if they diversify into the wrong areas. To make sure that your business diversifies successfully:

- Do not go into areas that you know nothing about.
- Choose a product or service that compliments what you already sell.
- Avoid allocating too much capital to new areas before you know if they will be profitable.
- Don't neglect your original product or service line.

Sue Ann would like to open a café in her store. She would have to make room in her store to do so. Sue likes the idea of a café, but she knows nothing about it. Her lack of experience and her concern about the effect on her main business convince her not to open the café.

 **CHECKPOINT** What are some ways you can expand your business?

THINK CRITICALLY

1. What are the negative consequences, if any, of not allowing your business to grow?

2. How might Joshua, the owner of Pegasus Books, have avoided closing both his stores?

3. Your friend owns a successful hair salon. She wants to expand and asks for your advice on a growth strategy. What will your advice be?

MAKE CONNECTIONS

4. MATH Tony Balducci owns a deli and sandwich shop. Total sales for his target market are $1.75 million per year. If he attracts 12 percent of the market, what will his sales be? What will sales be if he increases market share to 18 percent?

5. MATH Pete Wilson owns a sports center with an indoor track, driving range, and basketball courts. He has recently installed two batting cages at the facility. Last year his total sales were $325,500. If the batting cages take up 5 percent of the space and add 4 percent to total sales, how much will each batting cage contribute to total sales?

GOALS

IDENTIFY the different ways you can export and import.

DETERMINE whether international business is right for you.

EVALUATE trade regulations that will affect your business.

Global Trends *and* Opportunities

The global marketplace has dramatically changed the way businesses operate. It has made business more competitive, and it has opened up new opportunities for companies, including small entrepreneurial businesses. As the global marketplace continues to expand, entrepreneurs can take advantage of even more opportunities.

EXPORTS AND IMPORTS

International trade is one way you can become part of the global marketplace. This means you would export or import the products or services you sell or use in your business.

Exporting

Products and services that are produced in one country and sent to another to be sold are **exports.** The United States exports agricultural products, automobiles, machinery, computers, and more. These products are shipped to countries all over the world.

DIRECT EXPORTS You can find buyers or distributors in foreign markets and ship your products to them. This is called *direct exporting.* For direct exporting, you may need to hire salespeople who live in or travel to foreign countries.

Tiffany Wilson owns a mid-sized printing company. Last year, Tiffany decided to expand her business internationally. She hired a Dutch sales representative, Mieta Van Praag, to market her business in Europe. Mieta calls on customers in the Netherlands and France.

INDIRECT EXPORTS It can be hard to make contacts with buyers in other countries. Some businesses use *commissioned agents,* brokers who find foreign buyers for products and services. Exporting by using commissioned agents is *indirect exporting.*

USING THE WORLD WIDE WEB TO EXPORT Yet another way of exporting is through the World Wide Web. Businesses translate and modify their web sites to appeal to foreign customers.

Shahid Mahmoud's business manufactures puzzles. He recently began promoting his products abroad over the World Wide Web because research showed Japanese buyers like puzzles. To target that market, he created an e-commerce web site written in Japanese.

ⒼHECKPOINT What are some ways you could export your products or services?

Importing

Products and services that are brought in from another country to be sold are **imports.** The United States imports automobiles from Europe, Japan, and Korea. It imports oil from the Middle East.

Two main reasons for entrepreneurs to import products to sell are price and quality. Inexpensive imports sell because consumers like low prices. Expensive imports sell because consumers also enjoy quality.

Some entrepreneurs use imported products to make their own products. James Sutton owns a business that makes African-style clothing. He imports all of his fabrics from West Africa because of their unique colors and textures.

Exports and imports can be sent by ship.

ⒼHECKPOINT Why are exports and imports important for entrepreneurs?

IS INTERNATIONAL BUSINESS RIGHT FOR YOU?

Not every business can succeed internationally. You need to consider the pros and cons of competing globally. Then, you must determine whether there is a market for your business in other countries and write an international business plan.

> ## YOU CAN SAY THAT AGAIN!
> **When a company gives back to the community it markets to, it can only see its growth increase.**
>
> —*John Lopez Jr.,*
> *owner of Lopez Foods Inc.*

Pros and Cons of Competing Globally

Competing in the global marketplace can provide your business with many benefits, including increased profits. There are at least three good reasons to expand into other countries:

1. ***Increased sales.*** You will attract new buyers and widen your customer base. You may also import unique products that local customers can buy.

2. ***Reduced costs.*** Manufacturers in other countries can produce goods less expensively because of low labor costs or availability of raw materials. This can mean a savings for you on an item's price.

3. ***Decreased dependence on current markets and suppliers.*** If economic conditions in the United States suddenly worsen, foreign markets and suppliers might help keep your profits high. Selling products and services abroad can also help you stabilize seasonal market fluctuations or fluctuations caused by changes in the U.S. economy.

Point your browser to

http://www.ideas-in-action.swep.com

Complete the activity for Chapter 15.

RISKS OF GLOBAL COMPETITION Doing business in a foreign country can be difficult. You will encounter problems that you probably have not run into in the United States. These new challenges will arise for several reasons:

1. ***You may not speak the language of the countries you are targeting.*** If you cannot communicate with buyers or consumers, how will you be able to sell your service or product?

2. ***You may not be familiar with the laws, customs, and cultures of foreign countries.*** In the United States, looking directly at people while speaking to them is a sign of respect. In some other countries, it is a sign of disrespect and not an acceptable way to do business. Lesson 15.3 details some additional problems you may run into.

3. ***You may have to change your products or services to meet the needs of new markets.*** Consumers abroad have different needs and wants from consumers in the United States. What sells in this country will not necessarily appeal to foreign customers. You will need to consider this when you sell products or services into other countries.

4. ***Your travel and shipping expenses may be high.*** International flights can be very expensive. Sending or receiving packages from overseas can also be costly.

 **What are some of the risks and benefits of competing internationally?**

Analyze the Market

Analyzing whether there is an international market for your product will be very similar to analyzing your target market and target customers. In addition to the kind of analysis you learned about in Chapter 6, you will need to consider other factors, including political, economic, social, and cultural issues. Additional taxes and regulations, as well as cultural barriers, are also things to research and think about.

RESEARCH A variety of resources are available that can help you learn about doing business abroad. These include:

- trade fairs and seminars sponsored by the U.S. Department of Commerce
- Dun and Bradstreet's *Exporter's Encyclopedia*
- trade statistics from the Bureau of the Census, the Small Business Administration, and other sources
- federal or state government market studies on your industry's potential abroad

Mark Milowski owns a business that processes payroll records. He recently met with several Polish business owners who wanted Mark's company to handle their payrolls. Mark liked the idea of expanding globally, but he had many questions. He contacted the Department of Commerce to get information on doing business in Poland. The *Exporter's Encyclopedia* also told him what regulations he would face.

Write an International Business Plan

An international business plan is an extension of your business plan. It sets forth your goals for international expansion and defines the strategies for achieving those goals. Your plan should indicate:

1. why you want to expand your business into the global marketplace
2. which foreign markets you plan to enter and why
3. what revenues your venture is expected to bring in
4. how you plan to finance your global expansion
5. what costs (travel, shipping, marketing) you expect to have
6. how you plan to market and sell your products or services abroad
7. how you plan to deliver your products or services to foreign markets
8. what legal requirements you will need to meet to sell your products or services abroad

 **ECKPOINT** What are some sources of information that can help you find out about doing business abroad?

Some governments establish **trade barriers,** methods for keeping foreign businesses from competing with domestic producers. Quotas, tariffs, and qualitative restrictions are trade barriers. You will have to research the barriers that exist that may affect your global expansion.

Quotas

A **quota** is a limit on the amount of a product that can be imported into a country over a particular period of time. Japan places quotas on the number of foreign automobiles that can be imported. Quotas protect Japanese car makers from losing business to foreign competitors.

Tariffs

A **tariff** is a tax on imports. Governments use tariffs to protect domestic manufacturers of products that compete with imports. The United States places a tariff on imported sugar. Foreign companies that sell their sugar in the United States must pay a tax. This makes their products more expensive and more competitive with the U.S. market.

Qualitative Restrictions

A **qualitative restriction** is a standard of quality an imported product must meet before it can be sold. A qualitative restriction can be created to keep foreign businesses from competing with domestic producers. They are also set up out of concern for consumers. For example, the United States insists that all meat sold in this country meet certain sanitary regulations. It also insists that imported toys meet U.S. safety requirements.

In Class Activity

Think of five qualitative restrictions a government might place on imports. Name at least one product for each restriction. Share your answers with the class.

The North American Free Trade Agreement

In 1996, the United States, Mexico, and Canada signed the North American Free Trade Agreement (NAFTA). That agreement removed all barriers to trade between the three nations. This means that American businesses can sell their products and services in Canada and Mexico just as they would in the United States. It also means that the United States imposes no quotas or tariffs on imports from Canada and Mexico. NAFTA makes it much easier to export and import products and services within North America.

Government Assistance to Companies Operating Abroad

Dozens of different government agencies are available to answer your questions about doing business overseas. They include:

- *The U.S. Department of Commerce.* Promotes the sale of U.S. products and services overseas.
- *The Office of International Trade of the Small Business Administration.* Provides counseling and other services to small businesses interested in becoming exporters.
- *The International Trade Administration's Export Promotion Services.* Analyzes foreign markets, locates buyers and representatives overseas, and promotes U.S. products and services.
- *The Bureau of Export Administration.* Handles services related to export licenses. These licenses are required for some technologies, such as military equipment, that may affect national security.

In addition to these agencies, the federal government offers many programs that help U.S. businesses operate in foreign markets. The programs include export counseling, export financing, and technical assistance.

 **CHECKPOINT** Explain the ways the federal government regulates international trade.

THINK CRITICALLY

1. Sometimes foreign manufacturers are able to sell their goods at a low price because they pay low wages to their workers. Is it ethical to purchase products from such manufacturers? Why or why not?

2. Do you think it is in our country's best interest to have U.S. companies engage in international trade? Why or why not?

MAKE CONNECTIONS

3. MATH A government in an Asian country applies a 28 percent tariff to all electronic goods imported to the country. If it collects $24 million in tariffs for these goods, what was their total value?

4. RESEARCH Research the North American Free Trade Agreement and write a one-page report on what you find.

Culture and Business

As an entrepreneur, you will come into contact with all kinds of people. Many of these people will be from cultures different from yours. Whether your business operates only in the United States or all over the world, you will need to become familiar with and learn to respect other cultures.

WHAT IS CULTURE?

Culture is the set of customs, beliefs, and social attitudes that characterize a particular group of people. Every society has its own culture, and every culture has its own characteristics. Arab culture emphasizes traditional religious beliefs and family values. Chinese culture emphasizes respect for older people and commitment to family. Traditional Native American culture emphasizes respect for nature.

Cultures within the United States

The United States is a multicultural society. People from many different cultures live here. Entrepreneurs need to appreciate different cultures because:

- You need to be comfortable with your customers. If you are open to other cultures, you can attract more customers.
- People from different cultures may have different needs and wants. Understanding these can help you market your business more effectively.

RESPECT CULTURAL DIVERSITY As an entrepreneur, you may work with people from different cultures. You may also buy from and sell to people from different cultures. How can you develop good relationships with everyone you do business with? There are at least five things you can do to develop these relationships.

1. ***Avoid stereotyping people.*** Don't assume that all people from a particular ethnic or cultural group behave the same way or like the same things.
2. ***Focus on similarities rather than differences.*** Most people, regardless of their culture, want the same things in life.
3. ***Learn about different cultures.*** Learning about a different culture will make you more comfortable around people from that culture.
4. ***Make friends with someone from a different culture.*** This can help you begin to appreciate different cultures.
5. ***Try to understand and identify with other people's feelings.*** Try to see the world through the eyes of people from different cultures. Try to understand cultural views that are different from your own.

MARKET TO DIFFERENT CULTURES The United States represents a rich and diverse marketplace. This means you will have to identify the needs and wants of different cultures.

What Went Wrong

Expansion

Make-Up Test

Business: "Picture-Perfect" Brand, Los Angeles, CA • In business, 8 months

Sarah-Jane Stevens founded Charisma Cosmetics. Her company targeted professional dealers serving make-up artists in the film, TV, and theater industries. Charisma Cosmetics had an excellent reputation as a high-quality manufacturer, a loyal customer base, and a major share of the market. However, Sarah-Jane also saw new competitors slowly chipping away at her customer base. To remain competitive, she decided to expand her company. In the fall of 1999, she rolled out a separate brand, Picture-Perfect by Charisma. This brand was specifically designed to be sold in department store chains. This was a totally new market for Charisma Cosmetics, and Sarah-Jane was excited.

But the new strategy angered the professional make-up dealers who were the core customers of Charisma Cosmetics. Their competitive advantage had been to use better products that were not available elsewhere. With Charisma's Picture-Perfect brand cropping up in department stores, the make-up dealers felt betrayed. They could no longer use the same competitive edge when they resold Charisma Cosmetics.

"We were determined to grow, and we strayed from our root value of 'don't be bigger, be better,'" Sarah-Jane said. "Our customers told us point blank they didn't like what we were doing." Just eight months after getting into the department store market, Sarah-Jane and Charisma got out. "It was a huge loss and a big lesson," she said. The company ended up losing hundreds of thousands of dollars in developing and marketing the Picture-Perfect brand.

Think Critically

1. What problems were created by the "Picture-Perfect by Charisma" brand?
2. How might Sarah-Jane have avoided angering her dealers and yet still expanded distribution?

Phong Thieu is a Vietnamese-American who owns a clothing store. Phong has customers from many ethnic backgrounds, including Asians and South Americans. Phong has gotten to know her customers well and her familiarity with them helps her meet their fashion needs. Her respect for her customers has helped her business become very successful.

 **CHECKPOINT** Name two reasons entrepreneurs need to appreciate different cultures.

CULTURE AND THE GLOBAL MARKETPLACE

If you do business abroad, you will need to learn about the cultures of the countries in which you plan to do business. Learning about these cultures is important because culture affects what people buy. It also affects how people do business.

Familiarize Yourself with Other Cultures

Cultural values and cultural practices vary from country to country. To establish good business relationships with people in other countries, you will have to become familiar with their customs and learn to respect them.

SPEAK THE LANGUAGE Speaking a common language with another person is one important way of showing that you understand his or her culture. If you are doing a lot of business in a particular part of the world, you may want to hire someone who speaks the local language or learn it yourself.

You can take a course to learn another language.

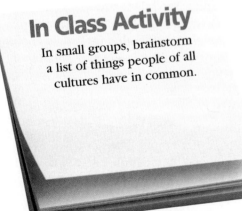
In Class Activity
In small groups, brainstorm a list of things people of all cultures have in common.

UNDERSTAND CULTURAL PRACTICES Becoming familiar with foreign cultural practices is important for doing business abroad. In Europe, many people buy their food at small shops and markets rather than at large supermarkets. Europeans also consume far less frozen and prepared food than Americans. Food exporters have to be aware of these differences in order to be successful.

Business practices also vary from culture to culture. In some cultures, businesspeople spend lots of money entertaining each other. In some countries, businesses close down in the early afternoon, when people go home to have lunch or take a nap. If you will be doing business globally, you will need to become familiar with these customs.

DEVELOP CULTURAL SENSITIVITY To avoid making a social blunder, you will need to learn about other people's cultures. You will also need to adapt the way you conduct yourself. Americans doing business abroad often inadvertently offend their foreign hosts because of lack of knowledge about or sensitivity to other cultures. In many foreign cultures, for example, referring to someone by his or her first name is a sign of familiarity. Some foreigners may be insulted by Americans who use their first name in conversation or correspondence.

RESEARCH DIFFERENT CULTURES There are many ways to learn about different cultures and their practices. Your local library and the Internet both have lots of information on different cultures. The International Chamber of Commerce may also have useful information for you. You can also talk to people from different cultures and learn first hand about their beliefs and the ways they live their lives.

Body language differs among cultures. In Egypt, people stand close to one another. In the Caribbean, people frequently touch one another. In the U.S., we stand a few feet apart and require the other person's permission to touch them.

 **How can you familiarize yourself with different cultures?**

THINK CRITICALLY

1. Why is it important to understand the cultural backgrounds of the people in your target market? Give examples of three products that have customers with different cultural backgrounds.

2. Give examples of three goods or services in which a person's culture influences its purchase. Write a sentence about each product.

MAKE CONNECTIONS

3. **RESEARCH** Use the Internet, the library, and other sources to find five interesting facts about a foreign culture of your choice. Present the facts orally to the class.

4. **COMMUNICATION** Interview someone from a different culture who lives in your area. Ask the person how his or her culture influences the products he or she buys.

Review

CHAPTER SUMMARY

Develop a *Strategy* for Growth

1. When expanding your business, you should consider the condition of your business and assess the economic conditions that affect your business.
2. You will need to create a plan for growth so that your growth is controllable. You might need to increase staff, obtain more financing, or obtain more resources for expansion.
3. You will choose a growth strategy when you expand your business. You can penetrate the market, expand geographically, or diversify with more products and services.

Global Trends *and* Opportunities

4. To get involved in international trade, you can export or import your products or services.
5. Some of the benefits of global competition are increased sales and reduced costs. Some of the challenges of global competition are that you may not speak the language of your customers, and your travel and shipping costs may be high.
6. You will need to analyze whether there is an international market for your product and write an international business plan.
7. Governments regulate international trade by establishing trade barriers, such as quotas, tariffs, and qualitative restrictions. The government also assists in international trade by making trade agreements with other countries and by creating agencies to help businesses compete abroad.

Culture and Business

8. Entrepreneurs need to appreciate people from different cultures so that they will feel comfortable with all customers and so that they will better market their products.
9. You can develop good relationships with people you do business with by avoiding stereotypes and learning about different cultures.
10. You should become familiar with the cultures of your targeted customers. You can learn to speak the language, understand cultural practices, develop cultural sensitivity, and research different cultures.

What Do You Know Now?

Read *Build a Business* again. Then answer the questions a second time. How have your responses changed?

VOCABULARY BUILDER

Choose the term that best fits the definition.
Write your answers on a separate sheet
of paper.

1. Limit on the amount of a product
   that can be imported into a country
   over a particular period of time
2. Standard of quality an imported
   product must meet before it can
   be sold
3. Strategy for expanding the target
   market of a business
4. Tax on imports
5. Increasing market share for a product
   or service within a given market in a
   given area
6. Methods for keeping foreign businesses from competing with domestic producers
7. Products and services that are brought in from another country
   to be sold
8. Products and services that are produced in one country and sent
   to another to be sold
9. The set of customs, beliefs, and social attitudes that characterize
   a particular group of people

a. **culture**
b. **exports**
c. **imports**
d. **market development**
e. **market penetration**
f. **qualitative restriction**
g. **quota**
h. **tariff**
i. **trade barriers**

REVIEW YOUR KNOWLEDGE

10. What signs may indicate that it is time to expand your business?

11. Are there consequences of growing your business too quickly?
    If so, what are they?

12. What is the difference between market penetration and market
    development?

13. What are some of the ways to increase your market share?

14. Name three ways to export your product.

15. Why might a business import products or services?

16. What are the advantages and disadvantages of competing globally?

17. Why do you need to analyze a foreign market before you begin sell-
    ing products and services?

18. What are some of the ways that governments regulate international trade?

19. Why do entrepreneurs need to appreciate different cultures?

20. What are some of the ways to familiarize yourself with other cultures?

APPLY WHAT YOU LEARNED

21. You publish a cooking magazine that circulates in your local metro area. How can you expand this business? What growth strategy will you employ? Write a plan for growth that includes measurable objectives, hiring managers, financing the expansion, and obtaining resources for expansion.

22. You own a clothing boutique and have recently expanded into catalog sales. Many of your products are sold abroad. What method of exporting will you use? What are some of the government regulations that will affect your business? How might you obtain further information about these regulations? What cultural issues are relevant to your business?

THINK CRITICALLY

23. Why do you think the economy plays a role in an entrepreneur's decision to expand? How can an entrepreneur control the growth of the business?

24. Using at least two growth strategies, name four ways a wedding photographer might grow his business.

25. What are the issues that an entrepreneur must consider before deciding to expand internationally? What factors determine which method of exporting an entrepreneur uses? How does an entrepreneur determine what trade barriers exist?

26. Why do you think it is important for business owners to be sensitive to and understand other cultures even if they only operate in the United States? Can you think of situations in which a lack of cultural sensitivity could hurt a business?

MAKE CONNECTIONS

27. MATH You have a business selling concrete to contractors. One of your suppliers in South America has quoted a price of $4.00 per 50 pound bag. Your U.S. supplier is charging $4.50 per 50 pound bag. The foreign company must pay a 12.5 percent tariff on each bag shipped and will pass that cost on to you. Which supplier will you buy from? Why?

28. COMMUNICATION Use newspapers, magazines, the Internet, and other tools to find a small business that has successfully expanded. Write a one-page report about the company. Include information about the growth strategy this business used and why you think the owner(s) chose this strategy.

29. RESEARCH Choose an industry or specific business that operates globally. Use the library and government agencies to find out what government regulations affect this business's global operations. Is the business subject to trade barriers? Are there cultural issues that affect this business? What are the specific challenges that this business faces? Is the business profitable?

This Is Your Business Project

1. What would indicate that you are ready to expand your business? Give specific examples, such as your sales growing by 20 percent or you are outgrowing your current location.

2. What effect does the economy have on your business? Write a growth plan that outlines your growth strategy and includes strategies for attaining measurable objectives, hiring managers, financing expansion, and obtaining resources for expansion.

3. What global opportunities exist for your business? Determine the best country for your business to expand into. List the specific benefits and risks of global expansion for your business.

4. Research the political, economic, and social/cultural issues of the countries in which you plan to do business. With this information, write an international business plan that outlines your goals for international expansion.

5. What are some other cultures you will be exposed to in your business? Research one of these cultures and find out information about their lifestyle and business practices. What cultural issues will affect your business? How will you market your product or service to this and other cultures?

Glossary

A

Account an accounting record that summarizes all the information for a particular business item (p. 239)

Advertising paid form of communication sent out by a business about a product or service (p. 196)

Advertising fees fees paid to support television, magazine, or other advertising of the franchise as a whole (p. 76)

Aptitude the ability to learn a particular kind of job (p. 11)

Assets items of value owned by a business (p. 142)

Audit an IRS investigation of a tax return (p. 271)

B

Board of directors group of people who meet several times a year to make important decisions affecting the company (p. 85)

Bonus financial reward in addition to a regular wage or salary (p. 222)

Brainstorming a creative group problem-solving technique that involves generating a large number of fresh ideas (p. 40)

Break-even point volume of sales that must be made to cover all of the expenses of a business (p. 266)

Business broker a person who sells businesses for a living (p. 70)

Business ethics application of the principles of right and wrong to issues that come up in the workplace (p. 306)

Business plan a written document that describes all the steps necessary in opening and operating a successful business (p. 94)

C

Cash flow statement accounting report that describes the cash that flows in and out of a business (p. 246)

Channels of distribution routes that products and services take from the time they are produced to the time they are consumed (p. 191)

Check register book in which you record the dates, amounts, and names of people or businesses to whom you have written checks (p. 240)

Code of ethics level of ethical behavior demanded by an individual, a business, or a culture (p. 305)

Collateral property that the borrower forfeits if he or she defaults on the loan (p. 146)

Commission percentage of a sale paid to a salesperson (p. 222)

Commission-based salary salary that varies from month to month, depending on how much of a product or service is sold (p. 222)

Competition-based pricing pricing that is determined by considering what competitors charge for the same goods (p. 195)

Computer hardware computers and the equipment used with them (p. 278)

Consensus agreement among a group of people (p. 41)

Copyright legal right to exclusive publication, production, sale, or distribution of a literary or artistic work (p. 300)

Corporation a business with the legal rights of a person and which may be owned by many people (p. 82)

Cost-based pricing price determined by using the wholesale cost of an item as the basis for the price charged (p. 194)

Cost of goods sold cost of the inventory a business sells during a particular period (p. 245)

Cover letter a letter that explains or provides more information about a document or set of documents (p. 106)

Culture the set of customs, beliefs, and social attitudes that characterize a particular group of people (p. 330)

Customer profile a description of the characteristics of the person or company that is likely to purchase a product or service (p. 118)

Customers the people who buy the products and services companies offer (p. 116)

$\overline{D}$

Debt capital money loaned to a business with the understanding that the money will be repaid, with interest, in a certain time period (p. 146)

Delegate to let other people share workloads and responsibilities (p. 228)

Demand individual's need or desire for a product or service at a given price (p. 52)

Demand-based pricing pricing that is determined by how much customers are willing to pay for a product or service (p. 195)

Demographics data that describe a group of people in terms of their age, marital status, family size, ethnicity, gender, profession, education, and income (p. 117)

Depreciation the lowering of the value of an asset to reflect its current value (p. 144)

Direct competition competition from a business that makes most of its money selling the same or similar products or services as another business (p. 127)

Discount a reduction in the retail or wholesale price of a product or service (p. 37)

Dividends distributions of profits to shareholders by corporations (p. 85)

$\overline{E}$

E-commerce selling products or services over the Internet; also called *electronic commerce* (p. 287)

Electronic mail used to send and receive electronic messages from anyone in the world; also called *e-mail* (p. 285)

Employees people who work for someone else (p. 4)

Enterprise zones areas that suffer from lack of employment opportunities (p. 172)

Entrepreneurs people who own, operate, and take the risk of a business venture (p. 4)

Entrepreneurship the process of running a business of one's own (p. 4)

Equilibrium price and quantity the point at which the supply and demand curves meet (p. 53)

Equity capital money invested in a business in return for a share in the business's profits (p. 151)

Ethics study of moral choices and values (p. 305)

Exports products and services that are produced in one country and sent to another to be sold (p. 324)

$\overline{F}$

Fixed costs costs that must be paid regardless of how much of a good or service is produced; also called *sunk costs* (p. 55)

Focus group an interview with groups of target customers who provide valuable ideas on products or services (p. 120)

Franchise a legal agreement that gives an individual the right to market a company's products or services in a particular area (p. 75)

Freelancers people who provide services to businesses on an hourly basis or by the job (p. 219)

$\overline{G}$

Gross profit profit before operating expenses are deducted (p. 264)

Gross sales dollar amount of all sales, including returns (p. 263)

$\overline{I}$

Imports products and services that are brought in from another country to be sold (p. 325)

Incorporate to set a business up as a corporation (p. 85)

Indirect competition competition by a business that makes only a small amount of money selling the same or similar products or services as another business (p. 127)

Industrial parks sections of land that can be used for industrial business locations (p. 172)

Initial franchise fee fee the franchise owner pays in return for the right to run the franchise (p. 75)

Interest an amount charged for borrowing money (p. 36)

Internet worldwide computer network that allows people to communicate with each other electronically (p. 284)

Internet Service Provider (ISP) a company that provides access to the Internet (p. 284)

Interns students who will work for little or no pay in order to gain experience in a particular field (p. 219)

Interoffice memo a memo from one person in a company to another (p. 26)

Inventory stock of goods a business has for sale (pp. 182, 248)

J

Job description written statement listing the duties and responsibilities of a job (p. 214)

L

Landlord person who owns and rents out buildings or space (p. 174)

Liability the amount owed to others (pp. 85, 142)

M

Marginal benefit measures the advantages of producing one additional unit of a good or service (p. 56)

Marginal cost measures the disadvantages of producing one additional unit of a good or service (p. 56)

Markdown an amount deducted from the retail price to determine the sales price (p. 36)

Markdown price price determined by subtracting an amount from the retail price of an item (p. 194)

Market development strategy for expanding the target market of a business (p. 322)

Marketing mix blending of the four marketing elements to satisfy a target market (p. 190)

Market penetration increasing market share for a product or service within a given market in a given area (p. 321)

Market research a system for collecting, recording, and analyzing information about customers, competitors, goods, and services (p. 119)

Market segments groups of customers that share common characteristics (p. 118)

Market share percentage of a market owned by a business (p. 205)

Markup an amount added to the cost price to determine the sales price (p. 36)

Markup price price determined by adding an amount to the wholesale cost of an item (p. 194)

Memorandum a short written form of business communication that has a set format (p. 26)

Modem an electronic device that allows information to be transmitted over telephone lines from one computer to another (p. 280)

Monopoly one company controls all of a market (p. 54)

N

Net cash flow the difference between cash receipts and disbursements (p. 246)

Net income from operations gross profit minus operating expenses (p. 264)

Net sales dollar amount of all sales after returns have been subtracted (p. 263)

Networking establishing informal ties with people who can help your business grow (p. 205)

O

Operating expenses expenses incurred by a business each month (pp. 140, 245)

Opportunity cost the cost of choosing one opportunity or investment over another (p. 57)

Organizational structure plan that shows how the various jobs in a company relate to one another (p. 215)

Owner's equity the difference between assets and liabilities (p. 244)

$\overline{P}$

Partnership a business owned by two or more people (p. 82)

Patent legal document that gives an inventor the sole right to produce, use, and sell an invention (p. 300)

Payroll a list of people who receive salary or wage payments from a business (p. 240)

Periodic inventory method inventory method that involves taking a physical inventory of your merchandise (p. 249)

Perpetual inventory method method used to keep track of inventory levels on a daily basis (p. 248)

Positioning placing a product in a certain market to get a desired customer response (p. 191)

Posting copying information from a journal entry to a ledger account (p. 239)

Press release written statement meant to inform the media of an event or product (p. 200)

Primary data information collected for the very first

time to fit a specific purpose (p. 120)

Principal amount of money borrowed in a loan (p. 36)

Pro forma financial statements financial statements based on projected revenues and expenses (pp. 101, 138)

Product mix different products and services a business sells (p. 190)

Psychographics data that describe a group of people in terms of their tastes, opinions, personality traits, and lifestyle habits (p. 117)

Public good a good from which everyone receives benefits, not just the individual consuming the good (p. 61)

Public relations act of establishing a favorable relationship with customers and the general public (p. 196)

Publicity free promotion generated by media coverage (p. 200)

$\overline{Q}$

Qualitative restriction standard of quality an imported product must meet before it can be sold (p. 328)

Quota limit on the amount of a product that can be imported into a country over a particular period of time (p. 328)

$\overline{R}$

Rate of interest the percent that is the basis for interest earned or paid (p. 36)

Rebate refund offered to people who purchase a product (p. 202)

Recruit to look for people to hire (p. 216)

Reorder point a predetermined level of inventory when new stock must be purchased (p. 183)

Royalty fees weekly or monthly payments made by the owner of the franchise to the seller of the franchise (p. 76)

$\overline{S}$

S corporation corporation organized under subchapter S of the Internal Revenue Code whose income is taxed as a partnership (p. 86)

Salaries payments for labor or services done on an annual basis (p. 221)

Sales the dollar value of the goods or services a business gives to customers over a certain period (p. 245)

Sales promotion act of offering an incentive to customers in order to increase sales (p. 201)

Secondary data data found in already published sources (p. 119)

Self-assessment evaluation of your strengths and weaknesses (p. 10)

Share of stock a unit of ownership in a corporation (p. 85)

Shoplifting   the act of knowingly taking items from a business without paying (p. 153)

Software   programs that control computer hardware and direct its operation (p. 280)

Sole proprietorship   a business owned exclusively by one person (p. 82)

Start-up costs   the one-time-only expenses that are paid to establish a business (pp. 76, 138)

Stock card   paper record for a single inventoried item (p. 248)

Stock turnover rate   rate at which inventory of a product is sold and replaced with new inventory (p. 251)

Supply   how much of a good or service a producer is willing to produce at different prices (p. 52)

T

Target market   the individuals or companies interested in a particular product or service and willing and able to pay for it (p. 116)

Tariff   tax on imports (p. 328)

Telemarketing   using the phone to market your product or service (p. 203)

Tenant   person who pays rent to occupy space owned by someone else (p. 174)

Term   number of years for which a loan is extended (p. 36)

Trade area   the area from which you expect to attract customers (p. 169)

Trade associations   organizations that promote certain types of businesses (p. 105)

Trade barriers   methods for keeping foreign businesses from competing with domestic producers (p. 328)

Trademarks   a name, symbol, or special mark that can be used only by certain businesses (p. 300)

Trade shows   special meetings where companies display their products (p. 14)

Transaction   a business activity that changes assets, liabilities, or net worth (p. 238)

V

Valuator   an expert on determining the value of a business (p. 72)

Variable costs   costs that go up and down depending on the quantity of the good or service produced (p. 55)

Vendors   companies that sell products and services to businesses (p. 180)

Venture capitalists   individuals or companies that make a living investing in start-up companies (p. 152)

W

Wages   payments for labor or services that are made on an hourly, daily, or per-unit basis (p. 221)

Web page   a file accessible through the World Wide Web which greets visitors and provides information (p. 285)

Index

A

AAMCO Transmissions, 206

Accident insurance, 224

Account, 239

Accountant, 247, 269

Accounting, 244–247

Accounting equation, 142, 244

Accounts payable
  as current liabilities, 143
  ledger, 239

Accounts receivable
  as current assets, 143
  ledger, 239

ACLU, 7

A Consumer Guide to Buying a Franchise, 75

ADA. *See* Americans with Disabilities Act

Addition. *See* Math skills

Advertising
  defined, 196
  direct-mail, 198–199
  magazine, 199
  newspaper, 198
  outdoor, 199
  radio, 197
  telephone directory, 198
  television, 197
  transit, 199–200
  want ads, 216

Advertising fees (franchise), 76

Agriculture
  businesses, 6
  product subsidies, 60

Allowance for uncollectible accounts, 143–144

Americans with Disabilities Act (ADA), 302

American Wholesalers and Distributors Directory, The, 192

AMTRAK, 54

Amway Corporation, 168

Antitrust legislation, 298

Apple Computer, Inc., 8, 168

Apply What You Learned, 20, 46, 66, 90, 112, 134, 162, 185, 210, 234, 254, 273–274, 294, 316, 336

Aptitude, 11

Arab culture, 330, 333

Arden, Elizabeth, 310

Assessment. *See* Self-assessment

Assets
  current, 143
  defined, 142
  fixed, 143

AT&T, *Business Buyer's Guide,* 192

Attorney, 268. *See also* Lawyer

Audit, 271

Averages. *See* Math skills

B

Balance sheet, 142–144, 244

Bankers, 268

Bank loans, 146–148

Bank statements, 239–240

Barron's magazine, 75

Beech, Olive Ann, 7

Beech Aircraft Company, 7

Benefits, employee, 223–224

Birdseye, Clarence, 7

Board of directors, 85

Bonus, 222

Boston Herald, The, 128

Bounced checks, 155–156

Bradley, Lydia Moss, 7

Brainstorming, 40–41

Break-even analysis, 266–267

Break-even point
  calculating, 267
  defined, 266

Browser, 285

Bugle Boy Industries, 286

Build a Business
  CDs and Records (Ch. 11), 237
  Cheryl's Day Spa (Ch. 6), 115
  Custom Car Center (Ch. 2), 23
  Darrell's Digs (Ch. 3), 49
  Delia's Dilemma (Ch. 1), 3
  Expanding and Moving (Ch. 8), 165
  Financing and Web Pages (Ch. 12), 257
  The Frazzled Photographer (Ch. 10), 213
  Gavin's Business Grows (Ch. 15), 319
  Getting Up to Date (Ch. 13), 277
  Importance of a Plan (Ch. 5), 93
  Mixing Up the School Store (Ch. 9), 189

One Day at a Time
(Ch. 7), 137
The Pastry Shop (Ch. 4), 69
Reasons for Regulations
(Ch. 14), 297

Bureau of Export Administration,
329

Business(es)
agricultural, 6
family, 72–74
manufacturing, 5
legal form of, 82–87
mining and extracting, 6
purchasing existing, 70–71
retailing, 5
service, 5
starting your own, 79–80
steps to purchase, 71–72
wholesaling, 5

Business broker, 70–71

Business Buyer's Guide **(AT&T),**
192

Business ethics, 306–308

Business letters, 24–26

Business license, 60, 102, 300

Business memos, 26–27

Business opportunities, 14–15

Business organization. *See* Legal
forms of businesses

Business plan
appendix, 109
basic elements, 98–102
defined, 94
effective, 103–109
importance of, 95–97
international, 327
introductory elements,
106–108
main body, 109
parts of, 105–108
purpose of, 94–95
research for, 103–105
table of contents for, 107

Business Start-Ups **magazine,**
75

Buying
space, 174–176
See also Purchasing

C̄

Canada, NAFTA and, 328–329

Capital, increasing, 260

Caribbean culture, body lan-
guage, 333

Carrying costs, 250

Cash budget, creating, 258–259

Cash drawer, 34

Cash flow
improving, 259–261
managing, 258–261
positive or negative, 246

Cash flow statement, 139–141
defined, 246
income statement vs.,
140–141

Cash payments journal, 238

Cash receipts, 246, 259

Cash receipts journal, 238

Cash register, 177

Casualty insurance, 157

Certified Public Accountant
(CPA), 247, 269

Chamber of Commerce, 105,
119, 303
International, 333

Channels of distribution
defined, 191
manufacturing businesses,
193
retail goods, 191–192
service businesses, 192–193

Check, bounced, 155–156

Check register, 240

Chinese culture, 330

Classified advertising, for job
openings, 216

Clayton Act, 298

Coaching, 227

Code of ethics
defined, 305
written, 307

Collateral, 146

College placement centers, 216

Command economy, 50–51

Commercial leases, 174–175

Commercials, 197

Commission
business brokers, 71
defined, 222

Commission-based salary, 222

Commissioned agents, 324

Communication skills, 24–29
listening, 28–29
speaking, 27–28
writing, 24–27
See also Make Connections

Community, responsibilities to,
310

Community shopping centers,
167

Compensation, employee,
221–222

Competition
direct, 127
global, 326
government and, 298–299
indirect, 127
with large businesses, 128
studying individual, 129
understanding, 118, 127–131
wages paid by, 221

Competition-based pricing, 195

Computer(s)
perpetual inventory method and, 249
record keeping using, 241–243

Computer consultants, 290

Computer hardware, 278–283
defined, 278
desktop computers, 278–279
modems, 280
portable computers, 279
printers, 279–280
purchasing, 289

Computer software, 280–282
See also Software

Computertots, 78

Conferences, employee training, 227

Consensus, 41

Consumer Product Safety Act, 301

Consumers
awareness of business ethics, 306
laws protecting, 300–301
See also Customers

Contracts
franchise agreements, 79
partnership agreement, 83–84

Copyright, 300, 307

Corporation, 85–86
defined, 82
disadvantages, 85
reasons to form, 85–86

Cost(s)
break-even point and, 266–267
inventory carrying, 250
concept of, 55–58
fixed, 55
franchise operating, 75–76

marginal, 56–57
opportunity, 57
start-up, 76, 138–139
of stock outages, 250
variable, 55

Cost-based pricing, 194

Cost of goods sold, 245, 264

County Business Patterns, 14

CPA. *See* Certified Public Accountant

Credit card
fraud, 155
Internet purchases using, 287–288

Creditors, responsibilities to, 310

Critical thinking. *See* Think Critically

Cultural diversity, 330

Culture(s)
business and, 330–333
defined, 330
ethics and, 305
familiarizing self with other, 332
global marketplace and, 332–333
marketing to different, 331
researching other, 333
sensitivity to other, 333
within United States, 330–333

Current assets, 143

Current liabilities, 143

Customer(s)
calculating rent per, 175–176
defined, 116
electronic customer base, 287
of existing business, 70
location and, 166–169

meetings with, 28
responsibilities to, 309
understanding, 116–117
See also Consumers

Customer loyalty, maintaining, 130

Customer profile, 118

D

Database software, 282

Debt capital, 146

Decision making
consensus-based, 41–43
See also Problem solving

Delegate, 228

Dell Computer Corporation, 168

DelSol Inc., 121

Demand
defined, 52
See also Supply and demand

Demand-based pricing, 195

Demand curve, 53

Demographics, 117

Demorest, Ellen Curtis, 218

Dental insurance, 224

Department stores, 167

Depreciation, 144

Desktop computers, 278–279

Deterioration, inventory, 250

Did You Know? 10, 25, 57, 71, 101, 126, 149, 168, 199, 228, 250, 265, 288, 299, 333

Digital Link, 13

Direct competition, 127

Direct exports, 324

Direct-mail advertising, 198–199

Disbursements, 246, 260

Discount, 37

Discount stores, 167

Discrimination, workplace, 301–302

Disney, Walt, 63

Distribution, 191–193
  on Internet, 192
  See also Channels of distribution

Diversification, 322–323

Dividends, 85

Division. *See* Math skills

Downtown location, 166

Drugstores, 167

Dun and Bradstreet, *Exporter's Encyclopedia*, 327

Duraclean, 78

E

Eastman, George, 285

Ebony magazine, 76

E-commerce
  defined, 287
  profitability of, 288

Economic Development Administration (EDA), 151

Economy
  command, 50–51
  growth strategy and, 320
  market, 51. *See also* Market economy
  scarcity in, 50
  small businesses in U.S., 10

EDA. *See* Economic Development Administration

Edison, Thomas, 260

EEOC. *See* Equal Employment Opportunity Commission

Egypt, body language in, 333

Electronic mail, 285

Electronic spreadsheet, for cash budget, 258–259

E-mail, 285

Employee compensation
  benefits, 223–224
  wages and salary, 221–222

Employees
  alternatives to adding, 219–220
  compensation packages, 221–224
  defined, 4
  description in business plan, 100
  desirable characteristics, 217
  dishonest, 154
  entrepreneurs vs., 4
  evaluating, 229–231
  family needs, 311
  hiring, 214–220
  leading, 225–227
  listening to, 228
  managing, 225–231
  motivating, 227–229
  need for, 214–215
  number in small businesses, 10
  policies, 226
  promoting, 231
  recruiting, 216
  regulations protecting, 301–303
  resistance to computers, 243
  terminating, 231
  training, 226–227
  what to look for in, 216–217

Employee theft, 153–154

Employment agencies, 216, 220

Enterprise zones, 172

Entrepreneurial Timeline
  A Beautiful Empire, 310
  A Business with Automatic Gains, 206
  An Electric Career, 182
  An Empire Build on Soap and Candles, 246
  A Pattern for Good Business, 218
  Airing Good Business Practices, 154
  British Business in 18th and 19th Centuries, 96
  First Woman Millionaire, The, 6
  From Computers to Clothing, 286
  Making Money in Colonial America, 51
  More Than Gold in California, 265
  Music to His Ears, 322
  Small Engines, Huge Profits, 41
  Stop the Presses! 76
  Vegetables Are Good for You, 128

Entrepreneurs
  characteristics of successful, 9–10
  defined, 4
  employees vs., 4
  present and past, 4–8
  skills for, 22–47
  today, 8
  See also Entrepreneurial Timeline, What Went Wrong?

Entrepreneurship
  advantages, 12
  defined, 4
  disadvantages, 12–13
  is it right for you? 9–13

Entrepreneurship magazine, 75

Environment
government regulation of,
313
respecting, 312-313

Environmental Protection Agency
(EPA), 313

EPA. *See* Environmental
Protection Agency

Equal Employment Act, 301-302

Equal Employment Opportunity
Commission (EEOC), 302

Equilibrium price and quantity,
53

Equipment, obtaining,
180-181

Equity capital, 151

Estée Lauder cosmetics, 8

Ethics
business and, 306-308
codes of, 305
culture and, 305
defined, 305

Europe, food shopping in, 332

Executive summary, business
plan, 107-108

Existing business
family business, 72-74
purchasing an, 70-72
running an, 70-74

Expansion. *See* Growth
strategy

Expenses, 31, 139, 261. *See
also* Costs

Experiences, assessing, 11

Experts, hiring, 268-271

Exporter's Encyclopedia
(Dun and Bradstreet), 327

Exports, 324

F

Fair Labor Standards Act, 303

Family businesses, 72-74

Family Medical Leave Act,
302-303

Fax machine, 283

FDA. *See* Food and Drug
Administration

Federal Food, Drug, and
Cosmetic Act, 301

Federal Trade Commission,
(FTC), 75, 299

File transfer protocol (FTP), 283

Financial advisor, 269

Financial goals, 15

Financial management, 256-273
analyzing financial
performance, 262-267
cash flow, 258-261

Financial plan, 138-144

Financial planners, 269

Financial planning, 270

Financial statements
analyzing, 262-265
balance sheet, 142-144,
244
cash flow statement,
139-141, 246
current and projected, in
business plan, 101
income statement,
141-142, 244-245
personal, 144-145
pro forma, 101, 138
start-up costs, 76, 138-139

Financing
bank loans, 146-148
obtaining, 146-152

Fixed assets, 143

Fixed costs, 55

Flexible work hours, 312

Floor plan, 176-177

Focus group, 120

Food and Drug Administration
(FDA), 301

Forbes magazine, 75

Ford, Henry, 7, 240

Ford Motor Company, 7, 72

Franchise
advantages, 77
agreements, 79
defined, 75
disadvantages, 77
evaluating, 78-79
initial fee, 75
operating costs, 75-76
ownership of, 75-79
small-investment, 78

Franchisee, 75

*Franchise Opportunities
Handbook, The,* 75

Franchisor, 75, 77

Franklin, Benjamin, 182

Fraud, credit card, 155

Freelancers, 219

FTC. *See* Federal Trade
Commission

G

General journal, 238

Geographic expansion, 321-322

Global marketplace, 324-329
exporting, 324-325
government regulation and,
328-329
importing, 325

Goals
business plan description,
99

financial, 15
marketing, 204–207
non-financial, 16
setting, 15–16

Goods
receiving, 192
retail channels of
distribution for, 191–192
See also Product(s)

Government
agencies protecting
competition, 299
effect on production, 59–60
as income redistributor, 62
international trade
assistance, 329
in market economy, 59–63
as public good provider, 61
as regulator, 60. *See also*
Government regulation
roles of, 60–62
as social programs provider,
61–62

Government regulation, 60
competition and, 298–299
of environment, 313
of international trade,
328–329
protecting business and
public, 299–301
protecting employees,
301–303

Graphics programs, 282

Great Britain, business in 18th
and 19th centuries, 96

Gross lease, 174

Gross profit, 264

Gross sales, 263

Group problem solving, 40–43
brainstorming, 40–41
consensus-based decision
making, 41–43

Growth rates, 35

Growth strategy, 320–323

Gupta, Vinita, 13

$\overline{H}$

Hardware. *See* Computer
hardware

Health insurance, 223–224

Health maintenance
organizations (HMOs), 223

Hewlett-Packard Company, 172

Hobbies, interests and, 11

Home business, 172–173

Honda, Soichiro, 41

Honda Motors, 41

HUD. *See* U.S. Department of
Housing and Urban
Development

$\overline{I}$

Ibanez, Maria Elena, 77

Imports, 325

In Class Activity, 5, 11, 15, 26,
36, 41, 53, 56, 61, 74, 80,
85, 95, 102, 107, 117, 123,
130, 140, 147, 155, 158,
170, 172, 178, 181, 193,
205, 217, 222, 229, 241,
245, 260, 266, 271, 280,
287, 291, 301, 308, 311,
322, 328, 332

Income statement, 141–142,
244–245

Income tax, 241. *See also*
Tax(es)

Incorporate, 85

Indirect competition, 127

Indirect exports, 324

Industrial business, location for,
171–172

Industrial parks, 172

Industry, description in business
plan, 99

Initial franchise fee, 75

Insurance
accident, 224
buying, 158–159
casualty, 157
dental, 224
as employee benefit,
223–224
health, 223–224
inventory and, 250
life, 157–158, 224
medical, 223–224
property, 157

Insurance agent, 158

Intel, 8

Interest
defined, 36
fees from suppliers, 250
payments, 36–37
rate of, 36

Interest assessment, 10–11

Internal Revenue Code, S corporation organization under, 86

Internal Revenue Service (IRS)
audit by, 271
home business deductions,
173

International business, 325. *See
also* International trade

International business plan, 327

International Harvester
Company, 7

International High Technology,
77

International trade, government
regulation of, 328–329

International Trade
Administration, Export
Promotion Services, 329

Internet
    business plan information
        on, 104–105
    defined, 284
    distribution on, 192
    promoting business on,
        286–287
    for technology purchases,
        291
    transacting business over,
        287–288
    See also World Wide Web

**Internet service providers
    (ISPs), 284**

Interns, 219

Interoffice memo, 26

Interview, job, 217–218

Inventory
    controlling, 260–261
    defined, 182, 248
    managing, 250–251
    for ongoing business, 183
    periodic method, 249–250
    perpetual method, 248
    physical, 249
    for start-up business,
        182–183
    tracking, 248–251
    turnover rates, 251

Investors
    responsibilities to, 310
    See also Venture capitalists

Invoices, 32–33

IRS. *See* Internal Revenue
    Service

J̄

Jani-King, 78

Job applicants
    checking references, 219
    interviewing, 217–218

    offering job to, 219
    screening, 217

Job attributes checklist, 11

Job description, 214

Johnson, John H., 76

Journals, 238–239

K̄

Knox, Rose, 7

Knox Gelatine Company, 7

Kodak, 285

Koplovitz, Kay, 154

L̄

Landlord, 174

Laws
    learning about, 303
    See also Government
        regulations

Lawyer
    hiring, 303
    See also Attorney

Layout, 176–179
    manufacturing business,
        179
    retail business, 177
    service business, 178
    wholesale business, 178

LCD projector/panel, 283

Leadership qualities, 225

Lease
    gross, 174
    net, 174
    percentage, 174

Leasing, space, 174–176

Ledgers, 239

**Legal forms of businesses,
    82–87**
    corporation, 82, 85–86

    partnership, 82–84
    sole proprietorship, 82–83

Legal requirements, 298–304

Lelia College, 6

Letter
    business, 24–26
    business plan cover, 106

Liabilities/Liability, 85
    current, 143
    defined, 142
    long-term, 143

Licenses, 60, 102, 300

Life insurance, 157–158, 224

Lighting, retail business, 177

Lillian Vernon Corporation, 157

Listening skills, 28–29, 228

Loans
    bank, 146–148
    long-term, 147
    other sources, 150–151
    secured, 146–147
    short-term, 147
    Small Business Administration,
        101, 148–150
    unsecured, 146

Location(s)
    advantages and
        disadvantages of, 168
    community shopping
        centers, 166
    comparing, 175–176
    of competitors, 129
    description in business
        plan, 100
    downtown, 166
    home business, 172–173
    industrial business, 171–172
    neighborhood shopping
        centers, 166
    non-retail business, 171–173
    regional shopping centers,
        167

retail business, 166–170
service business, 171
site selection, 169
standalone stores, 168
super-regional shopping
     centers, 167
warehouses, 168–169

Long-term liabilities, 143

Long-term loan, 147

Lopez, John, 325

$\overline{M}$

MAACO, 206

McCormick, Cyrus, 7

Macintosh computers, 279

Magazine advertising, 199

Mail-order companies, for technology purchases, 291

Make Connections
Communication, 8, 13, 17,
     20, 29, 43, 47, 54, 58, 63,
     67, 74, 87, 91, 97, 102,
     109, 113, 121, 126, 131,
     135, 145, 152, 159, 163,
     170, 173, 179, 183, 185,
     195, 203, 207, 211, 220,
     224, 231, 234–235, 243,
     251, 254, 271, 275, 283,
     288, 291, 294, 304, 308,
     313, 317, 329, 333, 336
Math, 8, 13, 17, 20, 37, 43,
     47, 54, 58, 63, 67, 81, 87,
     90, 102, 109, 113, 121,
     134, 145, 152, 156, 159,
     162–163, 179, 186, 195,
     207, 210, 211, 224, 234,
     243, 247, 251, 254–255,
     261, 267, 274–275, 283,
     294, 313, 323, 329, 336
Problem solving, 43, 58, 74,
     81, 97, 121, 126, 156,
     170, 203, 231, 235, 261,
     288, 291, 308

Research, 20, 47, 67, 81,
     91, 113, 135, 173, 185,
     211, 294, 186, 235, 275,
     304, 317, 333, 336

Mall of America, 167

Management, description in business plan, 100

Manufacturing businesses, 5, 179, 193

Marginal benefit, 56–57

Marginal cost, 56–57

Markdown, 36–37, 194

Markdown price, 194

Market
international, 326–327
prices and structure of, 54
target, 116–118

Market development, 322

Market economy, 51
government and, 59–63

Marketing, 188–211
information in business
     plan, 100–101

Marketing goals
long-term, 206
marketing plan and, 207
medium-term, 205–206
short-term, 204–205

Marketing mix
defined, 190
distribution, 191–193
price, 193–195
product, 190–191
promotion, 196–203

Marketing plan, 207

Market penetration, 321–322

Market research
defined, 119
how to perform, 122–125
primary data, 120–121

secondary data, 119–120
value of, 116–121

Market segments, 118

Market share, 205

Markup, 36

Markup price, 194

Martino, Anthony A., 206

Math skills, 30–37
addition, 30–31
averages, 31
basic, 30–31
division, 31
growth rates, 35
multiplication, 31
percentages, 34–35
sales transactions, 32–34
subtraction, 30–31

Medical insurance, 223–224

Meetings, with customers and suppliers, 28

Memo, 26–27

Memorandum, 26

Mentoring, 227

Mercado, Ralph, 322

Merle Norman Cosmetics, 78

Merry Maids, 78

MESBICs. *See* Minority
Enterprise Small Business
Investment Companies

Mexico, NAFTA and, 328–329

Microsoft Corporation, 8, 168

Mid-Delta Home Health, Inc., 99

Mining and extracting businesses, 6

Minority Enterprise Small Business Investment Companies (MESBICs), 150

Modem, 280

Monopoly, 54, 298

Mr. Rooter, 78

Mrs. Fields' Original Cookies, 8, 168

Multicultural society, 330

Multiplication. *See* Math skills

$\overline{N}$

NASA. *See* National Aeronautic and Space Agency

National Aeronautic and Space Agency (NASA), 59

Native-American culture, 330

Negro Digest, 76

Neighborhood shopping centers, 166

Net cash flow, 246

Net income after taxes, 264

Net income from operations, 264

Net lease, 174

Net profit before taxes, 245

Net profit on sales
    analyzing, 263
    importance of, 264

Net sales, 263

Networking, 205

Net worth, 142

Newspaper advertising, 198

Non-financial goals, 16

North American Free Trade Agreement (NAFTA), 328–329

$\overline{O}$

Observation, market research through, 120

Obsolescence, 250

Occupational Safety and Health Act, 302

Occupational Safety and Health Administration (OSHA), 60, 302

On-the-job training, 227–228

Operating costs
    franchise, 75–76
    See also Operating expenses

Operating expenses, 140, 245

Opportunities. *See* Business opportunities

Opportunity cost, 57

Organizational chart, 215

Organizational structure, 215

OSHA. *See* Occupational Safety and Health Administration

Outdoor advertising, 199

Owner's equity, 142, 244

$\overline{P}$

Paid advertisements, 197

Partnership
    agreement, 83–84
    defined, 82
    disadvantages, 83

Patent, 300

Payroll
    controlling, 260–261
    defined, 240
    records for, 24--241
    register, 240

Pension plan, 224

Pennsylvania Gazette, 182

Percentage lease, 174

Percentages. *See* Math skills

Performance appraisal, 229–230

Periodic inventory method, 249–250

Perpetual inventory method, 248

Personal computer, 278

Personal financial statement, 144–145

Personal selling, 202

Photocopier, 283

Physical inventory, 249

Pinkham, Lydia E., 128

Poor Richard's Almanac, 182

Portable computer, 279

Positioning, 191

Posting, 239

Prepaid legal plan, 304

Presentation software, 282

Press release, 200

Price
    of competition's products, 129
    determining, 193–195
    equilibrium quantity and, 53
    markdown, 194
    market structure and, 54
    markup, 194
    retail, 37
    setting objectives, 193
    See also Pricing

Pricing
    competition-based, 195
    cost-based, 194
    demand-based, 195
    See also Price

Primary data, 120

Principal, 36

Printers, 279–280

Problem solving
group, 40–43
process, 38–40

Procter and Gamble, 246

Product(s)
analyzing sales by, 262–263
description in business
plan, 99
positioning, 191
selecting features, 190–191

Production, government's effect
on, 59

Product mix, defined, 190

Professionals, hiring, 268–269

Profit
break-even point and,
266–267
equation to determine, 31
goals, 265

Profit and loss statement, 141
See also Income statement

Pro forma financial statements,
138

Projects. See This Is Your
Business Project

Promotion, 196–203
advertising, 196–200
personal selling, 202
publicity, 200
sales, 201–202
telemarketing, 203

Property insurance, 157

Psychographics, 117

Public good, 61

Publicity, 200

Public relations, 196

Purchase orders, 32–33

Purchases journal, 238

Purchasing
equipment and supplies,
180–181
government, 59
inventory, 182–183
See also Buying

Q

Qualitative restriction, 328

Quota, 328

Quotations. See You Can Say
That Again!

Quote, as purchase estimate,
181

R

Radio advertising, 197

Ramos, Carmen, 304

Rate of interest, 36

Rebate, 202

Receiving goods, 192

Record, database, 282

Record keeping, 236–255
accounting, 244–247
computerized, 241–243
inventory tracking, 248–251
setting up system for,
236–243
types of records, 238–241
See also Records

Records
bank statements, 239–240
journals, 238–239
ledgers, 239
payroll, 240–241
tax, 241

Recruit, 216

Regional shopping centers, 167

Regulations, government. See
Government regulations

Reorder point, 183, 248

Research
for business plan, 103–105
international market, 327

Retail business, 5
layout of, 177
location for, 166–170
technology purchase
through, 290–291

Retail goods, distribution of,
191–192

Retail price, 37, 194

Revenue, 139

Review Your Knowledge, 19, 45,
65, 89, 112, 133–134,
161–162, 185, 209–210,
233–234, 253–254, 273,
293–294, 315–316,
335–336

Robbery, 155

Robinson-Patman Act, 299

Rockefeller, John D., 7

Royalty fees, 76

S

Safety, employee training in, 227

Safe working conditions, 302

Salaries
defined, 221
See also Wages and salary

Sales
analyzing, 262–263
break-even point and,
266–267
defined, 245
gross, 263
net, 263
projecting, 35
total, 31

Sales journal, 238

Sales promotion, 201–202

Sales slips, 33

Sales tax
   figuring, 33
   records, 241

Sales transactions, 32–34

SBICs. *See* Small Business
   Investment Companies

Scanners, 126, 283

Scarcity, 50

Scheduling programs, 282

SCORE. *See* Service Corps of
   Retired Executives

S corporation, 82, 86

Secondary data, 119

Secured loans, 146–147

Self-assessment, 10

Selling, personal, 202

Seminars, employee training,
   227

Service business, 5
   channels of distribution for,
     192–193
   layout of, 178
   location for, 171

Service Corps of Retired
   Executives (SCORE),
   104–105, 169

Services
   description in business
     plan, 99
   positioning, 191

Shareholders, 85–86

Share of stock, 85

Sherman Act, 298

Shoplifting, 153

Shopping centers
   community, 167
   neighborhood, 166

regional, 167
   super-regional, 167

Short-term loan, 147

Sick leave, 223

Skills
   communication, 24–29
   for entrepreneurs, 22–47
   listening, 28–29
   math, 30–37
   problem-solving, 38–43
   speaking, 27–28
   writing, 24–27

Small business
   first jobs with, 228
   in U.S. economy, 10

Small Business Administration
   (SBA)
   entrepreneurial businesses
     chart, 5
   information published by,
     14, 103–104
   loans from, 101, 148–150
   Office of International
     Trade, 329
   secondary data from, 119
   web site, 104

Small Business Development
   Centers, 104–105

Small Business Investment
   Companies (SBICs), 150

Social programs, 61–62

Social responsibilities, 309–313
   to community, 311
   to creditors, 310
   to customers, 309
   environmental respect,
     312–313
   to investors, 310
   to suppliers, 310
   workplace changes and,
     311–312

Social security, 61

Software
   additional types, 282
   database, 282
   defined, 280
   e-commerce site, 287–288
   purchasing, 289
   spreadsheet, 258–259, 281
   word processing, 281

Sole proprietorship
   defined, 82
   disadvantages, 82–83

Southwest Airlines, 8

Space, lease or buy, 174–176

Speaking skills, 27–28

Spreadsheet software, 258–259,
   281

Staff. *See* Employees

Stand-alone stores, 168

Standard Oil Company, 7

Start-up costs, 76, 138,
   182–183

Stereotyping, 330

Stockbrokers, 269

Stock card, 248

Stockholders, 85

Stock turnover rate, 251

Strategic planning, 270
   competitors', 129

Subsidiary ledger, 239

Subsidies, government, 60

Subtraction. *See* Math skills

Supermarkets, 167

Super-regional shopping
   centers, 167

Suppliers
   credit terms, 261
   of existing business, 70
   identifying, 181

meetings with, 28
responsibilities to, 310
See also Vendors

Supplies, obtaining, 180–181

Supply, 52

Supply curve, 52

Supply and demand, 52–53

Survey, market research, 123–124

$\overline{T}$

Target market
competition and, 118
customer profile, 118
customers in, 116–117
defined, 116
identifying, 117
market segments, 118

Tariff, 328

Tax(es)
government and, 59
net income after, 264
net profit before, 245
sales, 33

Tax planning, 271

Team, working as, 228–229

Technology
Internet, 284–291
plan, 290
purchasing, 289–291
using, 276–295

Telemarketing, 203

Telephone conversation, 27

Telephone directory advertising, 198

Television advertising, 197

Temporary workers, 220

Tenant, 174

Term (loan), 36

Theft
bounced checks, 155–156
credit card fraud, 155
employee, 153–154
robbery, 155
shoplifting, 153

Think Critically, 8, 13, 17, 20, 29, 37, 43, 46, 54, 58, 63, 66, 74, 81, 87, 90, 97, 102, 109, 112, 121, 126, 131, 145, 152, 156, 159, 170, 173, 179, 183, 195, 203, 207, 210, 220, 224, 231, 234, 243, 247, 251, 254, 261, 267, 271, 274, 283, 288, 291, 294, 304, 308, 313, 316, 323, 329, 333

This Is Your Business Project, 21, 47, 67, 91, 113, 135, 163, 186, 211, 235, 255, 275, 294, 317, 336

Thomas, Dave, 39

Thomas Register, The, 192

Total sales, 31

Trade area, 169

Trade associations, 105

Trade barrier, 328

Trademarks, 300

Trade shows, 14

Training, employee, 226–227

Transaction, 238

Transit advertising, 199–200

Trust, 298

Turnover rates, 251

$\overline{U}$

U.S. Census, secondary data from, 119

U.S. Department of Agriculture (USDA), 60

U.S. Department of Commerce, 327, 329
Economic Development Administration of, 151
The Franchise Opportunities Handbook, 75
inventory costs, 250

U.S. Department of Housing and Urban Development (HUD), loans from, 151

U.S. Department of Justice, Antitrust Division, 299

U.S. economy, family businesses in, 72–74

U.S. Occupational Health and Safety Administration (OSHA), 60, 302

U.S. population, fastest-growing age group in, 57

UA-Columbia Satellite Services, 154

Uncollectible accounts, 143–144

Unishippers Association, 78

United States
body language in, 333
cultures within, 330–333
entrepreneurs in history of, 6–7. *See also* Entrepreneurial Timeline
NAFTA and, 328–329
small businesses in, 10
sole proprietorships in, 82

Universal product code (UPC), 126

Unsecured loans, 146

USA Network, 154

USDA. *See* U.S. Department of Agriculture

$\overline{V}$

Vacations, employee, 223

Variable costs, 55

Vendors, 180. *See also* Suppliers

Venture capitalists, 152. *See also* Investors

Vocabulary Builder, 19, 45, 65, 89, 111, 133, 161, 185, 209, 233, 253, 273, 293, 315, 335

Voucher checks, 241

W

Wages
defined, 221
laws governing, 303
See also Wages and salary

Wages and salary
compensation levels, 221
types of pay, 221–222

Walker, Madam C. J., 6, 223

Wall Street Journal, The, 75

Walt Disney Studios, 63

Want ad, 216

Warehouses
retail store, 168–169
wholesale business in, 178

Web page, 285

Web site, 192, 286–287

Wendy's Old Fashioned Hamburgers, 39

West Edmonton Mall, 167

What Went Wrong?
All Your Eggs in One Basket, 242
Be Sharp or Fall Flat, 16
Ice-Cold, 281
Let's Be Perfectly Franc, 32
Make-Up Test, 331
Modern Day Pirates?, 307
Pop Goes the Planning, 104
Price Wars, 125
Right Space, Wrong Place, 175
That Takes the Cake, 270
The Case of the Failed Ice Cream Shop, 62
Things Change, 144
Toothless in Seattle, 202
Who Do You Trust?, 226
With a Friend Like This . . ., 73

Wheeler-Lea Act, 299

Wholesaling businesses, 5, 178

Window displays, 177

Word processing software, 281

Workplace
discrimination, 301–302
ethical, 306

responding to changes in, 311–312

World Wide Web, 192, 285–286
exporting through, 324
recruiting employees with, 216
See also Internet

Writing skills, 24–27. *See also* Make Connections

Y

You Can Say That Again!
Disney, Walt, 63
Eastman, George, 285
Edison, Thomas, 260
Ford, Henry, 240
Gupta, Vinita, 13
Ibanez, Maria Elena, 77
Lopez, John, 325
Miller, Beverly, 200
Packler, David, 169
Ramos, Carmen, 304
Reed, Clara Taylor, 99
Sol, Carolos, 121
Thomas, Dave, 39
Vernon, Lillian, 157
Walker, Madam C. J., 223

Z

Zip compression utilities, 282

Zoning laws, 300–301

Photo Credits

Chapter 1

2, 15 ©EyeWire; 7 ©CORBIS/Bettman; 4, 9, 11, 12, 14, 16 ©1999 Photodisc

Chapter 2

22 ©EyeWire; 24, 27, 28, 29, 30, 31, 38, 42 ©1999 Photodisc

Chapter 3

48 ©EyeWire; 50, 52, 55, 56, 57, 59, 60, 61, 66 ©1999 Photodisc

Chapter 4

68 ©EyeWire; 72, 75, 77, 80, 82, 83, 85, 86 ©1999 Photodisc

Chapter 5

92 ©EyeWire; 94, 95, 97, 98, 99, 100, 105, 108, 109, 111, 112 ©1999 Photodisc

Chapter 6

114 ©EyeWire; 116, 117, 119,120, 123, 125, 128, 131 ©1999 Photodisc

Chapter 7

136 ©EyeWire; 38, 139, 141, 142, 146, 147, 148,150, 151, 152, 153, 154, 156, 159, 162 ©1999 Photodisc

Chapter 8

164 ©EyeWire; 167, 170, 173, 174, 177, 178, 181, 182, 186 ©1999 Photodisc

Chapter 9

188 ©EyeWire; 190, 191, 192, 194, 197, 198, 199, 201, 205, 207 ©1999 Photodisc

Chapter 10

212 ©EyeWire; 215, 217, 220, 222, 223, 224, 227, 228, 231 ©1999 Photodisc

Chapter 11

236 ©EyeWire; 251 ©Stockbyte; 239, 240, 245, 247, 249, 250 ©1999 Photodisc

Chapter 12

256 ©EyeWire; 259, 260, 262, 263, 266, 268, 269, 274 ©1999 Photodisc

Chapter 13

276 ©EyeWire; 279, 282, 284 ©1999 Photodisc; 286 ©CORBIS/Bettman; 287, 289 ©1999 Photodisc

Chapter 14

296 ©EyeWire; 299, 300, 301, 302, 305, 306, 307, 309, 312, 313, 316 ©1999 Photodisc

Chapter 15

318 ©EyeWire; 320, 321, 322, 325, 326, 327, 328, 330, 332, 337 ©1999 Photodisc